THE BOOM AND THE BUBBLE

THE BOOM AND THE BUBBLE

THE US IN THE WORLD ECONOMY

ROBERT BRENNER

VERSO

London • New York

First published by Verso 2002
© Robert Brenner 2002

Paperback edition first published by Verso 2003
© Robert Brenner 2003

1 3 5 7 9 10 8 6 4 2

Verso
UK: 6 Meard Street, London W1F 0EG
USA: 180 Varick Street, New York, NY 10014–4606
www.versobooks.com

Verso is the imprint of New Left Books

ISBN 1–85984–483–9

British Library Cataloguing in Publication Data
Brenner, Robert
  The boom and the bubble : the US in the world economy
  1. United States – Economic conditions – 1981–
  I. Title
  330.9′73

ISBN 1859844839

Library of Congress Cataloging-in-Publication Data
A catalog record for this book is available from the Library of Congress

Typeset in 10pt ITC New Baskerville
by SetSystems Ltd, Saffron Walden, Essex
Printed in the USA by R. R. Donnelley & Sons Limited

CONTENTS

LIST OF TABLES AND FIGURES

TABLES

FIGURES

AUTHOR'S NOTE

References for all variables in the book are, unless otherwise given, to be found in Appendix II (Main Sources of Data).

PREFACE

This book was essentially completed in July 2001. I have made no attempt to revise it to integrate more recent developments, although I have sought to take into account, at several points, newly released government data, including major revisions of corporate profits numbers for the years 1998, 1999, and 2000.

I have thus offered no assessment of the impact of the events of 11 September. The main short-, medium-, and long-run trends shaping the economy today were clearly operative long before that point, and I do not think that those events, however significant in other respects, have substantially altered them. The focus of this work is the US expansion of the 1990s, the stock market bubble which came to accompany it, and the ensuing bust and cyclical downturn. But my basic premise is that these conjunctural developments are comprehensible only in a much longer perspective. In particular, they must be understood in relation to those forces that made for the onset and perpetuation of the long stagnation of the world economy between 1973 and 1995, which followed the long boom of the first post-war quarter century. The aim of the book is to lay bare as clearly and concretely as possible the connections between the momentous, often tumultuous, economic developments that have taken place roughly since the start of the 1990s and this longer-term economic evolution.

I attempt to offer a conceptual framework that is at once theoretical and historical in order to interpret the boom, bubble, and bust. I am under no illusion that this is an easy task. But I am emboldened to make a start, out of a conviction that analyses of these recent events from the standpoint of orthodox economic theory have tended to be limited from the outset by their ahistorical character. As a rule, these make no reference whatsoever to the background of long-term international economic stagnation that framed the US expansion of the 1990s, let alone attempt to explain it, except with respect to the productivity slowdown and the weakening of innovation or exhaustion of technology allegedly behind that. It would be my view, in contrast, that, until the mechanisms behind the 'long downturn' are specified, and the degree to which they are still directly and indirectly at work has been determined, neither the real nature of the expansion of the 1990s, nor the economy's potential for getting beyond slowed growth, for avoiding serious crises, and for embarking on a new 'long upturn' can be adequately assessed. I should add that, in my view, the oft-heard notion that the US economy is essentially self-contained and can be analysed as such is profoundly misleading. The evolution of the US economy in the post-war epoch, all the more so in recent decades, is, I would argue, incomprehensible except in the context of the development of the world economy as a whole, and my interpretation proceeds from this premise.

It is my conviction, simply stated, that the problems that confront the world capitalist economy today, and thus the US economy, are deep-seated, and subject to no quick fixes. This is most directly evidenced by the inability of the advanced capitalist economies taken together to definitively transcend the long downturn during the course of the 1990s – or even to match their performance of the 1980s or 1970s, let alone the 1960s and 1950s. It is also manifest, I think, in the succession of ever deeper crises that have struck the world economy in recent years, culminating in the East Asian-cum-international crisis of 1997–98 – and indeed the one we are now entering – which had no counterparts during the 'long upturn' from the end of the 1940s to the early 1970s. To explain the persistence of incipient stagnation in the international economy, even through the US boom of the 1990s, and to bring out the economic dangers therein entailed, is the task of this book.

This work builds on the general account of the evolution of the post-war international economy that I presented in 'The Economics of Global

Turbulence: The Advanced Capitalist Economies from Boom to Stagnation', which appeared as the full issue of *New Left Review*, no. 229, May–June 1998. That work is being revised for publication in book form, and *The Boom and the Bubble: The US in the World Economy* is in a sense a first instalment. I owe, as usual, a huge debt to Perry Anderson, who provided careful critical readings of multiple drafts of this manuscript and offered invaluable suggestions. I wish also to extend my profuse thanks to Dick Walker, who followed the progress of the manuscript through each successive phase, not only offering detailed criticism at each point, but providing a bulwark of support and encouragement. Aaron Brenner, Andrew Glyn, Loren Goldner and John Buchanan also read several versions of the work, and I am deeply grateful to them for their superb critiques and ideas for improving it. Sebastian Budgen not only presented me with an excellent set of criticisms and suggestions on the substance of the manuscript, but gave it a thorough edit, which very much improved its style. I am profoundly grateful to Tom Mertes, who contributed in countless ways to the completion of this text, offering valuable critical commentary, an enormous amount of research help, and massive editorial and production work. I really cannot thank him enough. I want to express my appreciation to the editorial and production teams at Verso for their professionalism in seeing the work through to publication. My greatest debt is to Teri Edgar, not only for indispensable contributions on style and design, but for being there for me through the long and arduous process of producing this book.

Robert Brenner
November 2001

INTRODUCTION

ONLY YESTERDAY

In the autumn and winter of 1998–99, the international economy appeared to be stumbling. The crisis that had broken out in East Asia in summer 1997 was in the process of engulfing the rest of the world. Stock markets and currencies had crashed almost everywhere outside the capitalist core. Russia had declared bankruptcy. Brazil was falling into depression. The Japanese economy had slipped back into recession, having seen the entire disruption of its manufacturers' plans to extricate themselves from stagnation by means of a radical reorientation of trade, foreign investment, and bank finance to East Asia. The US economy was not immune. In response to falling profits during the first half of 1998, especially in the still pivotal manufacturing sector, equity prices fell alarmingly from July through September. By October, a severe liquidity crunch threatened to plunge the US economy, and thereby the world economy, into recession, or worse.

At that point, however, the US Federal Reserve – the 'Fed' – intervened. It bailed out the huge Long-Term Capital Management hedge fund, on the grounds that, had it been allowed to fail, the international economy risked financial collapse. The Fed also lowered interest rates on three successive occasions. This was not only to counter the credit crunch; it was also to make crystal clear that it wanted equity prices to rise. The idea was to raise the paper wealth of US households and corporations, in order to enable them to borrow more, and thereby to consume and invest more. Productivity and profitability would rise, it was hoped, and the demand would be provided to keep the US and the international economy turning over. But the outcome was contradictory in the extreme.

On the one hand, the economic expansion that had taken flight from the end of 1993 was enabled to continue. That expansion had gathered force against a background of two decades of deepening international stagnation on the basis of a dramatic recovery of profitability and competitiveness, especially in the manufacturing sector (although it had been deprived of one of its main props when the dollar rose precipitously from 1995). It ultimately delivered seven years of rapid growth of GDP, investment, labour productivity, and even real wages, while reducing unemployment and inflation to levels quite close to those of the post-war boom. Although wildly exaggerated in the business press, US economic performance during the second half of the 1990s was superior to that of any comparable period since the early 1970s (although, let it be noted, not better than that of the entire first post-war quarter century).

On the other hand, that very same period witnessed the inflation of the greatest financial bubble in US history. Equity prices exploded upwards and entirely lost touch with underlying corporate profits. This was no less so for technology, media, and telecommunications (TMT) firms at the heart of the 'New Economy' than for those of the old economy. Seeing their paper wealth expanding so rapidly, businesses and better-off consumers felt free to save less and borrow more, and household, corporate, and financial sector debt all ballooned to historically unprecedented proportions. The growth of debt made possible not only huge additions to the growth of both consumption and investment demand, but also stepped-up purchases by corporations of their own outstanding shares, aimed at driving their prices ever higher. The bubble was thus enabled to fuel itself and thereby to sustain and accelerate the boom of the economy. The fact remains that the continuation of the wealth effect, as well as the economy's ongoing capacity to realize the enormous increases in investment that the wealth effect made possible, depended upon the stock market's continuing ability to levitate in the absence of a parallel ascent of profits. Such defiance of gravity obviously could not be sustained for very long.

Meanwhile, although the fast-growing US demand for goods from overseas that accompanied the expansion did manage to keep the inter-national economy turning over, it signally failed to ignite an overseas boom of major proportions. Economic growth in the advanced capitalist economies taken together (including the US) during the decade of the 1990s failed to equal that of the 1980s, and proved, moreover, entirely dependent upon the US stimulus. On the other hand, the same exploding imports that drove the world economy brought US trade and current account deficits to record levels, leading to the historically unparalleled growth of US liabilities to overseas owners – and thus the historically unprecedented vulnerability of the US economy to the flight of capital and a collapse of the dollar.

In this context of underlying economic fragility, the Fed's dramatic rescue operation in autumn 1998, although phenomenally successful in its own terms, only increased the economy's vulnerability to crisis by forcing share prices to take a further leap into the stratosphere in the face of profits that were now actually falling significantly. The Fed's intervention thus made possible the last convulsive upward thrust of the equity price bubble, as information technology stocks rose to historic heights, with the imprimatur of the Fed chair. The resulting ascent of asset values allowed not only for the transcendence of the financial crisis, but also for the extension, indeed acceleration, of the ongoing US investment and consumption boom through the middle of 2000. It thereby enabled the US economy not only to save the world economy from depression, but also to trigger a new vibrant international cyclical upturn. The fact remains that because the final phase of the stock market run-up was so brutally mocked by a falling rate of profit in the real economy, its wealth effect could provide only temporary relief, a brief interregnum, for the US and the world economy. When the stock market plunged in the face of collapsing profits in 2000–01, the international economy entered once again into crisis – the extension, in a very real sense, of the international economic downturn of 1997–98.

The boom thus opened the way to the bubble; the bubble blew up the boom a good deal further; and the explosion of the bubble under its own pressure ultimately put an end to the boom. The fundamental question that is therefore posed is what is the real state of the US economy, underlying strength or serious weakness? The bubble-driven over-heating of the boom has been succeeded by an equal and opposite reaction downward. The major fall in share prices since summer 2000 has sent the wealth effect into reverse. It has forced corporations to cut back sharply on both spending and borrowing, and exposed to view a huge ledge of industrial capacity, legacy of the bubble, that cannot find a profitable outlet. The resulting drop-offs of both output and investment growth have been the steepest since World War II, and they have inevitably triggered the classical chain reaction by which corporate cutbacks in plant, equipment, and labour force make for declining corporate and consumer confidence and demand, rising unemployment, and increasing corporate and consumer debt defaults and bankruptcies, leading ultimately to cyclical downturn. Is a serious recession therefore in the offing?

Lurking behind that question is a bigger one, almost forgotten amidst the hoopla surrounding the 1990s boom. A long, debilitating stagnation held the US and the world economy firmly in its grip from the early 1970s right up to the middle 1990s, making for the snail-like growth of productiveness and declining living standards for more than a generation. Is this 'long downturn' by now only a bad and fading memory? Has the universally acclaimed 'New Economy' so transformed the underlying institutions, technological base, and industrial potential of the US economy that – whether or not a serious recession overtakes us in the short term – we are on the verge of a new 'long upturn' that will bring unprecedented international prosperity, much as did the post-war 'long boom' from the end of the 1940s to the early 1970s? Or, alternatively, are the major international slowdowns of 1997–98 and since summer 2000 not so much bumps along the road to long-term rapid growth as symptoms of unresolved weaknesses of the US economy and harbingers of things to come? Is the more compelling diagnosis, in other words, not only a return to slow growth over the longer term, but greater vulnerability to serious crisis than at any previous point during the long post-war epoch?

This work suggests answers to the foregoing questions. It distinguishes itself in so doing by virtue of its framework of analysis, which is the long downturn itself. Its defining premise is that there can be no serious analysis of the boom, bubble, and bust of the past decade without a specification of those forces that made for the continuation of the extended international economic stagnation of the two decades or more after 1973 – and the degree to which these continued to operate during the 1990s and perhaps beyond. Has the world economy transcended the forces that made for secularly slowed growth, or not?

The book's extended Chapter 1 provides a point of departure for the study as a whole by describing the unfolding of the long downturn, and by offering an interpretation of its origins and long continuation. It does so in terms of the quite paradoxical persistence of over-capacity and over-production – and thereby of persistently reduced profitability – in the international manufacturing sector, as well as problems of reduced aggregate demand and elevated cost of capital that derived from government and corporate attempts to cope with it. Chapter 2 explains how the US economy, in the course of the 1980s and early 1990s, established the conditions for its revival and ensuing boom, heavily on the basis of the striking turnaround of its manufacturing sector within the world economy. Chapter 3 explains why, on the other hand, the process of US economic recovery, taking place against a backdrop of continuing slowed growth internationally, was paralleled by deepening difficulties and descent into crisis for its leading trading partners and rivals in Germany, western Europe, and especially Japan – and thus brought no definitive escape from the long downturn even by the middle of the 1990s.

Chapter 4 hones in on what I believe to be the turning point for the world economy during the 1990s, the 'reverse Plaza Accord' of 1995, which took place in the wake of the worst half decade for the world economy of the post-war epoch. By that agreement, the big three powers bailed out a Japanese manufacturing economy that was slowing to a halt under the pressure of the record-breaking ascent of the yen. They did so by engineering a striking reversal of the steep decline of the exchange rate of the dollar that had taken place over the previous decade, a devaluation that had provided an indispensable basis for the US manufacturing revival. The dramatic consequences of that intervention, and of the resulting take-off of the US currency, are discussed in the next two chapters. Chapter 5 describes how, under the stress of the ascending dollar, the rise of profitability in the US manufacturing sector came to an immediate end, weakening one of the main planks of the US boom; explains why the stock market bubble simultaneously took off, egged on by the flooding in of massive funds from overseas in search of dollar-denominated assets, by the Fed's nurturing monetary policy, and by corporations' huge turn to buying back their own shares; and shows how the wealth effect of impetuously rising equity prices began to take over as the main engine driving the boom. Chapter 6 demonstrates, in turn, how the same rising dollar/declining yen that had been intended to bring about the revival of the Japanese economy triggered the East Asian crisis of 1997–98 and how the subsequent internationalization of the regional crisis ultimately threatened to de-rail both of the main engines of the US boom – the revitalization of US manufacturing and the stock market bubble.

Chapter 7 explains how the Federal Reserve's bailout of the US, and international, economy in autumn 1998 sent the stock market to historically unheard of and financially incomprehensible heights, thereby extending and deepening the expansion, but also opening up an historically unprecedented chasm between share prices and underlying returns on investment. Chapter 8 limns out the mechanisms by which the wealth effect of the stock market bubble accentuated the boom, especially from 1998 through the first half of 2000, while exploring the forces that were simultaneously succeeding in forcing down corporate profitability, even in the face of stunning contemporaneous increases in investment and consumption demand, as well as the growth of productivity.

Chapter 9 evaluates the strengths and weaknesses of the US expansion of the 1990s, in comparative and historical perspective. This prepares the ground for Chapter 10, which explores the mechanisms that moved the economy from the end of the bubble to the brink of recession, and for Chapter 11, which assesses future prospects.

CHAPTER 1

PERSISTENT STAGNATION, 1973–93

In order to assess the prospects for the US economy today, the point of departure must be the long downturn itself. It cannot be emphasized enough that the revitalization of the US economy from around 1993 took place against a backdrop of economic stagnation in the US and on a world scale lasting at least two decades, beginning in the early 1970s. During the long post-war boom between the end of the 1940s and the early 1970s, most of the advanced capitalist economies experienced rapid expansion, if not historically unprecedented rates of investment, output, productivity, and wage growth, along with very low unemployment and only brief and mild recessions. But during the long downturn that followed, between the early 1970s and the mid-1990s, the growth of investment fell sharply and issued in much-reduced productivity increase and sharply slowed wage growth (if not absolute decline), along with depression-level unemployment (if we leave aside the United States) and a succession of recessions and financial crises, the like of which had not been seen since the 1930s. Indeed, during the first half of the 1990s, the advanced capitalist economies displayed less dynamism and grew more slowly than they had during the 1980s, when they had expanded less rapidly than during the 1970s (not to mention the 1960s) (see Table 1.1; also p. 47, Table 1.10).

The initial question that must therefore be answered is: what were the forces that not only put an end to the long post-war boom, but also made for the continuation of economic stagnation for the following twenty years or more? Only once we have identified these forces, and determined whether or not they are still at work, directly or indirectly, in the world

Table 1.1 Comparing the long boom and the long downturn (average annual rates of change, except for net profit and unemployment rates, which are averages)

Manufacturing

	Net profit rate		Output		Net capital stock		Gross capital stock		Labour productivity		Real wage	
	1950–70	1970–93	1950–73	1973–93	1950–73	1973–93	1950–73	1973–93	1950–73	1973–93	1950–73	1973–93
US	24.35	14.5	4.3	1.9	3.8	2.25	–	–	3.0	2.4	2.6	0.5
Germany	23.1	10.9	5.1	0.9	5.7	0.9	6.4	1.7	4.8	1.7	5.7	2.4
Japan	40.4	20.4	14.1	5.0	14.5	5.0	14.7	5.0	10.2	5.1	6.1	2.7
G-7	26.2	15.7	5.5	2.1	–	–	4.8	3.7	3.9	3.1	–	–

G-7 net profit rate extends to 1990; German net capital stock covers 1955–93; Japanese net profit rates and net capital stock cover in manufacturing 1955–91.

Private business

	Net profit rate		Output		Net capital stock		Gross capital stock		Labour productivity		Real wage		Unemployment rate	
	1950–70	1970–93	1950–73	1973–93	1950–73	1973–93	1950–73	1973–93	1950–73	1973–93	1950–73	1973–93	1950–73	1973–93
US	12.9	9.9	4.2	2.6	3.8	3.0	–	–	2.7	1.1	2.7	0.2	4.2	6.7
Germany	23.2	13.8	4.5	2.2	6.0	2.6	5.1	3.0	4.6	2.2	5.7	1.9	2.3	5.7
Japan	21.6	17.2	9.1	4.1	–	–	9.35	7.1	5.6	3.1	6.3	2.7	1.6	2.1
G-7	17.6	13.3	4.5	2.2	–	–	4.5	4.3	3.6	1.3	–	–	3.1	6.2

G-7 net profit rate extends to 1990; German net capital stock covers 1955–93.

Sources: OECD, *National Accounts, 1960–1997*, volume II, Detailed Tables; OECD, *Flows and Stocks of Fixed Capital*, various issues; P. Armstrong, A. Glyn, and J. Harrison, *Capitalism Since 1945*, Oxford, Blackwell, 1991, data appendix, and their 'Accumulation, Profits, State Spending: Data for Advanced Capitalist Countries 1952–1983'; Oxford Institute of Economics and Statistics, July 1986 (updated by A. Glyn).

economy as a whole, will it be possible to begin to determine whether the re-strengthening of the US economy in the 1990s has prepared the ground, in the medium or long run, for a new long boom, or is more likely to prove partial and transient, opening the way to further serious economic difficulties.

FROM LONG BOOM TO LONG DOWNTURN

As it would be for the long downturn, the key to the long post-war boom from the end of the 1940s through the early 1970s was the trajectory of the profit rate. What made for the unprecedented economic expansion of the post-war epoch was the ability of the advanced capitalist economies to achieve and to sustain high rates of profit. High profit rates were fundamental above all because they enabled these economies to generate relatively large surpluses through the deployment of any given amount of plant and equipment (capital stock). Consistently large surpluses made it possible for these economies to maintain high rates of investment and thereby the rapid growth of productivity, permitting in turn the accommodation of rapid real wage growth without threatening profits. Because the average rate of return was high, moreover, relatively few firms were on the edge of bankruptcy, with the result that the advanced capitalist economies' vulnerability to economic shocks was, for a long period, much reduced, and recessions thus few in number and generally mild. Finally, because investors had little choice but to rely heavily on their realized rates of profit to assess their prospects (the expected rate of profit), the sustenance of high profit rates made for a generally excellent business climate throughout most of the first two post-war decades, again encouraging rapid capital accumulation (see below, p. 19, Figure 1.1).

Foundations of the post-war boom

US corporations from the end of the 1930s and Japanese, German, and other western European corporations from the end of the 1940s achieved the high rates of profit that constituted the fundamental precondition for their long post-war expansions. They did so, in the first instance, on the basis of the repression or containment of militant worker uprisings. These insurgencies broke out all across the advanced capitalist world and threatened capitalist rules of the game, first in the mid-1930s, then on the morrow of World War II, but they were everywhere brought under control, leaving labour in a subordinated position.[1] Real wages were thus forced down vis-à-vis the level of productivity, enabling manufacturers to net large surpluses with respect to their capital stock. The high rates of profit thereby secured opened the way to the high rates of capital accumulation that drove the boom by powering the rapid growth of productivity, of employment, and of real wages. The rapid acceleration of both investment demand and consumer demand naturally ensued, making for a virtuous upward spiral.

The US economy took off during the wartime years between the end of the 1930s and the middle of the 1940s. The way was prepared for the new epoch of growth by the huge reductions in the costs of production that were achieved during the course of the depression – by way of the enormous shakeout of obsolete capital stock, the strong downward pressure on real wages that resulted from record levels of unemployment, and the build-up of a great backlog of unused innovations, as well as the containment of the dynamic labour movement that had exploded onto the scene between 1934 and 1937. Under the stimulus of powerful wartime demand, the US economy was able to secure unprecedentedly high profit rates that made for a powerful expansion, and to increase its already impressive lead over all other national economies, at a time when the Japanese and western European economies were torn apart by war, only to be subsequently preoccupied with post-war reconstruction.[2]

Nevertheless, as a consequence of the very developments by which it consolidated its leading position, the US economy found it difficult to sustain the high levels of investment growth. Its initially advanced tech-

[1] Cf. P. Armstrong, A. Glyn, and J. Harrison, *Capitalism Since 1945*, Oxford, Blackwell, 1991.
[2] G. Dumenil, M. Glick, and D. Levy, 'The Rise of the Rate of Profit During World War II', *Review of Economics and Statistics*, vol. lxv, May 1993; R. Brenner, 'The Economics of Global Turbulence', *New Left Review*, no. 229, May–June 1998, pp. 48–9.

nology as embodied in great masses of sunk fixed capital; its more evolved socio-economic structure as manifested in its slender agricultural and small business sectors and consequently limited supply of surplus labour; its internationally hegemonic position as expressed in the internationalizing thrust of its multinational corporations, its great banks, and of course its state – all of these turned out to constitute significant barriers to its continued dynamism, as did the resistance of its residually powerful working class. The US economy was thus plagued, from end of the Korean War, by a loss of momentum, manifested in a slowdown of capital accumulation.

Already existing, already paid for – or *sunk* – fixed capital discouraged further capital accumulation, because it enabled firms to use their already existing plant and equipment free of charge, so long as they could make at least the average rate of profit on the expenditures on variable capital (wages, raw materials, and intermediate goods) required to put that fixed capital into motion. This enabled them to discourage entry by more technologically advanced potential rivals who could reduce unit costs below incumbents' total costs but not below their circulating costs per unit. The relatively reduced size of the US 'reserve army of unemployed' in the countryside and in traditionally over-staffed family businesses opened the way for the growth of employment to drive up wages relatively rapidly, because the demand for labour thus generated was unable to call forth a sufficient increase in supply. The major new profit-making opportunities offered by the boom in newly developing western Europe encouraged US multinational firms to rapidly increase investment abroad, while rising relative costs in international terms discouraged them from investing at home. Meanwhile, a slowdown in productivity growth resulting from the deceleration of investment growth, in combination with an uptick in real wage growth, squeezed profitability toward the end of the 1950s. The consequence was a strong tendency to economic torpor, which, though temporarily counteracted during the first half of 1960s, extended over the length of the first post-war quarter century.[3]

---

[3] H.G. Vatter, *The US Economy in the 1950s*, New York, Norton, 1963; Brenner, 'Economics of Global Turbulence', pp. 49–63.

What underlay the unprecedentedly sustained economic dynamism of the post-war global economy was thus the ability of the later-developing economies in particular – Germany and Japan, but also France, Italy, and others – to continue to achieve unparalleled rates of capital accumulation for an extended period. This they were able to accomplish by virtue of their capacity to maintain their initially high rates of profit, despite the powerful upward pressure of costs that was the unavoidable concomitant of their exceedingly high rates of economic expansion.

The producers of the later-developing economies had the capacity to cope with rising cost pressures, and thereby to bolster high profitability and international competitiveness, precisely by virtue of their belatedness. Due to their relative socio-economic backwardness, they could take advantage of huge pools of underemployed workers in their still relatively backward rural and small business sectors, so as to keep wage growth relatively low compared to productivity growth.[4] Owing to their position as technological followers, they were burdened by relatively little sunk fixed capital embodying obsolescent technology. They could, moreover, exploit the possibilities of catch-up, adopting cheap but advanced US technology, while succeeding, in many cases, in innovating so as to forge ahead, especially by means of the learning-by-doing and the economies of scale that they secured in the process of laying down huge quantities of new capital stock.[5]

The leading enterprises of the later-developing economies were also able to benefit from a series of institutional forms and government policies that were designed to promote growth and international competitiveness, but which were by and large either unavailable or of little interest to their rivals in the US, precisely because of the earlier development and dominant position of the latter. These enterprises thus maintained intimate ties – in

[4] C.P. Kindleberger, *Europe's Postwar Growth. The Role of Labor Supply*, Cambridge, Mass., Harvard University Press, 1967.
[5] M. Abramovitz, 'Rapid Growth Potential and its Realisation: The Experience of Capitalist Economies in the Postwar Period', in E. Malinvaud, ed., *Economic Growth and Resources*, Proceedings of the Fifth World Congress of the International Economic Association 1977, London, Macmillan, 1977; M. Abramovitz, 'Catch-Up and Convergence in the Postwar Growth Boom and After', in W.J. Baumol, R.R. Nelson, and E.N. Wolff, *Convergence of Productivity. Cross-National Studies and Historical Evidence*, New York, Oxford University Press, 1994.

a sense 'merged' – with great banks that were able to work closely with them and to monitor their operations, and, on that basis, provide them relatively cheap long-term loans, while catering to their changing needs in the face of fluctuating market conditions. They also participated in various forms of vertical and horizontal networks, which made possible greater inter-firm coordination and cooperation, and thereby allowed for greater planning, reduced input costs, and more secure markets.

The governments of the later-developing economies meanwhile sought, more or less systematically, to enhance the position of domestic producers on the world market, responding in so doing to powerful combined pressure from mutually supportive banks and manufacturers, which held a dominant position in the economy, as well as to their own self-interest in domestic economic development. They provided substantial levels of protection for home industry during a good part of the post-war epoch, while also offering it subsidies and securing for it undervalued currencies. These governments also saw to the 'repression of finance', strictly regulating the activities of lenders and speculators on the domestic front, while imposing sharp limits on the international mobility of capital, all with the goal of ensuring that financial activity would be harnessed to the needs of manufacturing expansion at home. The outcome was that the huge gains in productive effectiveness achieved by corporations of the late-comer countries redounded, for the most part, to the benefit of the domestic economies. This was in some contrast to the dominant trend in the relatively slow-growing, hegemonic US economy. There the penetration of overseas markets proceeded relatively less by way of the growth of exports than by way of the epoch-making internationalization of production by means of the relocation of industry, carried through by dynamic multinational corporations and banks. The US government strongly supported this effort and, throughout the period, constituted a powerful force for the liberalization of the world economy – not only free trade, but also the free movement of both long- and short-term capital – sometimes at the expense of domestically based manufacturing.[6]

---

[6] F. Block, *The Origins of International Economic Disorder*, Berkeley, University of California Press, 1977.

The later-developing economies were able to so effectively translate the advantages they derived from their socio-economic backwardness, followership, and hegemonized position as a consequence of the unparalleled speed with which they were able to expand their overseas sales and thereby to build disproportionately large, fast-growing domestic manufacturing sectors, sites of the most rapid productivity growth.[7] Their capacity to secure such rapidly expanding manufacturing exports depended in the first place on the unprecedentedly high rates of growth of world trade during the post-war boom. But it also rested on their ability to rapidly expand their shares of the world market. German and Japanese manufacturers, in particular, were able to achieve the extraordinary rates of export growth that drove their economies forward only by virtue of their ability to wrest ever greater fractions of world export markets from US and UK producers, as well as to penetrate the enormous US market itself.[8] In this context, they served as hubs for dynamic regional economic blocs in Europe and East Asia, respectively – supplying them with increasingly high-powered capital and intermediate goods and offering them huge and constantly magnifying markets for their output (although Japanese tolerance for manufactured imports was always limited).[9]

From the very beginning, then, uneven economic development did entail the *relative* decline of the US domestic economy. But it was also a precondition for the continued vitality of the dominant forces within the US political economy. US multinational corporations and international banks, aiming to expand overseas, needed profitable outlets for their foreign direct investment. Domestically based manufacturers, needing to increase exports, required fast-growing overseas demand for their goods.

---

[7] N. Kaldor, *Strategic Factors in Economic Development*, Ithaca, NY, Cornell University Press, 1967; N. Kaldor, 'Conflicts in National Economic Objectives', *Economic Journal*, vol. lxxxi, March 1971.

[8] A. Maizels, *Industrial Growth and World Trade*, Cambridge, Cambridge University Press, 1963, pp. 189, 200–1, 220; A.D. Morgan, 'Export Competition and Important Substitution', in *Industrialization and the Basis for Trade*, Cambridge, Cambridge University Press, 1980, p. 48; Brenner, 'Economics of Global Turbulence', pp. 46–7, 70, 88–90.

[9] R. Castley, *Korea's Economic Miracle. The Crucial Role of Japan*, New York, Macmillan, 1997; A.S. Milward, *The European Rescue of the Nation State*, Berkeley, University of California Press, 1992.

An imperial US state, bent on 'containing communism' and keeping the world safe for free enterprise, sought economic success for its allies and competitors as the foundation for the political consolidation of the post-war capitalist order, in the face of the anaemia of domestic ruling classes sapped by war, occupation, collaboration, and defeat. All these forces thus depended upon the economic dynamism of Europe and Japan for the realization of their own goals. This meant that they relied, paradoxically, for their own prosperity on the capacity of their rivals to increase export competitiveness, so as to appropriate growing shares of US producers' overseas markets and gain at least some access to the US domestic market. US producers could long cede, without too much cost, significant shares of their overseas markets because those markets were growing so rapidly in absolute terms during the long boom, and also because they constituted such a small proportion of their total markets. In any case, they could always fall back on the enormous US market, which they were long able to dominate as a consequence of their superior technology, as well as the deterrent effect of their sunk fixed capital on potential entrants into their markets.

Because US economic success turned out to be so tightly linked to the success of its rivals and allies, post-war international economic development within the advanced capitalist world could, for a brief time, manifest a relatively high degree of international cooperation – marked by high levels of US aid to and politico-economic support for its allies and competitors – even though dominated by the US state and mainly shaped by US interests. The US government, as well as its leading capitalists, were thus willing to tolerate their rivals' high levels of state interventionism, their trade protectionism, their undervalued exchange rates, and their shackling of finance because they themselves possessed such a strong interest in their rivals' national economic development – especially the growth of their domestic markets – and their political stability. One therefore witnessed, at least for a time, a symbiosis, if a highly conflictual and unstable one, of leader and followers, of early and later developers, and of hegemon and hegemonized.

The onset of over-capacity and the crisis of profitability, 1965–73

Nevertheless, uneven development through the growth of trade and the world division of labour did not long remain favourable only in its economic effects. From the end of the 1950s, currencies once again became convertible and trade barriers were lowered. The growth of commerce was thereby enabled to increase even more rapidly, but with highly contradictory effects. During the second half of the 1960s, producers in western Europe and Japan exploited gains from trade to secure the highest rates of economic expansion of the post-war epoch. But, at the same time, these producers began to supply, without warning, even larger fractions of the world market than before. They had previously been producing for their home markets bundles of goods that were quite similar to those already being produced by the US.[10] The goods that they now ended up exporting thus tended to duplicate, rather than complement, the products of US incumbents in existing markets, inviting redundancy and over-capacity and over-production.

Beginning in the mid-1960s, manufacturers based in the later-developing economic blocs – most notably in Japan, but also in Germany and in other parts of western Europe – were thus able to combine relatively advanced techniques and relatively low wages to sharply reduce relative costs vis-à-vis those required to produce the same goods in the earlier-developing US. On this basis, they not only succeeded in imposing their relatively low prices on the world market so as to dramatically swell their shares of that market, but also were able, precisely by virtue of their relatively reduced costs, to maintain their old rates of profit at the same time. US producers thus found themselves facing slower growing prices for their output, but were caught with inflexible costs as a result of their being lumbered with plant and equipment (fixed capital) that embodied production methods that had suddenly been rendered too costly, as well as with relatively high wage levels that could not quickly be squeezed downward. Those capitals that could no longer make the prevailing

[10] OECD, *Structural Adjustment and Economic Performance*, Paris, 1987, p. 267.

average rate of profit even on their circulating capital alone – i.e. on the labour power, raw materials, and intermediate goods that were needed to operate their fixed capital (plant and equipment) – had to shed productive capacity and/or reduce capital utilization. Others, in order to hold on to their markets, had little choice but to swallow significantly reduced rates of profit on their fixed capital, since they could not raise prices above costs as much as they had previously.

As a consequence of the unexpected irruption of lower-priced producers on to the world market, US manufacturers thus turned out to have over-invested, and were prevented from raising prices in line with labour and capital costs. The overall outcome was that, while the lower-cost, lower-price manufacturers of the later developing economies of Japan, Germany and western Europe succeeded in maintaining their profit rates, US manufacturers were unable to avoid reduced rates of return. A declining *aggregate* rate of profit in the international manufacturing sector, which manifested system-wide over-capacity and over-production, was the inexorable result. Between 1965 and 1973, the US manufacturing sector experienced a fall in the rate of profit on its capital stock of 43.5 per cent; the manufacturing sectors of the G-7 economies taken in aggregate, a surrogate for international manufacturing as a whole, a decline in profitability of about 25 per cent.[11]

The Japanese, German, and other European economies did not long remain untouched by this system-wide decline in aggregate manufacturing profitability. As an expression of declining manufacturing competitiveness, US trade and current account balances tumbled downwards (and German and Japanese trade and current account balances rose correspondingly). Simultaneously, rising foreign investment and bloated military expenditures associated with the Vietnam War brought about skyrocketing US balance of payments deficits. Because the number of dollars held abroad rose enormously, relative to demand for US products and assets, huge downward pressure was exerted on the US currency, and the world monetary system was propelled into crisis. Between 1971 and 1973, the Bretton Woods system of fixed exchange rates was jettisoned and the US dollar sharply devalued,

[11] Armstrong *et al.*, *Capitalism Since 1945*, p. 352, Table A1.

while the mark and the yen were correspondingly revalued. Owing to the increase in the value of their currencies, Japanese and German manufacturers were burdened with sharply rising relative costs of production vis-à-vis those of their US rivals and suffered very major declines in their rates of profit, assuming a much greater share than hitherto of the fall in aggregate profitability that had struck the G-7 manufacturing economies.

Testifying to the degree to which over-capacity and over-production had by this point gripped world manufacturing, US producers, though benefiting from the dollar's fall, were nonetheless unable to come close to restoring their boom-time profit rates. As an expression of the onset of the glut of capacity and output, world manufacturing prices had been unable to grow in line with wages and the cost of plant and equipment, resulting in a fall in manufacturing profit rates. It was the decline in the manufacturing rate of profit across the advanced capitalist economies that was primarily responsible for propelling the world economy from long boom to long downturn between 1965 and 1973 (see Figure 1.1).

The fundamental role of intensified international competition leading to manufacturing over-capacity and over-production in forcing down profit rates, both in the US and in the leading capitalist economies more generally, is evidenced by the fact that the decline in profitability was heavily concentrated in the manufacturing sector, composed mostly of tradables and therefore vulnerable to international competition. The decline touched only relatively lightly the non-manufacturing sector, composed mostly of non-tradables and therefore largely protected from international competition – even though costs rose substantially faster in non-manufacturing than in manufacturing in the years when profitability fell. Whereas manufacturing profitability fell by 43.5 per cent in the US between 1965 and 1973, non-manufacturing profitability fell by only 13.9 per cent in the same period (9 per cent, if no adjustment is made for indirect business taxes that weighed increasingly heavily on non-manufacturing, but not on manufacturing). Put alternatively, the average rate of profit in manufacturing in the business cycle between 1969 and 1973 fell by 29.5 per cent compared to that in the business cycles between 1948 and 1969, whereas the average rate of profit in non-manufacturing fell by just 5.4 per cent in that interval (see Figure 1.2 and Table 1.2).

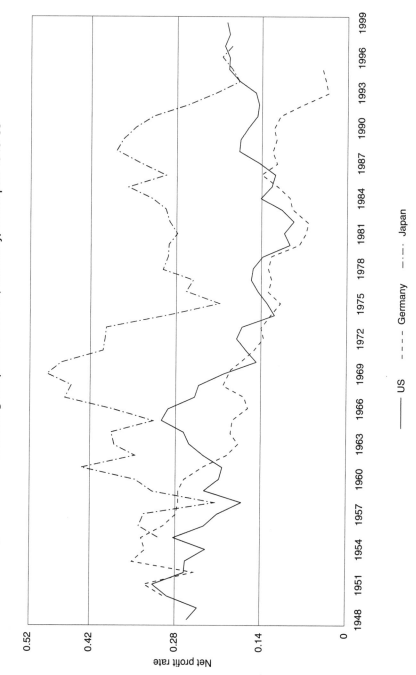

Figure 1.1 Manufacturing net profit rates: US, Germany, and Japan 1948–99

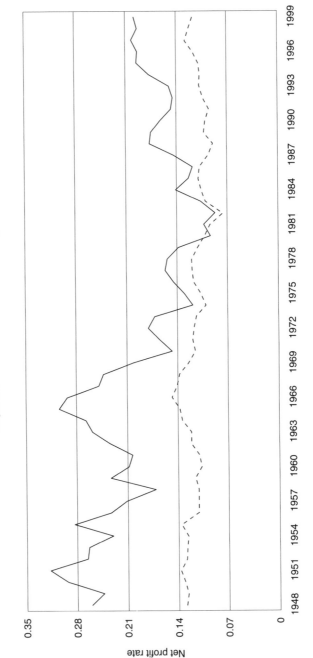

Figure 1.2 US manufacturing and non-farm non-manufacturing net profit rates, 1948–99 (adjusted for indirect business taxes)

——— Manufacturing   - - - - Non-farm non-manufacturing

Table 1.2 Profit rate trends in the manufacturing, non-farm non-manufacturing, and non-farm private sectors

Average profit rates (per cent)	1948–59	1959–69	1969–73	1973–79	1969–79	1979–90
Manufacturing	25.0	24.6	16.6	14.0	15.05	13.0
Non-farm non-manufacturing	11.0	11.1	10.4	10.3	10.3	9.1
Non-farm private	19.9	20.8	18.3	16.3	17.1	15.0

The foregoing was the case despite the fact that manufacturing labour productivity rose almost 50 per cent faster in this period than did non-manufacturing productivity and that manufacturing nominal wages increased more slowly than did those in non-manufacturing. What prevented manufacturers from maintaining their profit rates between 1965 and 1973 was clearly their inability to mark up their prices over costs at much more than half the rate of their non-manufacturing counterparts. Their prices rose at an average annual rate of 2.3 per cent, compared to 4.25 per cent for non-manufacturers (see Table 1.3) The same disparity between the profitability declines in manufacturing and non-manufacturing in these years can also be observed for the G-7 economies taken together (see below, p. 41, Figure 1.4).

It must be emphasized that the private economy *as a whole* saw its profit rate decline as a consequence of the fall in the rate of profit in the manufacturing sector, which had itself resulted from the relative repression of price increases in international manufacturing. Had firms outside of manufacturing succeeded in garnering *all* of the gains (reductions in cost of production) that were derived from the slowed growth of manufacturing prices, they would have recouped increases in profits sufficient to match the reductions in profits sustained by manufacturing firms; in that case, a rise in the non-manufacturing profit rate would have compensated for the fall in the manufacturing profit rate, and no fall in the aggregate profit rate for the private economy as a whole would have occurred. But, in view of the composition of manufacturing output, specifically the major place of consumer goods within it, it was a foregone conclusion that workers would share in these gains, increasing their real wages. Moreover,

Table 1.3 The growth of costs, prices, and profitability in the US, 1965–73: manufacturing versus non-manufacturing (percentage rates of change)

	Manufacturing	Non-manufacturing
Net profit rate	−5.5	−3.0
Net profit share	−2.7	−2.0
Real wage	1.9	2.7
Product wage	4.0	2.8
Labour productivity	3.3	2.35
Nominal wage	6.4	7.2
Unit labour costs	3.05	4.7
Product price	2.3	4.25
Output–capital ratio	−3.2	−1.1
Real output–capital ratio	−0.4	0.0
Capital stock price	5.2	5.6
Adjusted for indirect business taxes		
Net profit rate	−6.0	−1.7
Net profit share	−2.8	−0.7
Real wage	1.9	2.7
Product wage	4.2	2.7
Labour productivity	3.3	2.35
Nominal wage	6.4	7.2
Unit labour costs	3.05	4.7
Product price	2.1	4.4
Output–capital ratio	−3.4	−1.0
Real output–capital ratio	−0.4	0.0
Capital stock price	5.2	5.6
Not adjusted for indirect business taxes		

since employers outside of manufacturing did not suffer reductions in their own profit rates as a result of the increased real wages that their workers derived, they felt no added pressure to attempt to reduce wage growth. The upshot was that, between 1965 and 1973, the rate of profit in the private business economy fell by some 30 per cent in the US and by about 20 per cent in the G-7 taken in aggregate.[12]

[12] Ibid., pp. 352–3, Tables A1 and A2.

Implicit, finally, in this analysis is the conclusion that the fall in profitability in the US economy was *not* – as is widely argued – caused either by an exhaustion of technology leading to a squeeze on profits by way of a decline of productivity growth or by an increase in workers' power leading to a squeeze on profits by way of faster-growing real wages. A decline in productivity growth could not have been the source of the fall in profitability for the simple reason that, in the manufacturing sector, where the profitability decline was for the most part located, productivity growth actually rose during the years when profitability fell, increasing at an average annual rate of 3.3 per cent between 1965 and 1973, compared to 2.9 per cent between 1950 and 1965.

Moreover, had the decline in productivity growth, when it occurred, been primarily caused by the exhaustion of technological potentials, one would have expected a pattern of relatively slow and more or less continuous descent. In fact, not only in the US, but also in the other G-7 economies, productivity growth actually sped up in the 1960s and early 1970s, compared to the 1950s, then experienced a sharp and discontinuous fall-off from 1973. Indeed, in the US, productivity growth had maintained a fairly consistent pace for an amazing thirty-five years, before effectively collapsing between 1973 and 1979. This is hardly the trajectory one would associate with the (gradual) exhaustion of technological opportunities. As shall be seen, the reduction in productivity growth should be understood much more as a result than a cause of the long downturn (see Table 1.4).

By the same token, between 1965 and 1973, when the manufacturing profit rate first declined, average annual manufacturing real wage growth fell to 1.9 per cent, compared to 2.2 per cent between 1958 and 1965 and 3.6 per cent between 1950 and 1958. Indeed, had pressure from real wages been the source of the profitability problem, that problem should have been easily resolved over the subsequent period, for, as shall be seen shortly, real wage growth declined to the vanishing point during the subsequent decade and a half. The fact remains that the manufacturing profit rate was no higher in 1990 than it had been in 1973. The same conclusion can be reached through an alternative route. Real wage growth, at 2.7 per cent, was 42 per cent higher in non-manufacturing

Table 1.4 The pattern of productivity growth, 1938–79 (average percentage increase)

US	1938–50	1950–58	1958–65	1965–73	1973–79
Manufacturing	2.7	2.0	4.1	3.3	0.4
Non-farm economy	2.7	2.2	3.3	2.7	1.1

G-7 economies minus the US	Early 1960s	Late 1960s	Early 1970s	1973–79
Manufacturing	3.4	5.7	6.2	3.5
Non-farm economy	3.6	5.1	5.2	2.3

than in manufacturing between 1965 and 1973, but, in the same period, the fall in the rate of profit in non-manufacturing was not quite a third of that in the manufacturing sector (less than a quarter if no adjustment is made for indirect business taxes).[13]

STAGNATION IN THE WORLD ECONOMY, EARLY 1970s–MIDDLE 1990s

Producers' immediate, and quasi-universal, response to their sharply reduced profit rates was to attempt to compensate by reducing direct and indirect labour costs. Supported by increasingly sympathetic governments, employers across the advanced capitalist world unleashed an ever more aggressive attack on workers' organizations and workers' living standards. They succeeded, moreover, with surprising speed in asphyxiating the growth of real wages and social spending, very much alleviating, already during the 1970s, pressure from the growth of direct and indirect labour costs on profits (see Tables 1.5 and 1.6).

But the resulting redistribution of income away from labour and in

[13] It should be added that, except during the years 1973–79, which were marked by two major oil crises, manufacturing productivity growth failed to fall for any significant period during the post-war epoch. On the other hand, wage growth fell sharply and immediately after 1973, but failed to revive profitability.

Table 1.5 The growth of real wages (total economy, average annual percentage change)

	1960–73	1973–79	1979–90	1990–2000
US (per hour)	2.8	0.3	0.4	1.1
Japan (per person)	7.7	2.8	1.6	0.5
Germany (per person)	5.4	2.5	1.0	0.95
EU-11 (per person)	5.6	2.8	0.8	0.6

Source: 'Statistical Annex', European Economy, no. 71, 2001, Table 31.

Table 1.6 The growth of real social expenditures (average annual percentage change)

	1960–75	1975–80	1980–85
US	6.5	2.0	2.7
Germany	4.8	2.0	0.7
Japan	8.5	8.2	3.2
G-7	7.6	4.2	2.6

Sources: OECD, Social Expenditures 1960–89, Paris, 1985, p. 28; OECD, The Future of Social Protection, Paris, 1988, p. 11.

favour of capital did remarkably little to restore profit rates. Indeed, profitability failed to recover for the US, German, or the Japanese economies, or the G-7 economies taken in the aggregate, before some time in the 1990s, if then (see above, p. 19, Figure 1.1, and below, p. 39, Figure 1.3, and p. 41, Figure 1.4). The question, of course, is why?

International manufacturing at an impasse: worsening over-capacity, US counter-offensive, and the failure of Keynesianism, 1973–79

In view of its origins in over-capacity and over-production in international manufacturing industries, it might have been predicted that the decline of profitability would be easily transcended, especially in light of employers' success in cutting real wage and social spending growth. According to standard economic expectations, firms would thus naturally have responded to reduced profit rates stemming from intensified competition by reallocating means of production out of over-supplied lines into new ones, where potential profitability was higher. But, as it turned out, such a standard process of adjustment failed to take effect.

On the one hand, manufacturers across the advanced capitalist economies concluded that their most promising strategy in the face of the downward pressure on prices that resulted from too much output in their industries was to stand and fight rather than switch. In possession of huge masses of fixed capital that they had already paid for, they had every incentive to continue in their lines, even despite the reduction of the rate of profit on their total assets, so long as they could continue to make at least the average rate of profit on their further expenditures on variable capital (wages, raw materials, and intermediate goods). Beyond their sunk tangible capital (which would, of course, eventually be used up), they also held large quantities of hard-won 'proprietary' assets that, by definition, could not be transferred to other industries. These included not only long-established relations with suppliers and customers, but, above all, technological knowledge built up over many years in the business. Their best hope for maximizing profits seemed therefore to be to accelerate technical change by way of stepped-up investment in their own industries, rather than to reallocate capital to new ones.

On the other hand, even despite the crowding that prevailed internationally in many manufacturing lines, emergent low-cost producers based in still later developing regions found that they could profitably enter. They therefore ended up adding more and cheaper goods to many already over-supplied manufacturing lines, with the result that downward pressure on prices and profitability was further intensified. There was, in short, not only too little exit, but too much entry.

In the wake of the sharp fall in manufacturing profit rates that introduced the epochal shift from long expansion to long stagnation for the world economy, the US government over the course of the 1970s, and beyond, made great efforts to assist domestic producers to respond to the intensified international competition that had compressed their rates of return. In the context of what was, of necessity, an increasingly zero-sum game, dictated by the deceleration of the world market, it sought in particular to shift the costs of the system-wide slowdown to US manufacturers' overseas rivals. In August 1971, the Nixon administration closed the gold window, ending dollar convertibility. In February 1973, it forced the world economy to give up the Bretton Woods system of pegged exchange rates, and go to the float. Meanwhile, between 1970 and 1973, it resorted to ultra-expansionary monetary policy not only to stimulate the economy, but also to push down the value of the dollar.

By thus reneging on the US's obligation to convert dollars into gold and moving to floating exchange rates, Nixon freed the US government from the requirement to reduce its overseas deficits by deflating the economy in order to decrease imports and increase exports so as to hold the dollar at its assigned value. He thereby enabled it to pursue, untrammelled, expansionary monetary and Keynesian budget deficit policies aimed, at one and the same time, at stimulating domestic growth, devaluing the dollar in aid of manufacturing competitiveness, and depreciating the 'dollar overhang', the dollar reserves held abroad by foreign governments and individuals.[14] The foregoing steps by the US government marked the turning point in what turned out to be a pivotal shift. Henceforth, the relatively high level of international economic cooperation that had been achieved against the background of the great post-war economic expansion would increasingly give way to intensifying international politico-economic conflict in the face of a much slower growing world economic pie, especially over the rules of the game for international investment, trade, and money.

As part of the same process by which it ended dollar convertibility and forced the world economy to adopt floating exchange rates, the US government also put paid to the plans of its allies and rivals to strengthen national capital controls as part of a broader effort to revive pegged exchange rates and a Bretton Woods-type framework. US policy-makers saw the free mobility of both short and long-term investment as a top

---

[14] R. Parboni, *The Dollar and its Rivals*, London, Verso, 1981.

priority, for, in their eyes, it would provide a critical prop for the macroeconomic programme that they intended to implement. Speculative capital flows away from the dollar would force the further revaluation of the currencies of those of its rivals and partners that insisted on running current account surpluses, just as they had during the world money crisis of 1969–73. Currency revaluation, by reducing their competitiveness and by making their exports more difficult, would create, in turn, powerful pressures on those same rivals and partners to adopt expansionary mac-roeconomic policies that would facilitate higher US exports. Flows of funds in the opposite direction, into US capital markets, would, mean-while, allow the US to cover the ever higher budget deficits through which its government intended to stimulate the economy, as well as the rising current account surpluses that would inevitably result.

It was precisely because they wished to prevent the US from exploiting the dollar standard to inflate the US economy, run ever higher federal and current account deficits, and drive down the dollar that the other leading capitalist states, led by Germany, France, and Japan, sought through painstaking negotiations between 1972 and 1974 to secure a return to a system pegged exchange rates, to be buttressed by controls over the mobility of capital that would be made more effective by cooperative, international enforcement. But, while moving to end its own temporary capital controls in 1973–74, the US quashed its allies' and rivals' efforts to strengthen their own simply by refusing to play along. The reality was that capital controls could never work if the US refused to help enforce them, especially given how great an outlet was the US capital market for the world's flow of funds.[15]

The US government sought increased mobility of capital not only to facilitate its plans for the domestic economy, but also to strengthen domestic financial interests. During the first post-war quarter century, it had for the most part given strong support to the internationalization of US banks, which had followed their leading customers, the great multinational corporations, in expanding overseas, in Europe and else-

---

[15] For this, and the previous paragraph, E. Helleiner, *States and the Reemergence of Global Finance. From Bretton Woods to the 1990s*, Ithaca, NY, Cornell University Press, 1994, pp. 111–15.

where. Over the same period, it had reluctantly tolerated the tight controls over capital movements exercised by its allies and rivals. But, during the first half of the 1960s, it had taken a decisive step to nurture the re-emergence of free international capital markets when it sanctioned the rise of the unregulated Eurodollar market in London. When the Nixon administration eliminated temporary capital controls in early 1974, it sought to further that same process, especially to aid leading New York banks, which had, since the mid-1960s, been orienting an ever greater part of their lending business overseas. To the same end, it simultaneously quashed the initiative of its allies to have the IMF organize the recycling of Arab oil surpluses, especially to hard-hit third-world economies. A handful of US and other international banks were thus enabled to gain private control over this process. They ended up channelling hundreds of billions of dollars to the governments of a small number of leading Less Developed Countries (LDCs) – such as Brazil, Mexico, and a few others – enabling them, for a time, to accelerate their industrializing efforts, but opening the way to the LDC debt crisis of the early 1980s.[16]

The foregoing US moves to freer capital movements and exchange rates were accompanied by a sharp turn to greater trade protection. In 1973, the US entered into the International Multi-Fiber Arrangement, which, in open defiance of the GATT principle of non-discrimination, placed strong restrictions on textiles and clothing that were imported from LDCs. This was followed by the Trade Act of 1974, which authorized the US Trade Representative, under Section 301, to take punitive action against countries the US found to be 'unfair' traders. In practice, Section 301 was used to force the US's trading partners to accept 'voluntary export restraints' (VERS) under threat of total banishment from the US market. Over the remainder of the 1970s, Presidents Ford and Carter continued the policy of incurring growing public deficits so as to increase demand and, by inviting inflation, to reduce real interest rates

---

[16] Ibid.; M. de Cecco, 'International Financial Markets and US Domestic Policy Since 1945', *International Affairs*, vol. iii, 1976; J.D. Aronson, *Money and Power. Banks and the World Monetary System*, Beverly Hills, Calif., Sage, 1977.

below zero and, above all, to pull down the value of the dollar a great deal further. Meanwhile, they applied Section 301 to defend the domestic market, especially by placing limits on the import of Japanese steel and autos.[17]

In this more favourable context of increasing government demand stimulus, declining absolute and relative costs, and increasingly protected markets, US manufacturers sought to invest their way out of their profitability crisis, maintaining their rate of capital accumulation fairly close to that of the 1960s, while reducing dividend payments out of profits and stepping up borrowing to do so. (At the same time, foreign producers, especially from Japan and Europe, sharply increased their direct investment in the US, encouraged to do so by a falling dollar that made their exports to the US market more expensive and made US assets and means of production cheaper.) By boosting expenditures on plant and equipment, US manufacturers were able to maintain the growth of productivity fairly well in the face of two oil crises, and this had a positive effect on their ability to export and, ultimately, on their profit rates. With the help of the fast-falling dollar, US producers maintained export growth at 1960s levels, even in the face of the slowdown of world trade. Nevertheless, despite a major improvement in their relative cost position in international terms, US manufacturers were unable to increase either their rates of profit or their share of world manufacturing export markets during the 1970s. This was largely because their counterparts overseas refused, in turn, to politely cede the field to their US rivals (see above, p. 20, Figure 1.2, and p. 21, Table 1.2).

US manufacturers' main international trading partners and rivals, especially in Germany and Japan, were badly hurt by the slowed growth of world trade that accompanied the onset of the long downturn, as well as by the fast-rising mark and yen that represented the flip-side of the declining dollar. The fall of the dollar not only reduced their international competitiveness with respect to their US rivals; it also effectively slowed the growth of what was for them the critical US domestic market.

---

[17] R. Gilpin, *The Challenge of Global Capitalism. The World Economy in the 21st Century*, Princeton, Princeton University Press, pp. 80–2.

Between 1968 and 1975, under the combined stress of currency revaluation, intensified competition, and finally the temporary collapse of world demand during the oil-embargo recession, the German and Japanese manufacturing sectors were forced to endure deep declines in profitability from which full recovery still has not occurred, as well as profound labour force reductions that would turn out to be permanent.

The fact remains that, with the help of supportive financiers and governments, US manufacturers' leading rivals in these places were able to fight successfully to retain their shares of world export markets. This they accomplished by accepting lower prices and lower profit rates. They thereby limited the gains that US producers could accrue by means of the decline of the dollar, aggravating in the process system-wide over-capacity and over-production. Although manufacturers in Japan, Germany, and elsewhere in western Europe were obliged to reduce their rates of capital accumulation significantly below those they had become accustomed to during the long post-war boom, they still sought as much as possible to invest and improve. Indeed, in Japan, manufacturing firms, with the collaboration of their associated banks and other members of their industrial groups (*keiretsu*), unleashed an extraordinary process of across-the-board industrial restructuring, which succeeded, before the decade was out, in transforming the focus of Japanese industry from the 'heavy', energy-intensive, and labour-intensive lines to high-technology energy-efficient lines that combined electronics and machinery ('mechatronics').

Even while manufacturers throughout the advanced capitalist world strained to defend their competitiveness and profit rates by continuing to produce what they had produced before only at a lower cost, producers based in a limited number of LDCs – most especially in East Asia, but also, during the 1970s, in such places as Mexico and Brazil – were able to rapidly increase their exports so as to profitably enter a restricted number of manufacturing lines. This they accomplished by combining relatively low wages and relatively advanced plant and equipment, aided in so doing by enormous loans to their governments from the great international banks. They thereby followed the example set by their Japanese predecessors during the 1950s and 1960s, and with analogous results system-wide. International competition in manufacturing was thus further intensified, exacerbating the problem of redundant production.[18]

In sum, system-wide over-capacity and over-production failed to be alleviated because firms across the international manufacturing sector ended up producing in aggregate more of what was already being produced, aggravating the initial problem of superfluous means of production. Over the course of the 1970s, profitability in the manufacturing sectors of the US, Germany, Japan, and the G-7 countries taken together thus fell further (as did that in their private business economies as whole), and the growth of manufacturing output, capital stock, and labour force for the most part declined in tandem (see above, p. 19, Figure 1.1, and below, p. 39, Figure 1.3). On the other hand, attesting once again to the fact that the source of the problem was to be found mainly in intensifying competition leading to over-accumulation in the manufacturing sector, profitability in the *non*-manufacturing sector of the G-7 economies taken in aggregate, benefiting especially from the sharp reduction of wage growth, was actually able to increase somewhat (see below, p. 41, Figure 1.4). As a consequence, non-manufacturing output, capital stock, and labour force growth were sustained, or rose (see Table 1.7).

In the face of the reduced investment growth that was the unavoidable result of falling profit rates, manufacturers in the G-7 economies taken together were unable to avoid a significant fall-off in the growth of productivity over the course of the 1970s – to 3.8 per cent between 1973 and 1979, compared to 5.2 per cent between 1960 and 1973.[19] They were therefore obliged to press all the harder to reduce real wage and social spending growth in aid of defending profits. A major secular slowdown in the growth of investment plus consumption, thus aggregate private demand, was the unavoidable outcome. The latter was accompanied by a tendency to ever-deeper recessions, for, in the presence of reduced average rates of profit, an increased number of firms found themselves on the edge of bankruptcy, vulnerable to shocks. Major jumps in the price of

---

[18] For this, and the previous two paragraphs, Brenner, 'Economics of Global Turbulence', pp. 149–50, 167–72, 173–8.
[19] OECD, *Historical Statistics 1960–95*, Paris, 1997, p. 54, Table 3.10.

Table 1.7 G-7 manufacturing and non-manufacturing sectors on diverging paths (average annual percentage change)

	1960–73	1973–79	1979–89/90
Gross stock			
Manufacturing	5.5	3.8	3.25
Non-manufacturing	4.5	4.5	4.3
Gross output			
Manufacturing	6.4	2.5	2.1
Services	5.2	6.5	3.0
Labour force			
Manufacturing	1.3	0.3	– 1.2
Services	2.4	2.6	2.2

Sources: OECD, *Historical Statistics 1960–95*, Paris, 1997, pp. 32–3, 52, Tables 1.10, 1.11, 3.5, and 3.6; Armstrong *et al.*, *Capitalism Since 1945*, pp. 355, 356, Tables a5, a6.

oil were thus able to precipitate serious recessions in 1974–75 and again in 1979–80 (whereas oil and raw material increases of a similar magnitude had been easily absorbed during the boom time of the early 1950s).[20]

It was only the turn to large-scale Keynesian federal deficits, accommodated by easy credit, that made possible the subsidies to demand that enabled the advanced capitalist economies to transcend the oil crisis recession of 1974–75 and to continue to expand during the remainder of the decade. As it would for the next two decades, the massive growth of debt – especially public debt, which enabled parallel increases in private borrowing – constituted the indispensable key to international economic stability and expansion. Since only the US government was able, and willing, to sustain the ever larger budget deficits that turned out to be necessary – and the increased current account deficits that accompanied them – it was only US government borrowing that kept the world economy afloat during the following extended period of reduced private profitability and capital accumulation.

[20] J. Eatwell and L. Taylor, *Global Finance at Risk*, New York, Norton, 2000, pp. 106–7.

Nevertheless, the resort to Keynesian stimuli proved to be profoundly ambivalent in its effects. The subsidy to demand was unquestionably necessary to sustain growth on an international scale. But, by increasing demand, deficit spending and easy credit allowed many high-cost, low-profit manufacturers to continue in business and maintain positions that might otherwise have been eventually occupied by lower-cost, higher-profit producers. In this respect Keynesian remedies helped to perpetuate over-capacity and over-production, preventing the harsh medicine of shakeout, indeed depression, that historically had cleared the way for new upturns.

Moreover, given their low surpluses, firms with low rates of return could hardly undertake much capital investment or expansion. On the contrary, in response to any given increase in aggregate demand resulting from Keynesian policies, firms were rendered unable and unwilling, as a consequence of their reduced profit rates, to bring about as great an increase in supply as in the past when profit rates were higher. There was therefore 'less bang for the buck', with the result that the ever-increasing public deficits of the 1970s brought about not so much increases in *output* as rises in *prices*.

By the end of the 1970s, the manufacturing sector on an international scale was at an impasse, as was the Keynesian programme of demand management that had been implemented to revitalize the world economy. Ever greater government stimulus had been unable to prevent the further fall of manufacturing profitability *system-wide*. Meanwhile, the US macro-policy of federal deficits, extreme monetary ease, and 'benign neglect' with respect to the dollar's exchange rate – which had been designed to restore US manufacturing competitiveness and profitability – had brought not only runaway inflation, but also ever-increasing, record-breaking current account deficits. By 1977–78, the latter precipitated a devastating run on the US currency that threatened the dollar's position as an international reserve currency. The path was thus cleared for a major change of perspective.

The US had come up against the limit of its ability to take advantage of the dollar's role as key currency by running ever greater federal and current account deficits and devaluing, so as to achieve increased economic expansion and manufacturing competitiveness. It had done so precisely by endangering the dollar's very position as key currency and the international financial structure based upon it. Almost unbelievably, it was now the US economy that was obliged to accept a programme of 'stabilization', and the result was something of a revolution. The governments of the advanced capital world now turned to monetarist tight credit and so-called 'supply-side' measures aimed at cutting costs further. Since the debt-based subsidy to demand that had been keeping the world economy turning over was now suspended, a new deep recession was unavoidable.

The noose tightens: rising real interest rates, the slowed growth of aggregate demand, and the shift toward finance, 1979-90

The shift to Reaganism/Thatcherism throughout the advanced capitalist economies from the end of the 1970s brought unprecedentedly tight credit, as well as unparalleled austerity under the banner of 'supply-side economics'. It was intended, most generally, to raise profitability by further raising unemployment so as to dampen the growth of wages, as well as by directly redistributing income to capital through reduced taxes on corporations and diminished spending on social services. But it was designed, more particularly, to relieve the surfeit of capacity and production in manufacturing by provoking a purge of that great ledge of high-cost, low-profit manufacturing firms that had been sustained by the Keynesian expansion of credit, while clearing a channel to the profitable expansion of the low-productivity service sector by further reducing employee compensation. It was aimed, finally, at bringing about a revitalization of, and thereby shift into, domestic and international financial sectors – which had been hard hit during the 1970s by accelerating price increases and a plethora of loanable funds – by means of suppressing inflation, as well as rapid moves toward deregulation, especially the elimination of capital controls. It should be emphasized that, by this juncture, the control of prices was a priority not only for lenders, but also for manufacturers, who, just about everywhere, faced ever-intensifying international competition; in this respect, finance and manufacturing found common ground.

Nevertheless, the implementation of what might be termed pure monetarism turned out to be incompatible with the maintenance of even a modicum of economic stability. Starting in 1979–80, the imposition of record-high real interest rates brought about the worst recession since the 1930s and began to induce that large-scale shakeout of high-cost, low-profit means of production in manufacturing that was desired by the authorities and required to restore profitability. But by summer 1982, sharply restricted credit and a rising dollar had detonated the Latin American debt crisis, which, by endangering the solvency of some of the world's leading international banks, threatened to precipitate a worldwide crash, starting in the US. There was really no choice but to bring back Keynesianism with a vengeance, an outcome that had already fortuitously been assured, despite campaign rhetoric to the contrary, by Ronald Reagan's plan for cutting taxes and increasing expenditures on the military. Once again, the US would serve as market of last resort for the world economy.

The Reagan administration, as well as the Bush administration that followed it, thus implemented a monumental programme of military spending and tax reduction for the rich, and this partly offset the ravages of monetarist tight credit and kept the economy ticking over. The ensuing record federal deficits, and the unprecedented trade and current account deficits that accompanied them, proved indispensable, as had their predecessors of 1970s, in providing the injections of demand that were needed not only to pull the world economy out of the recession of 1979–82, but also to steer growth forward at home and abroad through the remainder of the decade in the face of what turned out to be the worsening stagnation of private capital accumulation. This was all the more the case since, from this point onward, most of the rest of the world increasingly eschewed Keynesian public deficits.

Manufacturing

The Reagan–Bush essay in Keynesianism, like those of the 1970s, did, then, bring about a new and lengthy cyclical upturn. But it could do little to restart dynamic capital accumulation, as it was unable to address the underlying problem of profitability. This was because the very step-up of government borrowing that headed off depression and kept the world economy turning over also slowed that major shakeout of high-cost, low-profit means of production that was required to restore the manufacturing profit rate. The mix, moreover, of record federal deficits and still restrictive monetary policy – which reflected the system's inability at this point to dispense with stabilizing Keynesian deficits – forced up real interest rates system-wide to historically unmatched levels. Firms in the US, and across the advanced capitalist world, did slough off great masses of redundant and obsolete manufacturing means of production, especially during the extended recession of the first part of the decade, pushing up profits through increasing productivity. This process of rationalization, as well as the further reduction in manufacturing investment growth that accompanied it, did, moreover, make for sharply rising unemployment, which further reduced wage growth and again raised profits. Still, this very real shakeout was, to a significant degree, counteracted by Asian producers' epoch-making entry into the world market. Between 1965 and 1990, the four East Asian Newly Industrialized Countries (NICs) increased their combined share of the world goods exports from 1.2 per cent to 6.4 per cent, matching Japan's performance in this respect between 1950 and 1975. By 1990, non-Japanese (non-OPEC) Asia held 13.1 per cent of world goods exports, a greater proportion than the US (11.7 per cent), Germany (12.7 per cent), or Japan (8.5 per cent). The advanced capitalist economies thus remained burdened throughout the decade by manufacturing over-capacity and over-production – made worse by record-high real interest rates – and thus mired in what turned out to be largely zero-sum struggles for over-supplied manufacturing markets.

The problem of over-capacity and over-production in the international manufacturing sector manifested itself at the start of the 1980s in the enormous haemorrhaging of manufacturing jobs that took place across the advanced capitalist economies. It continued to manifest itself throughout the decade, and indeed the one that followed, in the persistence of a kind of hydraulic dynamic in which the German and Japanese manufacturing sectors had difficulty in improving their profitability except at the expense of their US counterparts, and vice versa. It is true, and of fundamental importance, that, from the middle of the 1980s, after decades spent largely on the defensive, the US manufacturing sector did begin to turn the tables on its competitors in Japan, Germany, and the rest of western Europe and to secure ever higher rates of profit. But it did so, as shall be seen, largely by means of a declining dollar, exceptionally slow wage growth, and the shakeout of redundant means of production, while bringing about precious little increase in either investment or consumer demand (before 1994). As a result, it contributed little to the growth of the international economic pie, with the result that US gains in manufacturing profitability were achieved to a large extent at the expense of German and Japanese manufacturing.

Even by the end of the decade, despite further sharp reductions in the growth of compensation and social spending everywhere, neither for manufacturing, nor for the economy as a whole, had pre-tax profit rates in the US, Germany, Japan, or in the G-7 economies taken together risen above their already quite stunted magnitudes of the late 1970s, even though they did transcend the rock-bottom levels of the early 1980s (see Figure 1.3; also above, p. 19, Figure 1.1, and below, p. 41, Figure 1.4). To make matters much worse, counterbalancing a good part the limited rise of profitability that had taken place, real interest rates were still quite a few points above their level throughout the whole of the 1970s, when they had gone below zero. With investment growth plummeting in response to reduced rates of return, the advanced capitalist economies were left to depend heavily for their expansion upon 'external' subsidies to demand by means of public deficit spending, above all by the US government, or temporary financial bubbles and their associated 'wealth effect'.

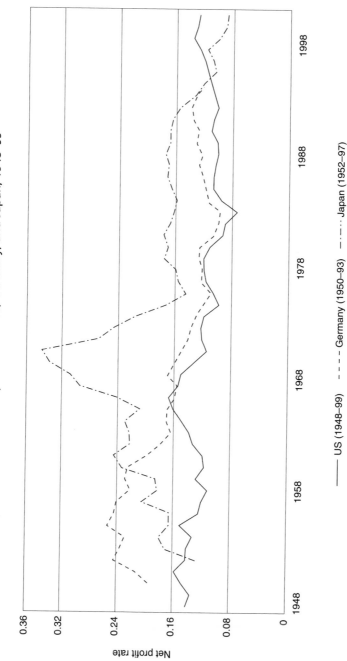

Figure 1.3 Business net profit rates: US, Germany, and Japan, 1948–99

Non-manufacturing

In the face of much reduced opportunities for profitable investment in manufacturing, there was, from the start of the 1980s, a sharp lurch toward the service sector. But this was strictly limited by the reduction in the growth of aggregate demand that resulted throughout the decade from the fall-off of manufacturing investment growth, the stagnation of wage growth, burgeoning unemployment (which in Europe reached figures reminiscent of the 1930s), and the reduction of government spending growth outside the US. Nowhere was it easy to secure decent rates of return. The degree to which the non-manufacturing sector could grow across the advanced capitalist world thus varied with the degree to which wages could be held down and government expenditures could be maintained: it expanded rapidly in the US, where unionization in services was just about non-existent and Keynesian deficits mushroomed, but very little in places like Germany, where union power prevented the proliferation of low-wage employment and the government remained committed to balanced budgets.[21] It is notable that neither outside manufacturing nor within it was there much of that expansion of new technology that would become such a prominent feature of the next decade's economy.

During the 1980s, the non-manufacturing profit rate for the G-7 economies taken together rose only slightly above its levels of the 1970s – remaining far below its levels of the post-war long boom – and the growth of non-manufacturing output, capital stock, and employment all fell to a greater or lesser extent (see Figure 1.4; also above, p. 33, Table 1.7). All told, economic growth in the 1980s was slower than in the oil-crisis-plagued 1970s (see below, p. 47, Table 1.10).

Finance

In response to the impasse of the international manufacturing sector at the end of the 1970s, resulting from the deepening of the crisis of

---

[21] See, for example, M.C. Burda and J.D. Sachs, 'Assessing High Unemployment in West Germany', *The World Economy*, vol. xi, no. 4, 1988.

Figure 1.4 G-7 manufacturing and non-manufacturing net profit rates, 1952–90

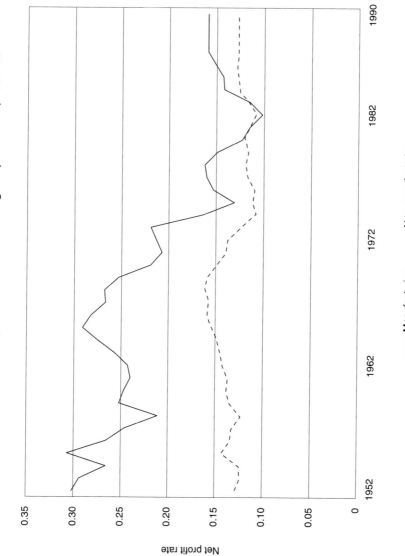

profitability throughout the previous decade, governments across the advanced capitalist economies sought to ease entry into financial activities and pave the way for higher returns. To do so, they initiated not only a permanent war against inflation, but also a far-reaching process of financial deregulation. Interest-rate ceilings and the like were cast away. Restrictions on cross-market access for financial institutions were scrapped. Capital controls were, almost everywhere, eventually eliminated. Even so, given how low was the average rate of profit throughout the real economy, profit-making, either through lending to private entities or through speculation, was no easy task – and securing high returns generally carried high risks.

The upshot was the return of financial cycles, which issued again and again in financial crises. These had been largely suppressed during the first three decades of the post-war epoch by systems of regulation that strait-jacketed financial institutions in terms of function and geographical area and restricted capital mobility (although even by the end of the 1960s, the latter were beginning to weaken under the impact of the rapidly expanding Eurodollar market). But with the unshackling of finance, the world economy was once again gripped by one credit-based speculative boom after another, issuing inevitably in devastating crashes.[22]

From the start of the 1980s, huge financial bubbles thus blew up all across the advanced capitalist economies, especially on the stock market, in mergers and acquisitions, and in commercial real estate, as speculative demand drove up asset values, as investors, in one line after another, made their purchases on the expectation that, having risen in the past, asset values would continue to rise in the future. But the outcome was mainly the unprecedented escalation of indebtedness on the part of non-financial corporations, which spent hundreds of billions of borrowed dollars on leveraged buyouts and the re-purchase of their own shares, and ever greater financial fragility on the part of banks, which largely financed

---

[22] Bank of International Settlements, *71st Annual Report, 1 April 2000–31 March 2001*, Basel, 11 June 2001, pp. 123–4. 'When financial systems were heavily regulated and central banks focused on controlling the monetary or credit aggregates [before the 1980s], the scope for damaging financial cycles was constrained. . . . [S]uch regulated environments . . . were less prone to the large cyclical swings seen in today's more liberalized environment.'

the speculative waves. In 1987, US equity markets crashed, severely shaking the system. But the flood of money that was then let loose by the leading capitalist governments to restore stability was heavily used to finance one last speculative fling. The climax came at the end of the 1980s and early 1990s, when governments in the US, Japan, and Germany successively took deflationary measures to rein in their respective financial expansions and thereby precipitated an explosion of bank failures and financial crises throughout the advanced capitalist world of an intensity not seen for almost sixty years, which very much exacerbated the recessions that immediately followed.

From investment-driven, export-oriented growth to international economic instability in the 1990s

With the new onset of recession internationally in the early 1990s, the world economy faced a deadlock. Another round of major US deficits appeared to be required to catalyse a new cyclical upturn domestically and internationally. Increasing US public deficits had, after all, been indispensable, not only to drag the world economy out of every international cyclical downturn since the start of the 1970s, but also to keep it growing between recessions, in the face of the slowed growth of private investment. But, given the enormous build-up of debt during the 1980s, a new spate of public borrowing threatened to precipitate a devastating credit crunch long before it generated a new cyclical upturn. In 1993, led in financial matters by its new economic czar, Robert Rubin, former CEO at Goldman Sachs, the Clinton administration shifted decisively toward balancing the budget and, in a sense, thereby completed the shift to monetarist austerity begun more than a decade previously.

The US's move to fiscal probity was of historic significance, because it eliminated what had hitherto constituted the most important counter-tendency to the contractionary trend unleashed in the late 1960s and early 1970s and exacerbated by the international turn to tight credit and increased austerity at the start of the 1980s: this was the sustained commitment of the US government to large-scale federal deficits, accom-

Table 1.8 The growth of real government final consumption expenditures (average annual percentage change)

	1960–73	1973–79	1979–89	1989–95
US	2.3	1.7	2.5	0.1
Japan	5.9	4.9	2.7	2.0
Germany	4.5	3.0	1.3	1.8
G-7	3.2	2.4	2.2	0.9

Source: OECD, *Historical Statistics 1960–95*, p. 61. The G-7 and US figures for the 1980s are inflated by the huge increase in US military expenditure in that decade.

panied by unparalleled trade and current account deficits. During most of the 1980s, the advanced capitalist economies outside the US had seen not only the imposition of tight money and progressively restricted wage growth, but also the slowed increase of government spending in the interest of reducing costs and raising profitability. But, by means of the Reagan–Bush version of military Keynesianism for the rich, the US government virtually single-handedly prevented the ever more bitter international austerity campaign from taking full effect, largely compensating through its increased growth of expenditures and its deficits for the reductions in the growth of government expenditures and deficits taking place almost everywhere else. When, in the early 1990s, the US, too, joined the international consensus behind fiscal as well as monetary constriction – at the very time when Europe was further tightening the noose both on the supply of credit and on the growth of state expenditures in preparation for monetary union – it put a further major brake on the growth of aggregate demand across the international economic system, while snuffing out its major source of stability (see Table 1.8).

The capitalist world economy was now obliged to begin to operate on an altered basis, one fraught with dangers. With the growth of government expenditures secularly declining, employment stagnant or falling, and wage growth plummeting, what had been standard sources of aggregate demand were increasingly enfeebled. It was therefore left to the growth of private investment, amplified by the increase of private debt, to drive the system forward virtually on its own. Nevertheless, to the degree that the international economy came to depend ever more exclusively on private investment and relinquished the source of stability hitherto provided by discretionary government spending, it became that much more urgently dependent upon the revival of profitability. Yet, during the first half of the 1990s, it was far from evident that profit rates had achieved a sufficient recovery system-wide to ignite a new boom in investment, especially in the manufacturing sectors of the big three economies that essentially drove the world economy. In the absence of such a recovery, firms across wide swathes of the system tended to attempt to restore their profit rates by means of shakeout, downsizing, and the suppression of wage growth, rather than through seeking increased productivity growth by means of capital accumulation. Their doing so not only made for further stagnation and deepening recession, but risked detonating a downward spiral in which declining investment demand fed upon itself.

To make matters more difficult, since domestic purchasing power was growing in such a sluggish manner, producers everywhere had little choice but to ratchet up their orientation to exports even further. During the 1990s, the ratio of the growth of exports to the growth of GDP reached its highest point during the post-war epoch (see Table 1.9). But, since manufacturers were thus for the most part simply directing a greater proportion of what they had already been producing toward the world market compared to the domestic market, the aggregate result could only be a further clogging of the system's arteries with redundant capacity, and an increased risk of serious crisis. In this situation, the struggle for export markets assumed an ever more central place, but perforce took on an increasingly destructive character, which continued to manifest itself in a slowly developing chain reaction in which sharply rising exchange rates swung one group of economies after another from manufacturing expansion to manufacturing crisis, sometimes accompanied by financial bubbles.

In the context of the already-existing surfeit of manufacturing capacity and production, the successive turns to credit tightening by the US, Japanese, and German governments between 1989 and 1991, plus the refusal of the US government to provide the accustomed fiscal stimulus, plunged the Japanese and western European economies into their worst

Table 1.9 Exports accelerate as output stagnates (average annual percentage change)

	1960–73	1973–79	1979–90	1990–97
OECD real exports (goods)	9.1	5.7	4.9	6.7
OECD real GDP	4.9	2.8	2.6	2.4
Ratio of exports to output	1.85	2.0	1.9	2.8

Source: OECD, *Economic Outlook*, no. 64, pp. A4 and A43, Tables 1 and 39.

recessions of the post-war epoch, while the US economy sustained a 'jobless recovery'. In fact, during the first half of 1990s, all three great capitalist economic blocs experienced their poorest economic performances by any standard measure for any five-year period since 1945 (see Table 1.10). The economies of East Asia, practically alone, did prosper in this period. But since their success was once again achieved through the breathtakingly rapid appropriation of still another huge chunk of the international market – Asia (excluding Japan) raised its share of world exports from 11.7 per cent in 1990 to 16.4 per cent in 1995 – it almost certainly exacerbated the underlying problem of too much manufacturing productive power system-wide. It is true that the ever more hesitant growth of aggregate demand in these years did much to accelerate that evacuation of high-cost, low-profit means of production that was so indispensable for the recovery of manufacturing profitability system-wide. It is also true that, precisely on the basis of wave after wave of shakeout, as well as the extreme repression of wage growth and big tax breaks for the corporations, the US manufacturing sector did make significant strides toward reviving its long-depressed profit rate and thereby investment growth, even while its counterparts in Japan and western Europe languished. The fact remains, however, that, even by mid-decade, there was little evidence that the advanced capitalist world had overcome its over-supply of manufacturing means of production and transcended the long downturn.

Table 1.10   Declining economic dynamism (average annual percentage change)

	1960–69	1969–79	1979–90	1990–95	1995–2000	1990–2000
GDP						
US	4.6	3.3	2.9	2.4	4.1	3.2
Japan	10.2	5.2	4.6	1.7	0.8	1.3
Germany	4.4	3.6	2.15	2.0	1.7	1.9
Euro-12	5.3	3.7	2.4	1.6	2.5	2.0
G-7	5.1	3.6	3.0	2.5	1.9	3.1
GDP per capita						
US	3.3	2.5	1.9	1.3	3.4	2.35
Japan	9.0	3.4	4.0	1.1	1.1	1.1
Germany	3.5	2.8	1.9	7.0	1.6	4.3
G-7	3.8*	2.1†	1.9	1.2	2.5	1.8
Labour productivity total economy (GDP/worker)						
US	2.5	1.3	1.15	1.2	2.3	1.8
Japan	8.6	4.4	3.0	0.7	1.2	0.9
Germany	4.3	3.0	1.5	2.1	1.2	1.7
Euro-11	5.2	3.2	1.9	1.9	1.3	1.6
G-7	4.8*	2.8†	2.55	1.7		
Real compensation total economy (per employee)						
US	9.7	2.7	0.7	0.6	1.9	1.3
Japan	7.3	5.0	1.6	0.6	0.2	0.5
Germany	5.1	4.3	1.1	2.0	0.1	0.95
Euro-11	5.6	4.0	0.8	1.0	0.3	0.6
Unemployment rate						
US	4.8	6.2	7.1	5.9	4.6	5.25
Japan	1.4	1.7	2.5	2.9	4.1	3.5
Germany	0.8	2.05	5.8	8.2	8.6	8.2
Euro-15	2.3	4.6	9.1	9.8	9.9	9.9
G-7	3.1*	4.9†	6.8	6.7	6.4	6.6
Non-residential capital stock (private business economy)						
US (net)	3.9	3.8	3.0	2.0	3.8	2.9
Japan (gross)	11.3	9.5	6.9	5.3	4.5	5.0
Germany (gross)	6.6	4.5	3.0	3.0	3.1‡	
G-7 (gross)	4.8	4.6	3.9			

* 1960–73   † 1973–79   ‡ 1990–93

Sources: OECD, *Historical Statistics, 1960–1995*, Paris, 1995, Table 2.15, 3.1, 3.2: 'Statistical Annex', *European Economy*, no. 71, 2000, Tables 11, 31, 32; OECD, *Economic Outlook*, no. 67, 2001, Annex, Table 21; IMF, *World Economic Outlook*, Washington, DC, May 2001, Database, Tables 1 and 4; Armstrong *et al*, *Capitalism Since 1945*, p. 356, Table A6.

CHAPTER 2

AMERICAN ECONOMIC REVIVAL

The US economy forged a major recovery against the background of ongoing international stagnation. Over the course of the 1980s and 1990s, a reversal of the pattern of uneven development that had hitherto marked the evolution of the world economy thus began to take place. During the first two post-war decades, manufacturers in Japan, Germany, and elsewhere in western Europe had achieved declining relative costs internationally and imposed ever greater competitive stress on their rivals in the US. But following the collapse of the Bretton Woods system between 1971 and 1973, and especially from the middle of the 1980s, a certain swapping of positions took place. The US manufacturing sector began at that point to enjoy a series of major cost advantages and to turn the tables on its rivals, vastly improving its competitive position and sharply increasing its export growth. In large part on that basis, starting in late 1993, it came to evince a new dynamism and to stimulate a broader revival in the US private economy as a whole. Just as the fall, and continuing depression, of the manufacturing profit rate had brought about the long downturn in the US and internationally, a rising manufacturing profit rate in the US underpinned a US economic recovery – although its effects on the international economy as a whole were far more ambivalent.

The recovery in the US manufacturing sector, and the US economy as a whole, was anything but straightforward. By the start of the 1980s, the attempt of US manufacturers during the 1970s to invest their way out of their problems with the help of the government's deficit spending, cheap money, and dollar devaluation policies had failed dismally. The US manufacturing sector could no longer avoid a profound crisis, which began in 1979–80 and reflected deeply depressed profit rates, ultimately resulting from international over-capacity and over-production. Masses of high-cost, low-profit means of production were eliminated over the course of the following half decade. This was mainly the effect of Volcker's high interest rates and recession, as well as the high dollar that accompanied them, but it was also the result of the conscious efforts of frustrated shareholders and financial entrepreneurs to plunder corporate assets, while attempting to drive up the value of corporate equity prices – especially by way of the huge movement toward mergers and buyouts made possible by the greatest binge of corporate borrowing in US history.

The manufacturing sector could thus launch its recovery in earnest only from 1985. At this point, the US government – initially with the help of Japan and Germany, but ultimately despite their resistance – set off a decade-long, deep fall of the dollar, which was accompanied by ten years in which real wage growth was held by employers almost to zero. Rates of taxation on corporations had already been drastically reduced in 1981. A major increase in US international competitiveness and a dramatically increased orientation of the US manufacturing sector toward exports was thereby facilitated, which enabled US manufacturers to launch an extended and decisive process of profitability recovery. Even then, manufacturing corporations had to pay a heavy price for their financial obsessions and excesses over the course of the 1980s. They were little able to raise the rate of growth of investment and suffered a serious debt crisis that considerably slowed their emergence from the recession of 1990–91. However, having weathered that storm with major assistance from Alan Greenspan and the Fed, the US manufacturing sector, from the latter part of 1993, entered into a period of prosperity and growth greater than any it had experienced since the early 1960s.

THE ROCKY ROAD TO PROFITABILITY RECOVERY
IN THE US NON-FINANCIAL ECONOMY

The crisis of manufacturing

The process of manufacturing revival found its roots in the deep recession of the early 1980s, which was not really transcended till after the middle of the decade. This ushered in an extended period, on the one hand, of brutal industrial rationalization, and, on the other, of sharply declining real wage growth, accompanied by major government-sponsored reductions of corporate taxation. The elimination of redundant high-cost, low-profit means of production and the large-scale redistribution of income from labour to capital that resulted were necessary preconditions for the recovery of international competitiveness and of profitability. But these were in themselves quite insufficient to power a recovery of a manufacturing sector confronting saturation of capacity and production, and shrunken growth of demand more generally, on an international scale.

Under the impact of Volcker's unprecedented tightening of credit between 1979 and 1982, interest rates in real terms rocketed from -2 per cent in 1979 to an average of 7.5 per cent between 1981 and 1985, the highest for any four-year period during the twentieth century. The resulting collapse of demand delivered a decisive shock to the manufacturing sector, setting it on a new trajectory, as massive means of production were disgorged by means of an explosion of business failures and layoffs on a scale unmatched since the 1930s and the parallel shedding of unprofitable plant and equipment. Between 1979 and 1982, manufacturing output decreased by 10 per cent, manufacturing investment fell by 8 per cent (and another 15 per cent in 1983), and capacity utilization thudded to a post-war low. Simultaneously, manufacturing employment (measured in hours), which had managed to continue to grow all through the 1970s to reach a post-war high in 1979, shrivelled by a shocking 13 per cent, as unemployment also reached a post-war high of over 11 per cent in 1982. The economy now paid the price for its success in fending off business failures during the Keynesian 1970s. By 1982, the annual bankruptcy rate was at its highest level since the depression, and it continued to arch sharply upwards beyond the middle of the decade (see Figure 2.1).[1] Even by 1989, the manufacturing labour force still remained almost 5 per cent below its 1979 level, and would be compressed once again during a new phase of industrial shakeout in the early 1990s.

With unemployment rising so sharply, workers found themselves all the more vulnerable to the rising assaults of employers, backed ever more directly by the government. An initial turning point came in 1980, when the Carter administration imposed major concessions on autoworkers at Chrysler as the condition for its bailout of that corporation. Not long thereafter, in 1981, the Reagan administration delivered the *coup de grâce* to the US labour movement when it dismissed striking members of the Professional Air Traffic Controllers union (PATCO). Henceforth unionization drives dwindled into insignificance, unfair labour practices committed by management during organizing drives pullulated, and union density collapsed. At 38.8 per cent as recently as 1973 and 32.3 per cent in 1979, the proportion of the manufacturing labour force in unions fell to 20.6 per cent in 1990 and 17.6 per cent in 1995 (see Figure 2.2). Themselves under pressure from declining profit rates, manufacturers had already succeeded between 1973 and 1979 in reducing the average annual growth of real hourly wages to 1 per cent, compared to 2 per cent between 1960 and 1973. Between 1979 and 1995, it flopped to 0.65 per cent.[2]

As pressure on profits from wages lessened, stress on profits from taxes was also lifted. Tax cuts were, of course, the centrepiece of Reagan's supply-side revolution, and the reductions introduced were indeed radical. As a consequence of the legislation of the early 1980s and subsequently,

---

[1] Time series on the business failure rate and liabilities of failed businesses, 1950–97, were constructed by M. Naples and A. Arifaj. I am grateful to Michele Naples for making them available to me. Cf. Naples and Arifaj, 'The Rise in US Business Failures: Correcting the 1984 Discontinuity', *Contributions to Political Economy*, vol. 16, 1997, pp. 49–60.

[2] L. Troy and N. Sheflin, *MS Union Sourcebook. Membership, Finances, Structure, Directory*, West Orange, NJ, Industrial Relations and Information Service, 1985, Table 3.63; BLS, *Employment and Earnings*, vol. xliv, January 1997, p. 211. I wish to thank Mike Goldfield for passing on to me data on unfair labour practices, supplied by the US Department of Labor.

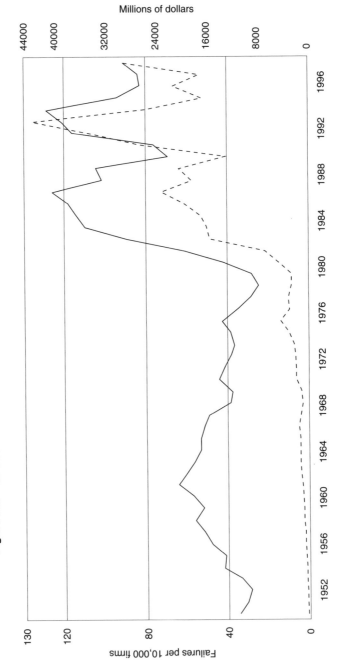

Figure 2.1 US business failure rate and liabilities of failed businesses, 1950–97

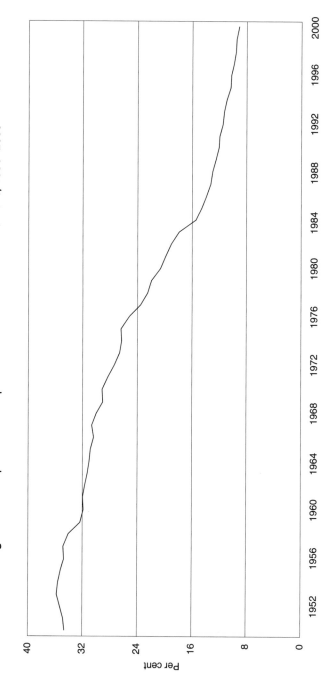

Figure 2.2 Proportion of US private sector labour force in unions, 1950–2000

corporate taxes as a proportion of manufacturing corporate profits dropped to just 28 per cent on average between 1981 and 1990, compared to 46 per cent on average between 1965 and 1981 (see Figure 2.3; also below, p. 72, Figure 2.10). When, beginning in 1981–82, the Reagan administration incurred unprecedented federal deficits in order to sustain record tax cuts and enormous increases in military spending, it was widely expected that already skyrocketing interest rates would go through the roof, sending the economy into a tailspin. But, with the encouragement of the Ministry of Finance, Japanese insurance companies and other institutions made huge advances to fund the US deficits, despite the high risks of future losses in the event of the devaluation of the dollar.[3] One thus witnessed the extraordinary spectacle of Japanese financiers providing the credit required by the US government to finance its budget deficits in order to subsidize the continuing growth of Japanese exports. US Keynesianism would thus ensure the expansion of the Japanese economy during the first half of the 1980s, but was itself made possible only by Japanese loans. It was difficult to determine who was more dependent upon whom – the US Treasury on Japanese lenders or Japanese manufacturers on US borrowers and their demand. What was clear, however, was the degree to which the two leading capitalist economies – and thus the world economy as a whole – were relying on the historically unprecedented growth of debt in the US and the willingness of the Japanese to help fund it.

Even despite the contributions of the Japanese, the elevated real interest rates that Volcker introduced in 1979–80 failed to fall very much during the following half decade (see below, p. 69, Figure 2.8). As a consequence, money poured into the US from all over the world. This was in keeping with the Reagan administration's desire to strengthen the US financial sector. But the outcome proved catastrophic for large sections of US manufacturing, because it naturally resulted in

---

[3] As Federal Reserve Chair Paul Volcker saw this development, '[T]he shortage of domestic savings was compensated in substantial part by an enormous inflow of mainly borrowed capital from abroad. That inflow was at one point at a greater rate than all the personal savings in the US and *turned out to be far larger than I had thought possible*' (emphasis added). Quoted in R.T. Murphy, *The Weight of the Yen*, New York, Norton, 1996, p. 148.

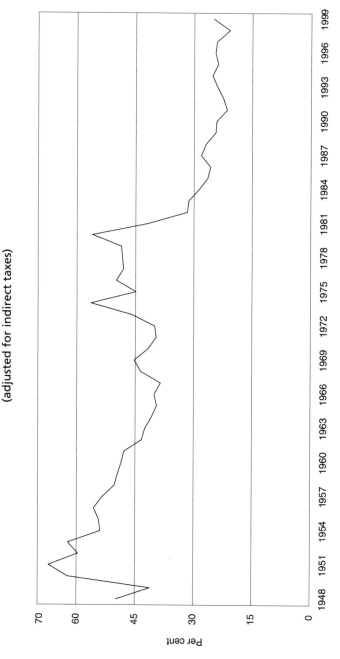

Figure 2.3 US manufacturing corporate taxes as per cent of corporate manufacturing profits, 1948–99 (adjusted for indirect taxes)

a surging dollar. Between 1978 and 1985, the real effective exchange rate of the dollar rose by 37 per cent, with the dollar's nominal value rising by 46.5 per cent and 15 per cent, respectively, against the mark and the yen in the same period (see below, p. 65, Figure 2.6, and p. 99, Figure 3.3). Already reeling from the record costs of borrowing and the sharp curtailment of demand, US manufacturers now faced unbearable competitive pressures from abroad, and their crisis deepened.

As late as 1981, the US current account was in surplus by $5 billion or 0.2 per cent of GDP, but by 1985, it was in deficit by $119 billion, a record 3 per cent of GDP (see below, p. 207, Figure 8.6). Almost the entirety of this negative turnaround was accounted for by the rise of the manufacturing trade deficit by $106 billion during the same four-year period. Between 1980 and 1985, the average annual growth of manufacturing exports collapsed to just 1 per cent (in nominal terms), while that of manufacturing imports leaped to 15 per cent and manufacturing import penetration climbed by close to one-third. Not only Japanese producers, but those from the East Asian Gang of Four, secured enormous increases in their share of the US import market, the Japanese quotient increasing from 12.5 per cent to 22.2 per cent of US imports between 1979 and 1986, the portion of the Gang of Four from 7.6 per cent to 15.3 per cent in the same period. Meanwhile, between 1981 and 1986, the US share of world goods exports dipped from 12.2 per cent to 10.5 per cent.

With the sacrifice of overseas sales growth and markets came a sharp fall in the rate of profit. By 1982, at the bottom of the cyclical downturn, the rate of profit in the manufacturing sector had fallen 43 per cent from its post-oil crisis peak of 1978, at which point it still remained about 20 per cent below its level of 1973, itself down 43.5 per cent from 1965. Even by 1986, after four years of cyclical recovery, the manufacturing profit rate still remained 23 per cent below its level of 1978. By contrast, the rate of profit outside of manufacturing, having fallen by 36 per cent, had bounced back to within 9 per cent of its level in 1978, and the reason is not far to seek. Unit labour costs between 1978 and 1986 grew much more rapidly in non-manufacturing than in manufacturing – as manufacturing labour productivity in these years grew at the average annual rate of 2.8 per cent, compared to just 0.4 per cent for non-manufacturing. But firms outside of manufacturing were able to compensate for their rising costs, and thereby to defend their profit rates, by increasing product prices at an average annual rate of 6.5 per cent, half again as fast as those in manufacturing. Manufacturers, by contrast, were clearly finding their margins squeezed between the rising costs in international terms that they had to incur due to the fast-rising dollar and downward price pressure emanating from overseas.

Under such unpromising conditions, it would have been futile for firms to seek to maintain, let alone increase, the growth of investment. Stockholders thus demanded draconian measures to eliminate high-cost, low-profit means of production in the interest of higher productivity, while also calling for major cutbacks in expenditures on new plant and equipment and research and development, so that the proceeds could be returned to themselves. In addition, they pushed for increased dividend payouts and/or more stock buybacks to force up share prices.

At the same time, encouraged by new tax breaks that ensured higher returns on unearned income and capital gains, by the looser enforcement of anti-trust laws, by the accelerating deregulation of the financial sector, and by the vulnerability of workers and suppliers, entrepreneurial speculators entered into implicit or explicit alliance with financiers, from whom they borrowed heavily, in order to purchase controlling interest in companies, with the goal of pillaging them. Under the euphemistic banner of 'increasing free cash flow', they sold off outmoded, inefficient means of production so as to increase productivity and accumulate funds, ran down capital stock and refrained from reinvesting the profits that accrued, and did everything possible to rearrange, if necessary unilaterally and by force, pre-existing relationships with employees, suppliers, and creditors so as to redistribute a greater share of total revenues to themselves. It need hardly be added that the unprecedented explosion of borrowing that made this all possible, which took corporate debt–equity ratios to historically unheard of levels, was for the purpose not of financing increased expenditures on plant and equipment, but of paying for share buybacks and mergers and acquisitions. Owners would presumably benefit from the forcing-up of asset values, financiers from the high interest rates on their loans.[4]

During the 1980s, dividends as a percentage of manufacturing corporate profits were raised by a third over their levels of the 1970s, having been cut back by a third during that decade from their levels of the first two post-war decades. At the same time, as a reflection of the increase in borrowing and the rise in interest rates, interest payments as a percentage of manufacturing pre-tax corporate profits (including interest) reached 26 per cent between 1982 and 1990, compared to 13 per cent between 1973 and 1979 and 1 per cent between 1950 and 1965. But only little of the borrowed money went to improve production. Between 1981 and 1989, of total funds borrowed by non-financial corporations, only 21 per cent was used for capital expenditures, which were for the most part covered out of cash flow (after-tax profits net of interest and dividends plus depreciation). By contrast, a full 50 per cent of the funds borrowed by non-financial corporations between 1983 and 1989 were used to finance net equity purchases.[5]

The paradoxical outcome was that, at the same time as borrowing and indebtedness by non-financial corporations reached its highest levels of the post-war epoch, investment by manufacturing corporations reached its lowest levels. Between 1983 and 1989, non-financial corporate borrowing as a proportion of non-financial corporate GDP averaged 8 per cent, compared to 5.5 per cent between 1973 and 1979, with the result that, by 1990, non-financial corporate debt as a proportion of non-financial GDP

---

[4] M.M. Blair, 'Financial Restructuring and the Debate about Corporate Governance', in M.M. Blair, ed., *The Deal Decade. What Takeovers and Leveraged Buyouts Mean for Corporate Governance*, Washington, DC, Brookings, 1993; J.R. Crotty and D. Goldstein, 'Do US Financial Markets Allocate Credit? The Case of Corporate Restructuring in the 1980s', in G. Dymski, G. Epstein, and R. Pollin, eds, *Transforming the US Financial System*, Armonk, NY, M.E. Sharpe, 1993.
[5] Board of Governors of the Federal Reserve System, *Flow of Funds Accounts of the United States, Flows and Outstandings* [henceforth FRB, *Flow of Funds*], Table F.102, Nonfarm Nonfinancial Corporate Business (flows), and Table F.213, Corporate Equities (flows). Thanks to Doug Henwood for calling my attention to this table.

had reached 80 per cent, up from 59 per cent just a decade before.[6] Nevertheless, between 1979 and 1990, the average annual growth of the manufacturing net capital stock was cut in half, falling to just 1.8 per cent, compared to 3.6 per cent between 1973 and 1979, and 4.65 per cent between 1960 and 1973. Over the same period, the average annual growth of manufacturing investment fell to 2.5 per cent, compared to 5.6 per cent between 1973 and 1979 and 6.3 per cent between 1960 and 1973.

The Plaza Accord, the recovery of competitiveness, and the beginning of recovery of profitability

The huge purging of redundant, high-cost means of production and labour that took place under the pressure of record high real interest rates, the Volcker recession, and the over-valued dollar – and which was very much helped along by the sharpened predation of stockholders and financiers – did bring about major gains in productiveness, even in the face of the huge parallel fall in investment growth. Manufacturing labour productivity grew at the remarkable average annual rate of 3.5 per cent between 1979 and 1985, well above the average for the long post-war boom. But this paradoxical process was ultimately unsustainable. The US economy was experiencing its worst crisis since the depression of the 1930s, and its continuation implied the radical hollowing out of the US manufacturing sector. By mid-decade, Congress was threatening to pass strong protectionist legislation and many of the country's leading corporate executives were undertaking a powerful lobbying campaign demanding relief from the runaway dollar.[7]

In the end, the Reagan administration, in order to respond to irresistible political pressure and to restore the viability of a crisis-torn US manufacturing sector, had little choice but to undertake an epoch-making reversal

---

[6] Ibid., Table F.102 and Table L.102, Nonfarm Nonfinancial Corporate Business (flows and levels). Data on borrowing by the manufacturing sector is not available, so is here given for the non-financial corporate sector.

[7] C.R. Henning, *Currencies and Politics in the United States, Germany, and Japan*, Washington, DC, Institute for International Economics, 1994, pp. 276–84.

of direction. On 22 September 1985, the G-5 powers, under US pressure, signed the Plaza Accord, agreeing to take joint action to reduce the exchange rate of the dollar to rescue a US manufacturing sector on its way to desolation. The very next day, Reagan attacked the 'unfair' trading practices of other countries, and went on to announce a further major shift in US trade policy in a barely concealed protectionist direction. This complemented the Plaza Accord itself, and resumed the aggressive policies of the Nixon, Ford, and Carter administrations during the 1970s, which had not only sought the radical devaluation of the dollar, but also initiated a powerful protectionist and 'market opening' thrust, in the International Multi-Fiber Agreement of 1973 and Section 301 of the Trade Act of 1974.[8]

Already in the early 1980s, the Reagan administration had imposed so-called 'voluntary export restraints' (VERs) upon Japanese automakers to slow the penetration of Japanese auto imports into the US market. Over the following decade, successive Reagan, Bush, and Clinton administrations would, again and again, use the threat of closing off the US market to US producers' leading rivals, especially in Japan and increasingly East Asia, as a bludgeon both to limit their imports and to force the opening of their markets to US exports and foreign direct investment. Landmarks in this effort included the Semi-Conductor Agreements of 1986 and 1991, which obliged Japan to agree, at least formally, to certain targets for the increase of US chip exports into the Japanese market; the Omnibus Trade and Competition Act of 1988 ('Super 301'), which sought to extend the reach of the Trade Act of 1974 to a much larger number of allegedly unfair traders, so as to limit their imports; the Structural Impediments Act of 1989, which sought a further opening of Japanese markets; and a series of ad hoc, increasingly hostile broadsides to force open the Korean and Taiwanese economies.

The Plaza Accord, and its sequels, proved to be the turning point in the US manufacturing turnaround, and a major watershed for the world economy as a whole. It set off ten years of more or less continuous, and

---

[8] For this, and the following, paragraph, see R. Gilpin, *The Challenge of Global Capitalism. The World Economy in the 21st Century*, Princeton, Princeton University Press, 2000, pp. 81–2, 232–6.

major, devaluation of the dollar with respect to the yen and the mark, which was accompanied by a decade-long freeze on real wage growth. It thereby opened the way simultaneously for the recovery of competitiveness, along with the speed-up of export growth, of US manufacturing, a secular crisis of German and Japanese industry, and an unprecedented explosion of export-based manufacturing expansion throughout East Asia, where economies for the most part tied their currencies to the dollar and thereby secured for their manufacturing exporters a major competitive advantage vis-à-vis their Japanese rivals when the dollar fell between 1985 and 1995.

It must be emphasized that little of this historic shift in trends of competitiveness or, in turn, of the accompanying rise in the manufacturing profit rate was attributable to productivity growth differentials among national economies, or any speed-up in US manufacturing productivity growth (before 1994). Almost all was owing to differences in wage growth and the exchange rate. Between 1986 and 1993, the growth of US manufacturing productivity averaged just 2.5 per cent per annum (although it did gather momentum soon after that, under the impetus of a new rise in investment growth). This was lower – in some cases significantly lower – than that of all of the other G-7 economies, except for Canada and Germany.[9] On the other hand, during the same period, the average annual increase of real hourly wages in the US manufacturing sector was the lowest among the G-7 economies, averaging 0.15 per cent per annum, compared to 2.9 per cent in Japan and 2.85 per cent in Germany. Consequently, while manufacturing real wages in Germany and Japan increased by about 35 per cent over the decade 1985–95 as a whole, in the US they inched up by little better than 1 per cent (see Figures 2.4 and 2.5).

Along with the relatively slow growth of real wages, the falling exchange rate was pivotal for the recovery of competitiveness and profitability in US manufacturing. Between 1985 and 1990 and then between 1990 and 1995,

[9] Average annual manufacturing productivity growth between 1986 and 1993 was as follows: UK 4.8 per cent; Japan 4.5 per cent; France 3.3 per cent; Italy 3.0 per cent; US 2.5 per cent; Canada 2.2 per cent; Germany 1.7 per cent.

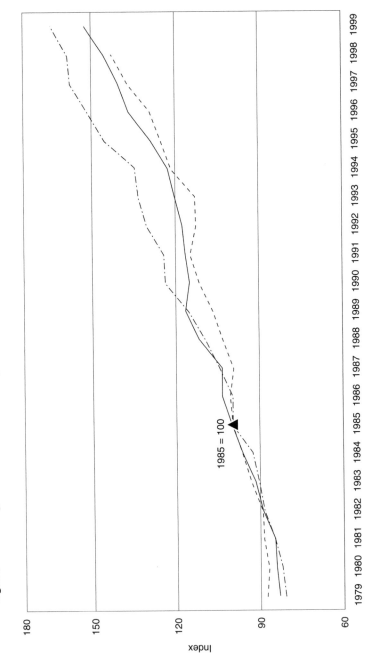

Figure 2.4 The growth of manufacturing labour productivity: US, Germany, and Japan, 1979–99

Figure 2.5 Real hourly wage growth in manufacturing: US, Germany, and Japan, 1978–99

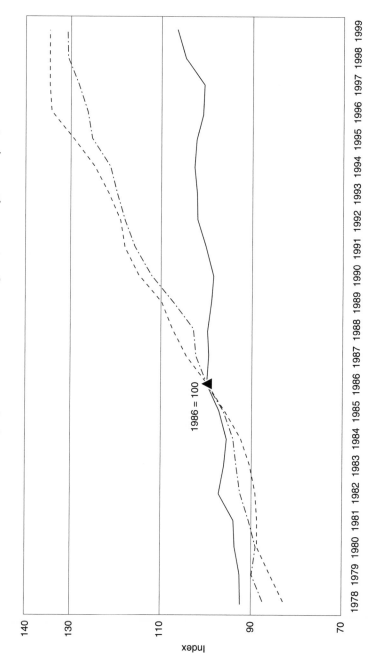

1986 = 100

——— US   – – – – Germany   –·–·– Japan

the exchange rate of the yen and the mark appreciated against the dollar at the extraordinary average annual rates of 10.5 per cent and 12.7 per cent, respectively, and then 9.1 per cent and 2.5 per cent, respectively (see Figure 2.6). Between 1985 and 1995, therefore, US nominal wages expressed in dollars rose at an average annual rate of 4.65 per cent, while those of Japan and Germany streaked ahead, respectively, at the average annual rates of 15.1 per cent and 13.7 per cent. Over the same ten-year period, manufacturing unit labour costs, expressed in the national currencies, rose at an average annual rate of 0.8 per cent in the US, 0.7 per cent in Japan, and 3.0 per cent in Germany. But, expressed in dollars, they mounted at an average annual rate of 0.8 per cent in the US, compared to 11.7 per cent in Japan and 11. 3 per cent in Germany. By 1995, hourly wages expressed in US currency for manufacturing production workers were $17.19 in the US, $23.82 in Japan, and $31.58 in Germany.[10]

The combination of industrial shakeout, wage repression, and dollar devaluation detonated a fundamental shift in the *modus operandi* of US manufacturing toward an increasing reliance upon exports. That shift had originated between 1971 and 1978, when the dollar's steep devaluation had opened the way for real goods exports to shoot up at an average annual pace of 8.7 per cent. But it had been brutally interrupted by the huge hike of the currency between 1979 and 1986, when the growth of real goods exports had sunk to an average annual rate of −0.7 per cent. The years between 1986 and 1997 witnessed a dramatic reversal: real goods exports grew at an average annual rate of 9.3 per cent, more than a third faster than between 1950 and 1971, and the ratio of manufacturing exports to manufacturing value added doubled, from 21 per cent to 42 per cent. Little by little, improved competitiveness and export growth enabled the manufacturing sector, and thereby the whole economy, to begin again to move forward, and thereby the whole economy (see Figure 2.7; also below, p. 98, Figure 3.2).

The recovery of international competitiveness facilitated a major recovery

[10] 'International Comparisons of Hourly Compensation Costs For Production Workers in Manufacturing, 1999', in US Bureau of Labor Statistics, *News*, 7 September 2000, p. 14, Table 2 (BLS website).

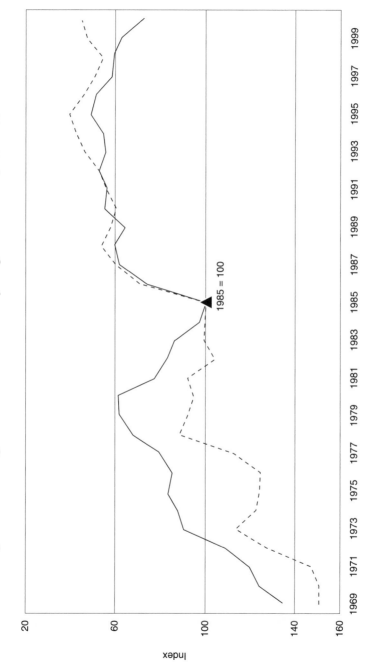

Figure 2.6 Exchange rate of the mark and the yen against the dollar, 1969–2000

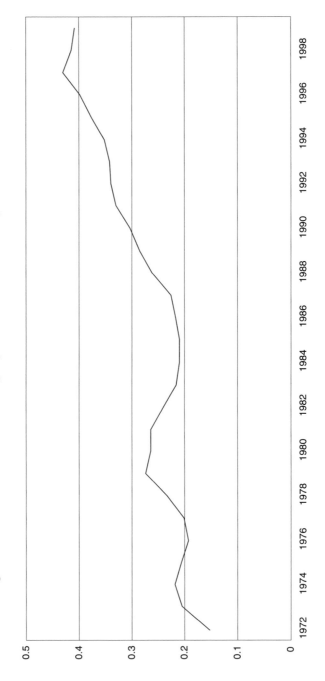

Figure 2.7 Ratio of US manufacturing exports to US manufacturing value-added, 1972–99

of pre-tax profitability in manufacturing. Between 1982 and 1986 and between 1986 and 1995, manufacturing unit labour costs grew at the same average annual rate of 0.8 per cent. But, between 1986 and 1995, goods export prices were enabled by the falling dollar to grow at an average annual pace of 2.3 per cent, compared to just 0.6 per cent in the face of the rising dollar between 1982 and 1986. As pressure on profit margins from international prices was thus eased, profitability was freer to head upwards, and between 1986 and 1989 the manufacturing profit rate did increase rapidly, by 49 per cent.

It must be emphasized, however, that, although it initiated a new and decisive longer run trend toward the recovery of manufacturing profitability, the initial step-up in the manufacturing profit rate that took place in the latter years of the 1980s was as yet unaccompanied by any significant improvement in US manufacturing dynamism. The manufacturing sector remained overwhelmingly dominated by the propensity to use financial resources for financial manipulation – above all borrowing for the purpose of leveraged mergers and acquisitions and stock buybacks, rather than for investment in new plant and equipment. Indeed, the huge expansion of international liquidity that was arranged by governments in the US, and across the advanced capitalist world, in response to the stock market crash of 1987 gave a new lease of life to the explosion of speculation. Between 1984 and 1989, expenditures by non-financial corporations on mergers and acquisitions reached an annual average of $184 billion, compared to an annual average of $84 billion spent on non-residential fixed investment.[11] By the end of the decade, manufacturing corporations had become burdened by debt to an historically unprecedented degree, with little real expansion of productive capacity to show for it.

The ascent of manufacturing profitability was interrupted by the recession of 1990–91, which dealt a major blow to wide swathes of the manufacturing sector left vulnerable by manufacturers' binge of borrowing and speculation in the face of their still much-reduced profitability.

---

[11] R. Pollin, 'Borrowing More but Investing Less: Economic Stagnation and the Rise of Corporate Takeovers in the US', unpublished manuscript, December 1994, p. 4. I would like to thank Bob Pollin for allowing me to refer to this text.

Indeed, although the recession was officially deemed over in 1991, in 1991, 1992, and 1993 the business failure rate reached and exceeded the previous record post-war levels of the first half of the 1980s (see p. 52, Figure 2.1). Had it not been for the bailout engineered at this point by the Federal Reserve, which imposed a huge reduction of the Federal Funds rate from 9.2 per cent in 1989 to 3.0 per cent in 1993 – from 5.3 per cent to 0.3 per cent in real terms – financially fragile industrial corporations, straining under the weight of hitherto unheard of liabilities, might have faced a much more devastating crisis, especially as financial institutions, possessing mountains of bad debts, were themselves in deep trouble, unable and unwilling to lend. It should be added that, by 1993, manufacturers were also reaping the benefits – directly and via its effect on the economy as a whole – from a major decline in the real cost of long-term borrowing, as the real interest rate on thirty-year US Treasury bonds fell from a crest of 8.1 per cent in 1984 to 4.9 per cent in 1988 to 3.6 per cent in 1993 (see Figure 2.8).[12]

Thus rescued from financial crisis, and enjoying the benefits of much lower borrowing costs, the manufacturing sector was enabled from 1993 to resume its upward trajectory. By 1995 it saw its pre-tax profit rate ascend to a level 65 per cent above that of 1986 and surpass for the first time in a quarter century its level of 1973. The manufacturing profit rate still remained a good 33 per cent short of its high, boom-time pinnacle of 1965, but it was only 20 per cent below its average for the long business cycle of the 1960s (1960–69) and indeed the post-war boom as a whole (1949–69).

It has become standard to downplay the importance of the manufacturing sector, by pointing to its shrinking share of total employment and GDP. But, during the 1990s, the US corporate manufacturing sector still accounted for 46.8 per cent of total profits accruing to the non-financial corporate sector (the corporate economy minus the corporate financial sector), and in 1999 it took 46.2 per cent of that total. The climb of

[12] B.S. Bernanke and C.S. Lown, 'The Credit Crunch', *Brookings Papers on Economic Activity*, 1991, no. 2 (see, especially, 'Comments and Discussion' by B.M. Friedman); D. Henwood, *Wall Street*, London, Verso, 1997, pp. 158–61.

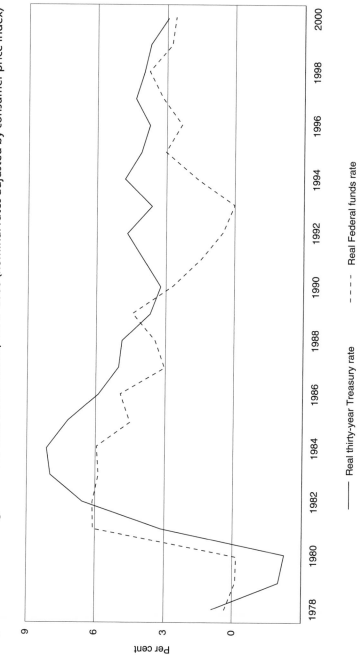

Figure 2.8 US real long- and short-term interest rates, 1978–2000 (nominal rates adjusted by consumer price index)

Real thirty-year Treasury rate   – – – – Real Federal funds rate

pre-tax manufacturing profitability was in fact *the* source of the parallel recovery of pre-tax profitability in the private economy as a whole. Between 1986 and 1995, the pre-tax rate of profit in the private economy as a whole lunged forward by 16.5 per cent, to surmount for the first time in a quarter century its level of 1973 and thereby approach its level at the end of the 1960s. Since the pre-tax rate of profit in the private non-farm non-financial economy exclusive of manufacturing failed to rise at all during this whole decade – sliding somewhat, then not quite recovering its 1986 level by 1995 – the entirety of this gain was accounted for by the increase in the rate of profit attained by the manufacturing sector (see Figure 2.9).

The revival of profitability was further amplified by the huge tax breaks that had gone into effect in the early 1980s, when Republicans and Democrats had vied with one another to offer the greatest handouts to the corporations. The burden of taxation on corporations had indeed been falling since the early- to mid-1960s. Between 1960 and 1965 manufacturing corporations had paid out 52 per cent of their pre-tax profits in taxes. But during the 1990s they paid just 23 per cent. By 1995, the *after-tax* profit rate for the corporate manufacturing sector had therefore been able to climb to within 24 per cent of its 1965 peak, and had just about come to *equal* its average level of the 1960s boom (1960–69), even while the pre-tax profit rate still remained 35 per cent below its 1965 peak and 25 per cent below its average level of the 1960s. The *after-tax* profit rate for the non-financial corporate economy as a whole had risen to within 23 per cent of its 1965 peak and 9 per cent of its average during the 1960s boom, although the pre-tax profit rate was still 34 per cent below its 1965 level and 24.5 per cent below its average level of the 1960s (see Figures 2.10 and 2.11).

Last but not least, during the first half of the 1990s, as they were being nurtured by the Fed's low interest rate policy, non-financial corporations went a long way to restore to health their battered balance sheets and in the process stanch the heavy outflow of net interest payments. After increasing their debt at the ferocious average annual rate of 10.6 per cent between 1980 and 1990, they tightly drew in the reins between 1990 and 1993, their debt rising by barely one per cent in total in these years. Meanwhile, after having been net purchasers of equities in every year

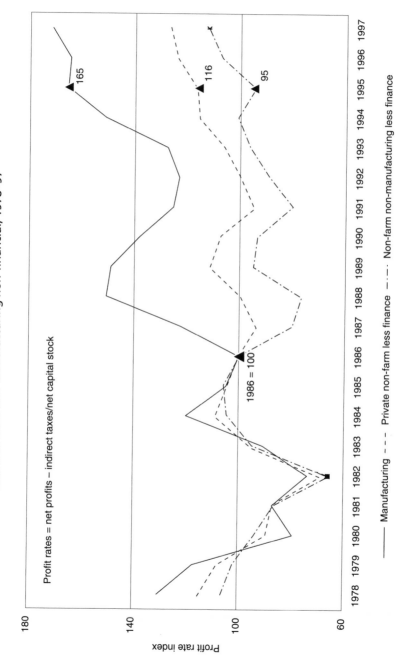

Figure 2.9 US net profit rate indices: manufacturing, non-farm non-financial, and non-farm non-manufacturing non-financial, 1978–97

Profit rates = net profits – indirect taxes/net capital stock

—— Manufacturing – – – Private non-farm less finance –––·– Non-farm non-manufacturing less finance

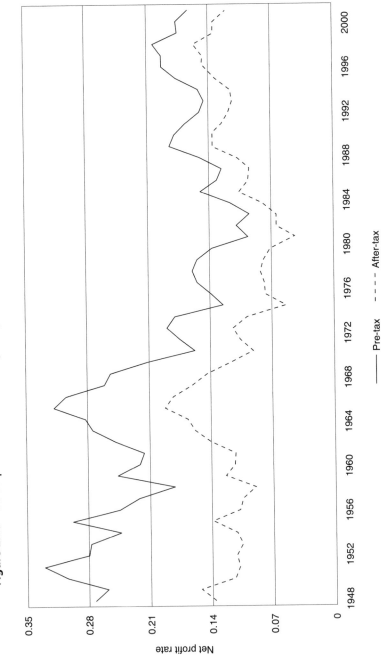

Figure 2.10 US corporate manufacturing net profit rates, pre-tax and after-tax, 1948–2000

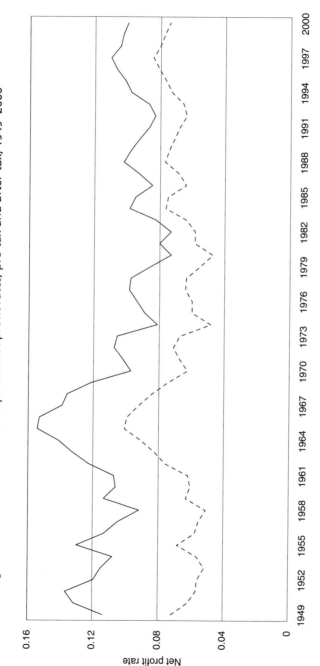

Figure 2.11 US non-financial corporate net profit rates, pre-tax and after-tax, 1949–2000

throughout the 1980s, they suddenly became net sellers in every year between 1990 and 1993, raising money by selling their own stocks rather than spending it to buy them back, the value of their equity issues rising above the value of their equity retirements through mergers and acquisitions and stock buybacks. Thus, whereas non-financial corporations had seen their net interest payments as a proportion of profits average 31.8 per cent between 1979 and 1991 and reach 37 per cent in 1991, they were able to bring that figure down to 20 per cent by 1995. It would average under 20 per cent for the remainder of the decade.[13]

FROM PROFITABILITY RECOVERY TO ECONOMIC REVIVAL

It was only in the aftermath of the slow recovery from the 1990–91 recession that the profitability revival in the manufacturing sector finally began to help stir the whole economy, its stimulating effects having hitherto been limited by the sector's inability during the last half of the 1980s to underwrite a significant increase in investment growth, in the face of high, if declining, real interest rates, the huge increase in the burden of debt, and the lure of speculation in mergers and acquisitions. Deriving major benefit from sharply rising potential profitability – itself an expression of the reduction of real wage growth to near zero and the spectacular fall of the dollar, as well as the Fed-sponsored reduction of interest rates between 1989 and 1993 and the consequent reduction of the weight of interest payments on their profits – manufacturers were perhaps better placed to drive the economy forward than at any time since the early 1960s. Even so, the subsequent economic revitalization had to take place against a new backdrop of government macroeconomic restrictiveness, and was indeed powerfully shaped by it – as well as by the state's continuing encouragement of exports.

Virtually from its inception, the Clinton administration thus combined

---

[13] *Flow of Funds*, Table D.1, Debt Growth by Sector; Table F.102, Nonfarm Nonfinancial Corporate Business (flows).

a commitment to fiscal stringency and monetary hawkishness that was something of a throwback to the days of Eisenhower, at least until the recovery of business profitability could be better assured. It not only eschewed recourse to the sort of deficit spending that had pulled the US, and the international, economy from every recession since the start of the 1970s, but it also embarked on a budget-balancing crusade. At the same time, it sought to encourage the economy's increasing dependence on exports, by talking down the dollar, especially against the yen, and between the end of 1992 and the first quarter of 1995, the dollar/yen exchange rate plunged by more than one-third.[14] Meanwhile, the Federal Reserve stood ready to intervene the moment the unemployment rate threatened to fall below its 'natural rate' and to set off the more rapid rise of prices. The focus of state policy on the control of costs, the restriction of demand, and the containment of the currency could not have been aimed more explicitly at repressing wage growth, while eliminating the economy's reliance on government deficits and forcing it to depend on investment and export growth. Between 1992 and 1997, the federal deficit as a proportion of GDP did in fact fall from 4.7 per cent to zero. Over the same period, the average annual growth of real wages in manufacturing was kept to − 0.2 per cent.

The take-off of manufacturing

From the last quarter of 1993, under the impetus of the ongoing revival of manufacturing competitiveness and exports – which began to take off once again at this point – the manufacturing sector finally began to experience robust growth, and the economy as a whole expanded with it. GDP was suddenly rising at a 4.5 per cent clip, and 'expectations for real GDP growth ... were continuously revised upward.' Had the economy been left to its own devices, the expansion of the 1990s would have

---

[14] B. Eichengreen, *Globalizing Capital. A History of the International Monetary System*, Princeton, Princeton University Press, 1996, p. 152; Henning, *Currencies and Politics*, pp. 304–5 ; OECD, *Economic Survey. United States 1995*, Paris, 1995, p. 55, Figure 25.

gathered force from 1993–94. But the Fed could not tolerate such economic dynamism, especially because 'the economy was still picking up steam and full employment was generally thought to be achieved or to be imminent' – even though the unemployment rate was barely under 6 per cent! Between February 1994 and February 1995, the Fed engaged upon an 'aggressive path of tightening monetary conditions', raising interest rates by a full three percentage points. This step interrupted the acceleration of the cyclical upturn for a full year – from the end of 1994 through the end of 1995.[15]

Nevertheless, from the end of 1995, following the Fed's return to easier credit earlier in the year, the economy did regain its momentum and, over the following two years, though at first haltingly, the accelerating expansion took up where it had left off in 1994. Between 1993 and 1997, after having wilted somewhat during the early 1990s, manufacturing export growth resumed its torrid pace of the later 1980s, averaging 11.2 per cent between 1993 and 1997 and raising the ratio of manufacturing exports to manufacturing value added by 20 to 25 per cent in the interim (see above, p. 66, Figure 2.7, and below, p. 98, Figure 3.2). As manufacturing export growth accelerated, manufacturing output growth leapt forward in tandem, averaging 5.7 per cent per annum from the fourth quarter of 1993 through 1997 (5.1 per cent through 1999), after having failed (on average) to grow at all during the previous five years and having plodded along at an average annual pace of just 1.9 per cent between 1979 and 1992. The key to growth was clearly a major step-up in the rate of increase of manufacturing investment. Having increased at an average annual pace of just 1.3 per over the previous thirteen years (4.1 per cent on average between 1982 and 1990), it jumped ahead at an average annual pace of 9.5 per cent between 1993 and 1997 (and 10.2 per cent through 1999). In that same period the manufacturing net capital stock grew at an average annual rate of 2.4 per cent (and 2.7 per cent through 1999), compared to just 1.3 per cent between 1982 and 1990.

---

[15] OECD, *Economic Survey. United States 1995*, pp. 14, 48–9; 'Industry Analytical Ratios and Basic Industry Data for the Manufacturing Sector, 8 August 2000', unpublished folder, provided by the US Bureau of Labor Statistics.

In view of its timing, the ascent of the profit rate, by way of the augmented growth of investment that it engendered, seems clearly to have been the main force behind the parallel gearing-up of the rate of productivity increase. From the start of the 1980s, labour productivity in manufacturing had been experiencing quite decent progress, despite faltering investment growth. The long-term extrusion of obsolete means of production and the huge, parallel downsizing of the labour force had, throughout the period, and especially during the crisis of manufacturing of the first half of the 1980s, directly kick-started the improvement in the growth of productiveness. The introduction of Japanese-style 'lean produc-tion' had worked to the same end by bringing about an intensification of labour on the shop floor, as had also the reorganization of the production chain through out-sourcing, mainly by bringing about the reallocation of labour into the non-unionized sector where workers lacked even minimal protection. Firms did begin, in these years, to apply information tech-nology to manufacturing production in significant ways – as in computer-aided production and computer-aided design – but the impact remained limited by the low level of investment. Between 1982 and 1990, despite the slowing of the growth of the capital stock to an average annual pace of 1.3 per cent, compared to 3.8 per cent between 1973 and 1979, manufacturing labour productivity thus increased at the average annual rate of 3.1 per cent, about the same speed as it had grown over the long post-war boom.

It was only with the spurt of new plant and equipment spending from the last quarter of 1993 that manufacturing productivity growth acceler-ated, averaging 4.4 per cent per annum between 1993 and 1997 (5.1 per cent through 2000). Nor was the increase in productivity growth simply an expression of equipping workers with greater capital stock per person. Since between 1993 and 1999 the average annual growth of capital productivity (the real output–capital ratio) mirrored its pace between 1982 and 1990 (2.6 per cent) – while labour productivity of course outdistanced it – it is evident that overall productiveness (taking into account both labour and plant and equipment inputs) was growing significantly faster in the later than in the earlier period. The rise of manufacturing productivity growth – which was, again, the result of the increase in investment growth that resulted from the clambering upwards of the rate of profit – itself contributed significantly to the further ascent of the manufacturing profit rate. The average annual growth of manufacturing unit labour costs thus tumbled down to an impressive −2.2 per cent between 1993 and 1997, compared to 1.8 per cent between 1986 and 1993, and this opened the way to a 33 per cent increase of the manufacturing profit rate over those years (although almost all of this was secured by 1995, when the dollar began to rise precipitously once again).

The revitalization of the economy outside manufacturing

As the manufacturing sector evinced increased vitality, it shot out greater demand impulses to the non-manufacturing sector. This is composed of the service sector – which includes wholesale trade, retail trade, FIRE (finance, insurance, and real estate), and a large number of heterogeneous 'service industries' – plus the non-manufacturing industrial sector – which includes construction, mining, and transportation and public utilities. Non-manufacturing had lost considerable steam from the early 1980s, experiencing its most difficult years of the post-war epoch, after having long avoided the sort of difficulties that had beset manufacturing from 1965 onwards.

The non-manufacturing sector had sustained nothing remotely like the profound slump in profitability that hit manufacturing in the later 1960s and 1970s. Indeed, during the 1970s, the economy outside of manufacturing seems to have benefited significantly from manufacturers' efforts to invest and expand their way out of their profitability problems. In the business cycles between 1969 and 1979, the profit rate in the non-manufacturing sector was, on average, only about 10 per cent below its level in the business cycle between 1959 and 1969 – whereas the profit rate in manufacturing was on average 39 per cent below that level – and there was no palpable fall-off in the growth of the non-manufacturing capital stock. On the other hand, the manufacturing sector's crisis of the early 1980s and the only hesitant revival of manufacturing investment and output growth during the second half of the decade – with the resulting fading away of manufacturing sector demand – appears to have dealt the non-manufacturing sector a significant setback (see above, p. 21, Table 1.2).

From the early years of the 1980s, the rising demand imparted by the explosive growth of military spending and parallel cuts in taxes did drive the non-manufacturing economy forward. Firms outside of manufacturing were, moreover, able to exploit the stagnation of real wages – and for much of the labour force absolute real wage decline – which was, to an important extent, an expression of the increasingly 'union-free' environment. Between 1979 and 1989, workers in all of the bottom seven percentiles (70 per cent) of the labour force suffered declining real wages, and workers in the bottom four percentiles (40 per cent) saw their real wages plunge on average by 9 per cent.[16]

With wages flat or actually falling, employers had every incentive to substitute labour for capital. Capital–labour ratios thus ascended only slowly in the non-manufacturing sector over an extended period from the end of the 1970s, and, while employment increased spectacularly, non-manufacturing labour productivity growth stagnated in a manner that was historically quite unprecedented, averaging just 0.5 per cent per annum between 1979 and 1990. 'The great American jobs machine' of the 1980s was thus almost literally just that: the rapid growth of employment taking place without the benefit of a parallel increase in the plant and equipment at the disposal of each worker. The huge expansion of the non-manufacturing sector was indeed a symptom of the broad economic decline that accompanied the crisis of manufacturing in the US economy, which can usefully be called 'de-industrialization', with all its negative connotations.

Between 1986 and 1993, the non-manufacturing sector, undercut by a falling dollar that rendered the inputs that it imported more expensive, as well as by recession and the delayed expansion of the manufacturing sector, saw its rate of profit plummet to its lowest levels of the post-war epoch – about 20 per cent on average below its levels of the 1960s and 10 per cent below its levels of the 1970s. Simultaneously, the average annual

[16] L. Mishel, J. Bernstein, and J. Schmitt, *The State of Working America 1998–99*, Ithaca, NY, Cornell University Press, 1999, p. 131, Table 3.6.

increase of the non-manufacturing capital stock declined by 40 per cent with respect to that of the previous twenty years. Nevertheless, from the last part of 1993, with the call for its goods increasing and its own profitability on the upswing, the non-manufacturing sector saw its output growth swerve sharply upward in tandem with that of manufacturing – as industries such as wholesale trade and retail trade, as well as construction, were all suddenly gathering speed at between 6 and 7 per cent per year. The rate of growth of non-manufacturing output would continue to increase every year during the remainder of the decade (with the exception of 1995).

Meanwhile, from its nadir during the 1990–91 recession, the non-manufacturing profit rate floated steadily upwards, although it was not until 1995 that it reached its level of 1986. As profitability rose, non-manufacturing investment growth rose in concert, galloping forward at an average annual pace of 11.2 per cent between 1991 and 1997 (11.7 through 1999), compared to 4.3 per cent between 1982 and 1990.

The germination of productivity growth outside of manufacturing had to wait until 1996. Unlike in manufacturing, where solid productivity growth had been occurring long before the acceleration of the 1990s, productivity increase in the non-manufacturing sector had pursued a truly dismal trajectory for almost two decades, creeping forward at an average annual pace of 0.6 per cent between 1977 and 1995. But after 1995, in delayed response to investment that had been expanding rapidly along with rising profitability since 1992, non-manufacturing productivity growth finally careered forward, increasing at an average annual pace of about 2.4 per cent over the next five years, compared to around 2.7 per cent during the post-war boom between 1950 and 1973.[17] How to interpret this discontinuity is a point to which it will be necessary to return below. But, the increase of non-manufacturing productivity growth certainly acceler-

[17] I wish to thank Brian Moyer of the Bureau of Economic Analysis for providing me with the non-farm, non-manufacturing value-added series, from which I derived the productivity figures, using hours provided by the Bureau of Labor Statistics. These numbers are no doubt several tenths of a percentage point too high, as very recent data revisions have brought total GDP growth for 1998, 1999, and 2000 down by about one-half a percentage point per annum. Revised disaggregated figures are as yet unavailable.

ated the rise of non-manufacturing profitability: after finally reaching its level of 1985 in 1995, the latter hauled itself up a further 17.5 per cent during the next two years. As a consequence, by 1997, the (pre-tax) profit rate for the non-farm economy as a whole had risen to within 22 per cent of its 1965 peak, and to within 9 per cent of the average rate of profit during the 1960s boom (the business cycle 1960–69) (see above, p. 39, Figure 1.3).[18]

FROM ECONOMIC REVIVAL TO THE ASCENT OF FINANCE[19]

The return of the real economy to more rapid growth opened a path for a parallel ascent of finance. But, just as the road to recovery for the real economy proved rocky, the rise of finance was achieved only through the transcendence of a succession of serious crises.

As the US manufacturing sector entered into deep recession at the start of the 1980s, there took place a major reallocation of capital in the direction of financial activity. This shift had been delayed during the 1970s by inflationary macroeconomic policies that were designed to bring down both the dollar and real interest rates with the goal of reviving the manufacturing sector, but which naturally proved more than problematic for lenders. But it was now facilitated by late Carter and Reagan administration moves toward financial deregulation, aiming to break down hitherto existing barriers that confined financial institutions to specialized functional and restricted geographic spheres. Between 1975 and 1990, the proportion of total private plant and equipment investment devoted to FIRE (finance, insurance, and real estate) doubled, from around 12–13 per cent to 25–6 per cent; between 1982 and 1990, almost a quarter of all private plant and equipment investment was in FIRE (see Figure 2.12).

[18] In 1997, *after-tax* non-financial corporate and corporate profit rates came within 15 per cent and 9 per cent, respectively, of their 1965 highpoints. In that year they were, respectively, 8 per cent *above* and equal to *average* non-financial corporate and corporate profit rates during the 1960s boom (1960–69).

[19] I wish to thank Jim Crotty, Gary Dymski, Jerry Epstein, and Bob Pollin for very valuable help and advice on the material in this section.

Figure 2.12 FIRE investment as a proportion of total private investment, 1947–97

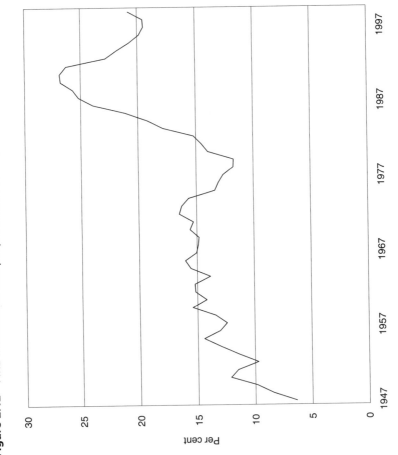

It was, however, one thing to free up the flow of capital and for capital to lurch sharply in the direction of finance; it was quite another for investors to make a satisfactory profit from so doing at this juncture in the evolution of the post-war international economy. The problem was straightforward. In a situation in which the real economy was producing such a sharply reduced aggregate surplus with respect to its total capital stock, how could lenders and speculators – rentier interests more generally – make a killing, given the dependence of their own returns on successful profit-making in the real economy? In the face of the stagnating economic pie throughout the 1980s, lenders and speculators were offered only limited options by a real economy that was cutting back on capital investment. They were obliged to rely for their best profit-making opportunities on the more or less forceful redistribution of income and wealth by political means. This was achieved most strikingly through direct action by the state, though also via class struggle at the level of the firm, as well as by means of the plundering of the corporations themselves.

The Reagan regime, in its early years, could hardly have catered more directly to the needs of lenders and speculators. The deep reduction of corporate tax rates in 1981, followed by the Fed's partial easing of interest rates in 1982, ensured that the stock market, and thus returns to investors in equities, would escalate, especially once the government's programme of massive deficit spending on the military stimulated the rapid growth of demand.[20] The imposition of unprecedentedly tight credit, certainly the defining policy departure of the period, was designed to break the back of inflation so as to restore the stability of returns on lending. Unquestionably it achieved its purpose, as commercial banks' profits clearly benefited almost immediately (see below, p. 90, Figure 2.13). Finally, with the gap between falling federal taxes and rising federal expenditures producing record federal deficits that had to be financed, with real interest rates at historic highs, and with the value of the dollar rising inexorably, financiers from the US and abroad could (at least for a time) make huge profits on the purchase of US Treasury bonds, and money poured into US financial

---

[20] See, especially, W. Greider, *Secrets of the Temple. How the Federal Reserve Runs the Country*, New York, Simon and Schuster, 1987.

markets. In his state of the union message of January 1985, Ronald Reagan welcomed all these developments, calling for the construction of the US as 'the investment capital of the world'.[21]

Nevertheless, the contradictions entailed by such decided state support for finance in a period of profitability crisis in the real economy, especially in manufacturing, manifested themselves almost immediately. The obverse side of the Carter–Volcker–Reagan lurch toward finance was thus, as emphasized, the increasing desolation of the manufacturing sector under the impact of the same high real interest rates, elevated dollar, and semi-recession that was proving so favourable to rentiers. By 1985, the administration was obliged to bring down the dollar.

The Plaza Accord, however, entailed contradictions of its own. As US policy-makers talked down the currency and US interest rates fell relative to those abroad, the dollar's real effective exchange rate slumped unexpectedly sharply – by close to one-third from its high point in early 1985 to spring 1986 – and the value of US assets in international terms came under threat (see below, p. 99, Figure 3.3). Just as international capital had hitherto flowed inexorably toward the US as interest rates and the dollar had risen, it now began to recoil from it as interest rates and the dollar fell, threatening US equity and bond markets with disaster. US policy-makers were caught in a bind, needing relatively low interest rates and a low dollar to protect the manufacturing sector, and quite the opposite in order to offer security to financiers and speculators.

In early 1987, with the Louvre Accord, the G-7 powers – most especially the Japanese – sought to prevent a collapse of the dollar. This was not just to head off the crisis of the German and Japanese manufacturing sectors under the pressure of an overvalued mark and yen, but also, and especially, to prevent a potentially destructive international financial breakdown. The stability of the currency could not, however, be secured, in the face of investors' attempts to exit from the dollar. In fact, during most of 1987, private capital ceased to flow to the US on a net basis, and foreign central banks were obliged to finance roughly two-thirds of the $163.5 billion US current account deficit. In autumn 1987, the Fed raised

---

[21] Quoted in Henning, *Currencies and Politics*, p. 273.

interest rates in a further effort to stem the dollar's fall and calm the financial markets. However, the Germans and Japanese offset the Fed's action by following suit and the resulting flight of capital from US financial markets triggered the October stock market crash.[22]

Only intervention in the equity markets – not only by the US Federal Reserve, but also by the Japanese authorities – saved the day in the short run. Had it not, moreover, been for the willingness of the Japanese government to further press down their already historically low interest rates – as well as to pressure Japanese investors to augment their placements of capital in the US, despite the high probability of further major exchange rate losses resulting from further declines of the dollar – a truly serious financial crisis in the last years of the decade might not have been staved off. These initiatives came at great cost to the Japanese economy: they much exacerbated the 1980s financial bubble and they led to staggering Japanese losses reaching into the hundreds of billions of dollars when the US currency did in fact fall significantly further with respect to the yen during the first half of the 1990s. They were only undertaken on the premise that, in their absence, the equilibrium of the US economy was in jeopardy, and with it *the* indispensable market for Japanese exports, as well as the stability of the world economy as a whole.[23]

The inconsistencies entailed in seeking to secure profits for lenders and speculators in a period when the real economy was stagnating were exhibited not only in government policies, but also in the projects of private investors. Thus, where financial activity sought to be self-sustaining – i.e. independent of more or less direct state support – it almost always had to assume a highly risky form, and typically ended in disaster – although the government rarely failed to throw a life jacket.

---

[22] Ibid., pp. 285–7.

[23] Murphy, *Weight of the Yen*, pp. 229–32; C.F. Bergsten, 'International Aspects of Financial Crises', in M. Feldstein, ed., *The Risk of Economic Crisis*, Chicago, University of Chicago Press, 1991, pp. 109–15. See especially the testimony of Richard Koo, chief international economist of Nomura Securities, on the Japanese government's pressuring of Japanese investors to make placements in the US, irrespective of their apparent potential for profits, during the mid to late 1980s, in the interest of maintaining order in international financial markets ('Japanese Investment In Dollar Securities after the Plaza Accord', in US Foreign Debt, Hearing before the Joint Economic Committee, US Congress, 13 September 1988).

Just how problematic it was to try to profit through lending in the teeth of international over-capacity and over-production in manufacturing had been forcefully brought home at the start of the 1980s when the explosion of lending to third-world producers that had taken place during the previous decade issued in the Less Developed Countries' (LDCs') debt crisis, which shook the system to its foundations. The US government had opened the way for the massive increase of third-world lending by leading US banks when it had insisted in 1973–74 that the recycling of Arab oil surpluses be carried out privately, and not by public agencies like the IMF. But the developing economies' boom of the 1970s had been precarious from the start. It depended on the maintenance of high prices for their raw materials and an expanding US market for their low-end manufacturing exports, both of which relied, in turn, on the continuing implementation of Keynesian expansionary policies. It also had to proceed in the face of a manufacturing profitability crisis in the core, which LDC exports tended to exacerbate. It was thus catastrophically deflated by the Volcker–Thatcher monetary tightening. In the wake of the ensuing LDC debt crisis, a number of the world's greatest banks were brought to the brink of bankruptcy. But, of course, the leading capitalist governments swooped in to rescue the international banks, using the IMF to impose the most crippling terms on the developing economies, so to ensure (as far as possible) that their loans would ultimately be repaid

The foray by US savings and loan (S&L) institutions and commercial banks into commercial real estate followed a similar pattern. It ended in the crash of the commercial real estate bubble and the collapse of many S&Ls and commercial banks by the end of the decade. The resulting bailout of the S&Ls cost US taxpayers the equivalent of three full years of US private investment in new plant and equipment.[24]

Nor did the leveraged mergers and acquisitions craze, without doubt the characteristic financial trend of the era, ultimately prove very different. During the first half of the decade, leveraged mergers and acquisitions did offer big profits, as the potential for gain through new productive investment in manufacturing reached its lowest point. Having

---

[24] R.E. Litan, *The Revolution in US Finance*, Washington, DC, Brookings, 1991, p. 6.

used borrowed funds to gain a controlling interest in a firm, financial entrepreneurs could make a fortune by tearing up union contracts and abrogating long-term arrangements with suppliers, by cutting back on investment and simply appropriating to themselves the residual 'free cash flow', and by downsizing redundant, low-profit factories and employees. But this field's potential for gain was soon reduced by intense over-crowding, yielding steadily diminishing returns as the decade wore on and investors were obliged to pay ever more inflated prices for their mergers and acquisitions.[25] The shipwreck of the mergers and acquisitions boom at the end of the decade contributed mightily to the enfeebled condition of commercial banks, many of which had been deeply involved in financ-ing it. They were already suffering sharply reduced returns as a conse-quence of intensifying competition from a variety of non-bank lending institutions such as insurance companies and finance companies, of manufacturers' increasing recourse to the money market instead of com-mercial banks for their borrowing, and of the trend to securitization.[26]

There can be no doubt of course that, during the 1980s, the very rich got very much richer and did so in large part by means of lending and speculative activity. On the other hand, just about no one else did. Of the total growth in family income that occurred between 1977 and 1989, the top one per cent of all families by income secured no less than 70 per cent, while the next 9 per cent secured virtually all of the rest.[27] It must be stressed, in addition, that those who prospered in this decade typically did so by means not only of spectacular redistributions of income by political means away from working people, but also of a phenomenal milking of the corporations and financial institutions themselves – which were, as a result, often left in a desperate condition. Although a road to recovery, through the repression of real wage growth, a sharply declining dollar, and corporate tax relief, had begun to open up for US manufac-turing, the corporations' borrowing binge left them, by the end of the decade, with record-high debts, manifested in unprecedentedly high

---

[25] W.F. Long and D.J. Ravenscraft, 'Decade of Debt: Lessons from LBOs in the 1980s', in Blair, ed., *The Deal Decade.*
[26] Litan, *The Revolution in US Finance.*
[27] P. Krugman, *Peddling Prosperity*, New York, Norton, 1994, pp. 134–8.

debt–equity ratios and interest obligations that as a percentage of pre-tax profits (including interest) had reached an all-time record level of 37 per cent, compared to 23 per cent in 1979. The difficult straits into which financial institutions had meanwhile fallen found expression in the sharp fall in the rate of return on equity and assets sustained by commercial banks at the end of the 1980s, which opened this way to a wave of bank failures on a scale not seen since the Great Depression (see below, p. 90, Figure 2.13).

The condition of both the banks and the corporations was made much worse with the onset of the recession of 1990–91, which was itself aggravated by the inability of lending institutions to advance funds to debt-strapped businesses. It was only the dramatic government rescue operation of the Federal Reserve in reducing short-term real interest rates to zero that prevented financial collapse and enabled banks to restore their balance sheets and resume profitable lending activity.[28]

As it turned out, financiers' problems of the 1980s were dissolved with astonishing rapidity in the early 1990s. It was the era of Bill Clinton, Robert Rubin, and Alan Greenspan, much more than that of Ronald Reagan and Donald Regan, that witnessed the true ascendancy of finance. The Fed's deep reduction of short-term interest rates enabled banks both to make windfall profits on the bonds that they owned and to carry on their basic business of borrowing cheap short-term in order to lend dear long-term with unparalleled success. When Clinton promised to balance the budget by refraining from undertaking new expenditures that were not balanced by spending cuts, he offered insurance to lenders that inflation would not eat into their profits. To remove all doubt about the latter, in 1994 Alan Greenspan sharply raised interest rates by three percentage points to slow the nascent expansion.

Still, the ultimate foundation for the economic recovery of lenders, as well as speculators, was the recovery of the profitability and financial health of the non-financial economy as a whole as the 1990s expansion progressed. The banks in particular achieved a stunning turnaround.

---

[28] L. White, *Why Now? Change and Turmoil in US Banking*, Washington, DC, Group of Thirty, 1992, p. 13.

Loan demand grew rapidly, and loan losses plummeted. Whereas in 1990, just 30 per cent of all bank assets were officially classified as 'well capitalized', 97 per cent were so labelled by 1996. As the economy began to prosper, moreover, banks were finally able to successfully exploit the process of deregulation under way since the end of the 1970s, expanding revenues from off-balance sheet activities, such as fees from the sale of mutual funds. Meanwhile, the movement toward bank concentration, begun in the 1980s, accelerated, as the share of bank assets held by the top fifty bank holding companies reached 64 per cent in 1996, up from 57 per cent in 1986, while the number of commercial banking organizations was trimmed to 7500 from 11000 a decade earlier. Perhaps most important, the Fed ensured that the gap between what the banks paid for their short-term borrowing and what they received for their long-term lending remained 'unusually wide'.[29]

The outcome was epoch-making. During the 1990s, US commercial banks achieved their highest rates of return on equity and assets in the post-war era, and did so by a decent margin. Indicative of the new state of affairs, the financial sector profits came to constitute a greater percentage of total corporate profits than at any previous time in post-war history. To put the icing on the cake, equity prices went through the roof, a point to which we shall return shortly (see Figures 2.13 and 2.14).

THE US ECONOMY ON A NEW FOUNDATION?

By the middle of the 1990s, US corporations had significantly improved their condition compared to a decade previously largely by means of extended and brutal processes of rationalization and redistribution. Manufacturers had, over a decade and a half, engaged in wave after wave of shakeout, scrapping masses of outdated and redundant plant and equipment and ejecting tens of thousands of employees, achieving in the

[29] OECD, *Economic Survey. United States 1997*, Washington, DC, 1997, pp. 71, 176, n. 26. I depend here, as well, on personal correspondence from Jerry Epstein and Bob Pollin on the bases for the banks' recovery in the 1990s.

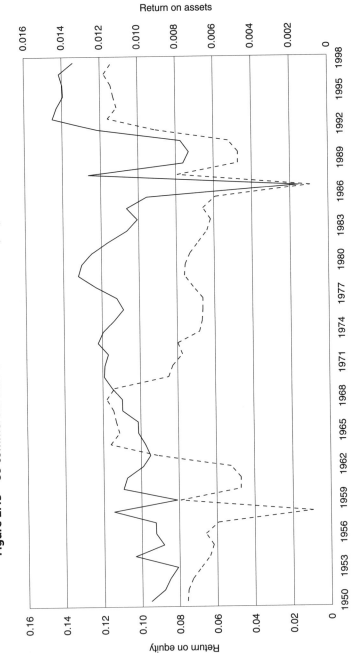

Figure 2.13 US commercial banks: rates of return on equity and assets, 1950–98

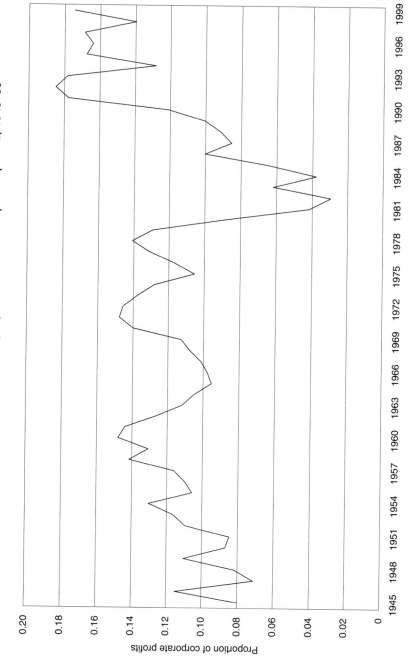

Figure 2.14 Financial sector profits as a proportion of total corporate profits, 1945–99

process substantial improvements in productiveness. They had, meanwhile, hugely amplified their profits at the expense of workers by means of a decade-long freeze on the growth of real wages, and at the expense of their overseas rivals via a decade-long devaluation of the dollar. Only near the end of this recovery process did they begin to substantially ratchet up capital accumulation, and thereby productivity growth, to achieve further significant gains in their profit rate. Nevertheless, operating for the first time in almost forty years in a context of both declining government deficits and stagnant real wages, they came from the end of 1993 to depend for their continuing expansion on investment growth – and export growth – to an extent greater than at any previous time during the post-war epoch. Between 1979 and 1990, the growth of investment had been responsible, in growth accounting terms, for just 12.4 per cent of the increase of GDP, the growth of consumption for 71 per cent. But between 1993 and 1997 the contribution of investment to GDP growth jumped to 30.5 per cent and that of consumption sank to 63 per cent. In the same period, the growth of exports continued to account for between 25 and 30 per cent of GDP growth, as it had since the time of the Plaza Accord. On this transformed basis, the US manufacturing sector boomed as it had not for a quarter century between 1993 and 1997.

It was the revival of profitability in the manufacturing sector, significantly magnified by the major reduction of taxes on corporate profits, along with the strengthening of corporate balance sheets that resulted from the sharp decline in the burden of interest payments, that underwrote the profitability recovery for the *non-financial sector as a whole* up until 1995. After 1995, the non-manufacturing profit rate finally rose above previous, reduced, levels and brought profitability in the non-financial business economy as a whole still closer to the high peaks of the long post-war boom. Driven to an important degree by the recovery of demand from the revived manufacturing sector, the non-manufacturing economy prospered along with it.

With the real economy on a firmer footing, the financial sector could finally exploit deregulation, as well as unstinting government subsidy and support. It did so to achieve a major, and unexpected, turnaround. If this symbiosis among the manufacturing, non-manufacturing, and financial sectors could be maintained, it offered the potential to place the US economy on a new foundation, and perhaps finally to leave definitively behind the long downturn. Even were this potential realized, however, a critical question would still linger. Would a newly revived US economy carry the rest of the world with it toward a new long boom, or would it itself be pulled down by the continuing weakness of the system as a whole?

CHAPTER 3

JAPAN AND GERMANY, 1980–95

The US economic recovery took place against the background of worsening international stagnation system-wide, which it did little or nothing to alleviate. Indeed, before the mid-1990s, the US profitability revival not only imparted little increased dynamism to the world economy, but also came to a large extent at the expense of the economies of its leading competitors and trading partners, especially Japan and Germany. This was because, right up until the end of 1993, US producers secured their gains primarily by means of the falling dollar and essentially flat real wages, as well as reduced corporate taxation, but with the benefit of little increase in investment. They therefore raised their rates of return by attacking their rivals' markets, but generated in the process relatively little increase in demand, either investment demand or consumer demand, for their rivals' products. When the US government moved in 1993 to balance the budget, the growth of US-generated demand in the world market received an additional negative shock.

As the opposite side of the same coin, from 1985 the manufacturing economies of Japan, Germany, and elsewhere in western Europe faced an ever-intensifying squeeze. Rising currencies, as well as relatively fast wage growth, made for declining competitiveness, thus increased downward pressure on already reduced profit rates and capital accumulation. Meanwhile, falling investment, consumer, and government demand growth issued in stagnating purchasing power for their goods at home and abroad, most especially in the US. These economies could thus avoid neither intensifying problems during the second half of the 1980s, nor severe crisis during the first half of the 1990s.

As a consequence of the reduced system-wide investment growth and output growth that resulted from the reduction of profitability in the advanced capitalist economies taken in aggregate – which was itself ultimately rooted in systemic over-capacity and over-production in international manufacturing – the struggle for export markets increasingly assumed a zero-sum character. Throughout the 1980s and indeed the 1990s, export-led expansions on the part of a leading economy, or a group of leading economies, usually founded on declining exchange rates, would thus tend to find their counterpart in crises of exports and manufacturing downturns on the part of others, dragged down by correspondingly rising exchange rates. At the same time, those same rising exchange rates were disposed to precipitate financial expansions, sometimes fuelled by capital imports. With gains through exports in one or several regions tending to be counterbalanced by losses elsewhere, system-wide growth inclined towards dependence on exogenous additions to demand growth – in particular, ever greater US federal deficits (paralleled by ever larger US trade and current account deficits), but also stock market and land bubbles and their associated subsidies to both household and corporate spending via the 'wealth effect'.

The US economy itself, and particularly its manufacturing sector, had of course been a victim of this dynamic, when the dramatic shift from negative real interest rates during most of the 1970s to record-high real interest rates at the start of the 1980s introduced an extended period of skyrocketing exchange rates; the latter incited both a spectacular financial expansion and a devastating manufacturing crisis, while record US federal deficits pulled Japan, Germany, and much of the rest of the world economy from recession. But with the Plaza Accord of 1985 and the ensuing long, steep fall of the dollar – and parallel sharp ascent of both the yen and the mark – the tables were turned, as pressure was lifted from US manufacturers and shifted to their competitors in Japan and Germany, and elsewhere in western Europe. The revival of the US manufacturing sector thus found its reflection internationally in downward stress on profit rates, growing instability, and, ultimately, the worst recessions of the post-war epoch for Japan, Germany, and much of the rest of western Europe during the first half of the 1990s, exacerbated by declining US federal deficits (see Figures 3.1, 3.2, and 3.3).

JAPAN

The 1980s: from manufacturing
impasse to bubble economy

The irrepressible yen and the predicament of Japanese manufacturing

During the long post-war boom, the Japanese economy had depended for its historically unprecedented dynamism, in the last analysis, on the expansion of exports. It thus relied for its success not simply on the rapid growth of world export markets in that period, but, even more, on the ability of its manufacturers to appropriate growing shares of those markets, especially from US producers, ultimately in the US itself.[1] But, from the start of the long downturn around 1970, Japanese producers' reliance on exports, and especially on increasing their share of world markets, proved their Achilles' heel, as they were hit with ever greater force both by the slowed growth of world trade and their own secularly declining competitiveness, which stemmed from an irrepressibly rising yen.

In Japan, institutional relationships among the great manufacturing corporations, between manufacturers and banks, and between investors and consumers, all strongly buttressed by state intervention, were organized so as to increase the growth of investment while repressing household consumption and to accelerate exports while holding down imports. The dominant 'city' banks stood at the core of great groups of manufacturing

---

[1] A. Maizels, *Industrial Growth and World Trade*, Cambridge, Cambridge University Press, 1963, pp. 189, 200–1, 220; A.D. Morgan, 'Export Competition and Important Substitution', in R.A. Batchelor, R.L. Major, and A.D. Morgan, eds, *Industrialization and the Basis for Trade*, Cambridge, Cambridge University Press, 1980, p. 48.

Figure 3.1 Manufacturing net profit rate indices: US, Germany, and Japan, 1978–99

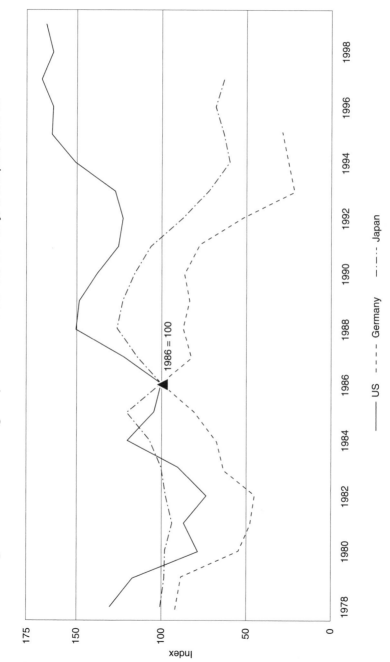

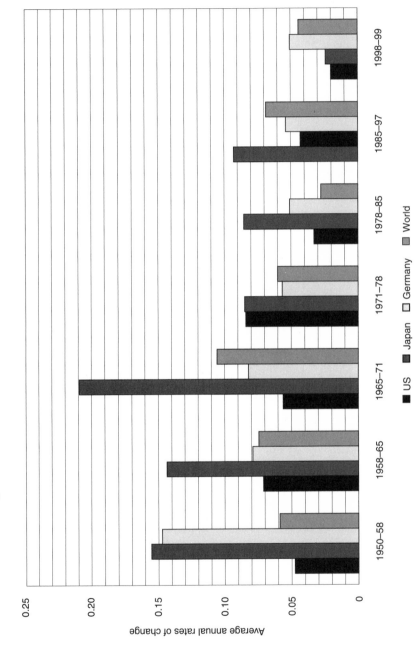

Figure 3.2 Growth of real exports of goods and services, 1950–99

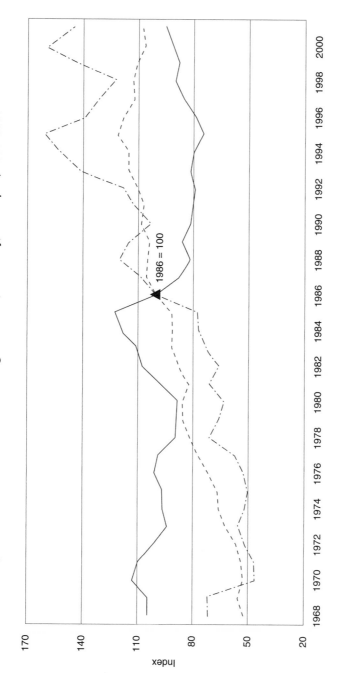

Figure 3.3 Nominal effective exchange rates: US, Germany, and Japan, 1968–2001

corporations (*keiretsu*), enjoying intimate ties with their individual member manufacturers that enabled them to offer them loans at a major discount. The government, meanwhile, maintained tight control of credit markets, with the goal of keeping interest rates low for those same manufacturers: it protected capital markets from foreign penetration, prevented capital exports, and directly rationed credit, advancing cheap funds to the banks on the condition that they on-lend it to the leading industrial firms. On the other hand, consumers were largely deprived of credit, and thereby obliged to put aside money in their bank and postal savings accounts over many years at low interest rates, before buying big-ticket items, especially housing. The price of housing was intentionally pushed up by means of zoning and other regulations, in order to force more savings and further repress consumption. As the opposite side of the same coin, the Ministry of Finance, in close collaboration with the Ministry of International Trade and Industry, funnelled money from those postal savings accounts into favoured industrial and infra-structural projects, under the Fiscal Investment and Loan Programme (FILP). Last but not least, firm-based unions tied their fate to the success of 'their' firms, so keeping the growth of wages behind that of net income, in order to safeguard the growth of profits. The outcome was that Japan enjoyed not only the highest household savings rate by far, but also the highest rate of investment growth, among the advanced capitalist economies throughout the post-war epoch.[2]

Nevertheless, with investment hot-housed in this manner – through the provision of cheap credit, the nurturing of profits by labour, and the government's more or less permanent commitment to the health and

---

[2] For the foregoing analysis, see I. Nakatani, 'The Economic Role of the Financial Corporate Grouping', in M. Aoki, ed., *The Economic Analysis of the Japanese Firm*, Amsterdam, North Holland, 1984; C. Johnson, *MITI and the Japanese Miracle. The Growth of Industrial Policy 1925–1975*, Palo Alto, Calif., Stanford University Press, 1982; K. Yamamura, 'Success that Soured: Administrative Guidance and Cartels in Japan', in K. Yamamura, ed., *Policy and Trade Issues of the Japanese Economy*, Seattle, University of Washington Press, 1982; M. Shinohara, *Industrial Growth, Trade, and Dynamic Patterns in the Japanese Economy*, Tokyo, University of Tokyo Press, 1982; R.T. Murphy, *The Weight of the Yen*, New York, Norton, 1996; A. Mikuni, *Japan: The Road to Recovery*, Washington, DC, Group of Thirty, 1998. I wish also to thank Dic Lo for valuable suggestions on these issues.

safety of first-tier industrial corporations – the economy faced a chronic tendency to excess-production in multiple manufacturing lines. This was so even despite the government's investment and depression cartels, which were designed precisely to counter the immanent stress on profits by maintaining prices and adjusting capacity. Manufacturers' drive to raise overseas sales so as to alleviate the pressure on profits resulting from otherwise superfluous capacity was thus built into the system, and rising exports were therefore essential for its smooth functioning. This was especially so since multiple mechanisms, ultimately defended by the state, tended both to prevent leading corporations and banks from going out of business and to stand in the way of layoffs, with the result that the reallocation of means of production and labour from more oversupplied and less profitable (or non-profitable) industries into more profitable ones could not easily occur through bankruptcies and layoffs, but had to take place directly, through existing firms' (and industrial groups') real-location of resources via new investment. The latter could not easily occur against a background of slow growth or, worse, recession – when firms' retention of excess means of production and labour would force down profitability and make new investment difficult to undertake – but required the continual expansion of demand, placing an even greater premium on export growth to keep the economy turning over.

Upward pressure on exports was paralleled by institutionalized repression of imports. The great manufacturing corporations went to great lengths to purchase their inputs from other members of their *keiretsu*, which cut down hugely on overseas purchases of industrial inputs. There was, moreover, a good deal of informal protectionism. As a result, throughout the post-war epoch, Japan maintained, by a good distance, the lowest ratio of manufactured imports to GDP, or manufacturing output, among the advanced capitalist economies.

From the accelerated exports and restricted imports at the heart of the Japanese growth model there has flowed an inexorable tendency to large and growing trade surpluses, and the latter have tended to lead to a more or less permanently rising yen. Especially as the dollar fell secularly under the impact of apparently uncontrollable US current account deficits, bringing about both increasing US competitiveness and a more slowly growing US domestic market, the inability of the Japanese economy to break from its established pattern of export-based growth thus led it into ever greater difficulty. This was made all the worse when the US ultimately moved away from the Keynesian deficits that stabilized the international economy through most of the length of the long downturn.

The restraining force that was to increasingly fetter the Japanese economy began to take effect from the point at which the US manufacturing sector initially entered into its crisis of profitability between 1965 and 1973. Throughout the whole of the post-war boom – and indeed through much of the long downturn that followed it – Japanese manufacturing had relied heavily on its ability to increasingly penetrate the huge American market, as well as to appropriate an ever greater share of world export markets from US producers. As growing Vietnam-induced federal deficits both extended the US boom in the years after 1965 and gave rise to accelerating inflation, Japanese export growth, driven upward by the red-hot US market and the reduced competitiveness of US producers, reached its post-war zenith, and Japanese profit rates, investment growth, productivity growth, and wage growth all reached their post-war peaks. The apex of the 'Japanese Miracle' was attained around 1970.

Nevertheless, the process of investment-led, export-dependent growth soon began to prove self-limiting. In the last years of the 1960s, US trade and current account deficits – forced up to a large extent by Japanese manufacturing imports – exploded out of control. Simultaneously, the Japanese economy produced trade and current account surpluses for the first time in its post-war history, and, as these rapidly expanded, the yen became ever more seriously undervalued. One wave of speculation against the dollar after another ensued, and, in the end, a very major devaluation of the US currency could not be avoided. With the Smithsonian Agreement of 1971 and ultimately the turn to floating exchange rates in the early part of 1973, Japanese authorities were obliged to give up the rate of ¥360/$ that had prevailed since the start of the 1950s. Between 1970 and 1973, as the dollar's value was forced down, the yen appreciated by 24.5 per cent and Japan's 'era of high-speed growth' was brought to an abrupt conclusion. Henceforth, the Japanese economy would have to run to stay in place, as it sought to increase its productiveness sufficiently quickly to keep up with the ever-inflating yen.[3]

The rise of the yen precipitated an immediate sharp decline of Japanese manufacturing competitiveness and a near-collapse of Japanese export growth, which fell by three-quarters between 1971 and 1973. The Japanese economy was plunged into crisis. Japanese authorities responded, as they would again after 1985, with a huge stimulus programme, flooding the economy with cheap credit. This was aimed, in part, to enable the growth of domestic demand to compensate for the fall-off of overseas demand. But it was intended, even more, to inflate the value of land and equities owned by Japanese corporations, so as to enable them to fund an investment surge of sufficient magnitude to increase productivity and reduce domestic costs enough to counteract the rise of the currency and thereby restore international competitiveness. An investment boom did materialize, but, especially in the context of runaway inflation, it was nowhere near sufficient to prevent manufacturing profitability from falling by more than 20 per cent between 1969 and 1973. When, in the wake of the deep oil-crisis recession of 1974–75, the bottom dropped out of the world market, returns from overseas sales collapsed and the Japanese manufacturing profit rate plunged a further 50 per cent, making for a total decline of 60 per cent between 1969 and 1975 (see above, p. 19, Figure 1.1). During the same years, the Japanese manufacturing labour force, which had grown ceaselessly throughout the length of the long post-war boom, fell by close to 15 per cent.[4]

From 1975, the US economic recovery, driven as usual by rising Keynesian federal deficits, pulled the Japanese economy from its recession. But the cyclical upturn was once again accompanied by sprouting US trade and current account deficits, which brought in their train a new period of declining dollar and elevating yen. Between 1975 and 1979, the yen rose at an average annual rate of 7.6 per cent against the dollar.

The Japanese manufacturing economy responded to this enormous

[3] For this, and the previous paragraph, see Y. Kosai, *The Era of High-Speed Growth. Notes on the Postwar Japanese Economy*, Tokyo, University of Tokyo Press, 1986; T. Uchino, *Japan's Postwar Economy. An Insider's View of its History and its Future*, Tokyo, Kodansha International, 1983.

[4] Kosai, *Era of High-Speed Growth*; Uchino, *Japan's Postwar Economy*.

burden of rising costs by unleashing an extraordinary process of self-transformation. It almost doubled the share of investment devoted to technology-intensive lines. It focused ever more obsessively on general machinery, electrical machinery, transportation equipment, and precision instruments, while leaving behind the 'heavy' chemical, petroleum, and metal industries, as well, of course, as labour-intensive textile and food industries. It hugely improved its efficiency in the use of raw materials, especially oil. In order to accomplish all this, it maintained a rate of growth of capital stock, which, though vastly lower than that of the 1960s, was a third higher than that achieved by US manufacturing in the same period. On that basis, it continued to secure the highest rate of labour productivity growth among the advanced capitalist economies. Meanwhile, its 'cooperative' labour force acceded to quite massive reductions in the growth of real wages. Between 1975 and 1979, Japanese manufacturing unit labour costs fell at an average annual rate of 2 per cent.[5]

Between 1973 and 1979 Japan did succeed in increasing its exports at the average annual rate of 9 per cent and raised its share of world exports by 10 per cent. Nevertheless, the burden of the exploding yen proved difficult to fully overcome, and in 1978 and 1979 export growth was grinding to a halt. In order to compensate for the resulting reduction in the growth of demand, the government turned to Keynesian deficits, and the manufacturing profit rate did climb significantly above the depths to which it had descended at the bottom of the oil-crisis recession. Nevertheless, with manufacturing producers subjected to unprecedented downward stress on their prices as a consequence of the runaway yen, manufacturing profitability remained 25 per cent below its level of 1973 and 40 per cent under that of 1969. When the new oil crisis struck at the end of the decade, Japan slid, along with the rest of the world economy, into a new (if mild) recession.

---

[5] K. Imai, 'Japan's Changing Industrial Structure', in Yamamura, ed., *Policy and Trade Issues of the Japanese Economy*, pp. 58–9; OECD, *Economic Survey. Japan 1981*, Paris, 1981, pp. 37–61; OECD, *Economic Survey. Japan 1985*, Paris, 1985, pp. 54–77; OECD, *Economic Survey. Japan 1989*, Paris, 1989, pp. 67–82.

Economic recovery via the bubble?

The Japanese economy was enabled to emerge from the world recession of the early 1980s thanks to record US federal and current account deficits and, especially, an exploding dollar. The latter made possible a new Japanese export-led cyclical upturn, just as they had following the international cyclical downturn of 1974–75. At the tail-end of the 1970s, under the stress of the ascendant yen, Japanese exports had fallen off precipitously. But, stimulated by the yen's new decline that began in 1979, they sprang forward at the average annual rate of 9.5 per cent between 1979 and 1985 (see above, p. 98, Figure 3.2). Between 1982 and 1986, Japanese exports to the US grew at the spectacular average annual rate of 23 per cent (in nominal terms). In just that short period, moreover, Japanese exports to the US as a percentage of total Japanese exports increased from 26.4 per cent to 38.9 per cent. The Japanese current account surplus, at 0.4 per cent of GDP in 1981, reached 4.2 per cent of GDP by 1986.

By 1984–85, the manufacturing rate of profit had jumped almost 20 per cent above its level of 1978, and had come within 10 per cent of its level of 1973. Japanese economic growth was back up above 4 per cent, and the capital stock was swelling at the average annual rate of above 6 per cent. The Japanese economy seemed to have regained, at least for the moment, its traditional, export-oriented path (see above, p. 19, Figure 1.1).

The US federal and current account deficits that supported Japan's economic expansion during the first half of the 1980s were historically unprecedented, and they soon transformed the US into the world's largest debtor, with major implications for the US–Japan relationship (see above, p. 54). The Japanese henceforth became the US's leading, and most reliable, creditor. The US government therefore acquired an interest in the continued health of the Japanese economy, for this was a precondition to the continued supply of money to fund its external imbalances. The Japanese, for their part, were only too happy to cover the widening gap between US exports and imports, for their so doing enabled US firms and households to keep buying Japanese exports.[6]

---

[6] Murphy, *Weight of the Yen.*

Nevertheless, Japan's fundamental problem of the tendency of the yen to rise remained very much unresolved, although it was temporarily obscured by a levitating US currency that was itself kept aloft by rocketing US real interest rates. Rising Japanese trade surpluses, the obverse side of rising US trade deficits, were thus bound to place continuing upward pressure on the yen. Henceforth, moreover, Japan's growing returns from its investments in US dollar-denominated assets would tend to magnify this. The tendency for the yen to rise was all the more threatening given the unlikelihood that the world economy would, for the foreseeable future, regain its dynamism of the first post-war quarter century. Assuming an unchanging background of repression of the Japanese import market and effective stagnation of the world market, the export-dependent Japanese economy had effectively but one route of escape, and that was via a high dollar. The Reagan administration, with its willingness to tolerate high interest rates in order to attract an ever-increasing inflow of money from abroad, did provide precisely this. But the resulting sacrifice of the US manufacturing sector to the needs of international finance was unsustainable in any longer run.

By the middle of the 1980s, the combination of record-breaking Japanese trade surpluses and record-breaking US trade deficits was thus creating ever-increasing pressures for precisely the same sort of adjustment that had undermined Japanese expansions after 1970 and again after 1975. In 1985, the Japanese government was obliged to accept the Plaza Accord, despite the grave danger it posed to continued Japanese export-oriented growth. In reality, Japanese authorities had little choice, for signing this agreement was the only way to secure continued access for Japanese producers to the indispensable US market against a rising tide of US protectionism, motivated by the crisis of US manufacturing under the stress of the high dollar. Nevertheless, the resulting ascent of the yen, the third wave of yen appreciation since 1971, was far greater than Japanese authorities had expected. Between 1985 and 1988, the yen's value vaulted upward by 56 per cent in trade-weighted terms and by 93 per cent against the dollar, a much greater appreciation than those of either 1971–73 or 1975–78. By 1988, the yen–dollar exchange rate, at 260/$ as late as March 1985, had reached 120/$, almost double the value of its previous peak of 210/$ in the late 1970s and triple its value before December 1971, when the rate was 360/$ (see above, p. 65, Figure 2.6, and p. 99, Figure 3.3). The Japanese economy, and especially its export-dependent manufacturing sector, was now subjected to unprecedented levels of stress, much as had the US manufacturing sector during the previous half decade when the dollar had skyrocketed.[7]

Already by 1986, the Japanese economy was confronting what was potentially its most severe crisis since 1950. The effective exchange rate of the yen had increased by 46 per cent, with devastating impact. Having risen by 15.5 per cent and 4.0 per cent, respectively, in 1984 and 1985, annual Japanese nominal goods exports suddenly collapsed by 15.9 per cent. Manufacturing output also fell, private business growth slipped to 1.2 per cent, and the economy seemed headed for a major recession. To meet the challenge, much as it had in the early 1970s, the government launched a policy of extreme monetary ease, aiming not only to stimulate the economy, but also to drive up asset values. It reduced the interest rate from 5 per cent to 3 per cent and, in 1987, to a post-war low of 2.5 per cent. Simultaneously, it promoted the massive extension of bank lending to real estate companies and brokerages in order to artificially inflate equity and land prices. The goal was not only to lower corporations' cost of borrowing; it was also to directly increase their wealth by puffing up the value of the substantial blocs of land and equities in their possession. The wealth effect of higher share prices would also push up consumer spending by inflating the value of household assets, especially land, and thereby encouraging dis-saving. If all went according to plan, Japanese manufacturers would acquire both the wherewithal and the incentive to raise investment growth sufficiently not only to increase international competitiveness by another order of magnitude so as to neutralize the effect of the rising yen, but also to reorient the Japanese economy away from exports and toward the home market.[8]

---

[7] For this, and the previous, paragraph, C.R. Henning, *Currencies and Politics in the United States, Germany, and Japan*, Washington, DC, Institute for International Economics, 1994, pp. 144–7.

[8] For this, and the following, paragraph, see Murphy, *Weight of the Yen*, pp. 209–18; T. Taniguchi, *Japan's Banks and the 'Bubble Economy' of the Late 1980s*, Princeton University,

The government's essay in ultra-cheap money did provoke runaway speculation, as was apparently hoped, and the unprecedented financial bubble that ensued powered a strong new cyclical upturn that lasted through the end of the decade. Real estate companies and brokerages borrowed massively to buy land and equities with the intent to sell at a higher price. Land prices thus rocketed, with both residential and commercial prices doubling between 1986 and 1989. Share prices on the Tokyo Stock Exchange reached their historic high at the end of 1989, also having doubled over the previous two years. Consumers reduced their savings rate and stepped up their spending, and residential construction boomed. Corporations at first exploited the tremendous increase in the value of their shares and land to reduce their reliance on debt finance, as well as to engage in financial manipulation ('zaitech'), raising funds very cheaply on the money market and depositing them at higher rates of return in interest rate deposits. But eventually, as the government had intended, they took advantage of the enormous increase in their wealth, as well the growth of consumer demand, to carry through a wave of plant and equipment investment on a scale not seen since the 1960s. Between 1986 and 1991, the economy boomed, as private business plant and equipment investment shot up at an average annual rate of 10.5 per cent and the growth of GDP averaged 4.8 per cent per annum.

Japanese manufacturers made Herculean efforts to improve and transform production so as to maintain exports in the face of a new rise of the yen after 1985, much as they had during the years of currency revaluation of the mid- to late 1970s. Between 1985 and 1991, they sustained an average annual rate of growth of the gross capital stock of 6.7 per cent. US manufacturers, who were benefiting at this juncture from a collapsing dollar, increased their own capital stock in these years less than one-third as fast. Japanese manufacturers were thus able to propel hourly labour productivity forward at an average annual rate of 5.4 per cent, compared to 2.2 per cent in the US. Indeed, by the end of the 1980s, Japanese

Center for International Studies, Program on US–Japan Relations, Monograph Series, no. 4 Princeton, 1993, p. 9; Y. Noguchi, 'The "Bubble" and Economic Policies in the 1980s', *Journal of Japanese Studies*, vol. xx, no. 2, Summer 1994.

manufacturers had succeeded in increasing the proportion of their output that was either high-tech or mixed high-tech and capital-intensive to about 85 per cent, catching up with the US in its degree of specialization in high-tech and high-wage lines, and becoming even more emancipated than was the US from low-wage and low-tech production.[9]

The failure of the bubble

Nevertheless, despite their multifaceted effort at adjustment, Japanese manufacturers found it difficult to offset the increase in costs entailed by the huge revaluation of the yen by means of improving manufacturing efficiency and entering new, technology-intensive industries where competition was less ferocious. In the end, therefore, they failed either to avoid a sharp fall in the rate of growth of manufacturing exports or to achieve a significant increase of manufacturing profitability. The bubble did enable Japanese producers to ward off, for a time, the sort decline of profitability and fall-off of capital accumulation that would undoubtedly have taken place in its absence, and to achieve the appearance of an enormous economic boom. But Japanese manufacturers had, in the longer run, to pay a heavy price for the bubble's temporary stimulus.

Between 1985 and 1991, Japanese producers succeeded, by means of the huge increment in investment growth and the resulting augmentation of productivity growth, in limiting the average annual growth of manufacturing unit labour costs *in national terms* to just 0.3 per cent. But because the yen's effective (trade-weighted) exchange rate rose in this period at the devastating average annual rate of 6.9 per cent, they could not prevent unit labour costs *in international terms* (in terms of the currencies of its trading partners) from shooting up at an average annual rate of 5.5 per cent. Japanese producers held down the *yen* prices of their exports at an average annual rate of − 3.5 per cent, but this meant that these prices still rose *in international terms* at an average annual rate of 3.4 per cent. During the years 1985–91, Japanese average annual export growth withered to 3.0 per cent, less than one-third as fast as between 1979 and 1985, and would

[9] OECD, *Industrial Policy in OECD Countries*, Paris, 1994, pp. 117, 134.

have been even lower had it not been so strongly supported by gargantuan US budget and trade deficits. As a share of the world total, Japan's exports plunged sharply from a peak of 10.3 per cent in 1986 to 8.5 per cent in 1990. By comparison, US exporters, who enjoyed a 50 per cent devaluation of the dollar against the yen in these years, were able to raise their prices in national terms at an average annual rate of 2.3 per cent and still achieve a rate of growth of exports that was more than double that of their Japanese counterparts, while slightly expanding their share of world exports.

Nor were Japanese producers able to trade off reduced export growth against a significant increase in their rate of profit. With export prices in yen terms pressed down so hard with respect to costs, profitability on manufacturing exports was naturally squeezed. According to the OECD, Japanese exporters could pass through, as price increases, only about 75 per cent on average of the rise in costs attributable to the higher yen.[10] Since, in these years, the ratio of manufacturing exports to manufacturing value-added had hit 45 per cent, one can see what Japanese producers were up against. Despite the advantages in terms of the cost of capital and subsidy to demand bequeathed to them by the bubble, manufacturers were thus unable to raise their rate of profit above its level of 1985, which was itself about 10 per cent below the already substantially reduced level of 1973. Since those advantages were bound to be temporary, disappearing once the bubble had burst, the implication was that they had failed to re-establish the conditions for sustaining reasonably rapid capital accumulation.

Thanks to the bubble – and the very cheap capital and huge growth of domestic demand that the bubble afforded – Japanese manufacturers had succeeded, despite the highly unfavourable relative cost conditions endowed by the rising yen, in maintaining their profit rates, in underwriting a huge wave of investment, and in supporting an economic expansion that was the envy of the world. But, as should perhaps have been more evident at the time, precisely because of its dependence on the bubble,

[10] OECD, *Economic Survey. Japan 1989*, pp. 93, 95. OECD, *Economic Survey. Japan 1988*, Paris, 1988, pp. 55–7.

the boom had faulty foundations that made it unsustainable. It relied upon runaway equity and land prices that increased the paper wealth of corporations (and some households), capital that was rendered almost free by record-low interest rates and enormously inflated share values, and a consumption boom helped along by the wealth effect, as well as the ability to borrow at record-low rates. But once the bubble deflated, all of these stimuli were bound to disappear or go into reverse, so the investment and consumption growth that depended on them was bound to give way.

The Japanese manufacturing sector would, at the point that the bubble imploded, still have to come to terms with the rising yen and declining international competitiveness, but its profits would no longer be held up by the amplification of demand for their goods and the reduction in the cost of their capital that had been temporarily endowed by rising share and land values. Their situation would be rendered that much more difficult, moreover, by the huge over-capacity that was bound to be the residue of virtually free finance; by the fall-off in domestic demand growth that could not but result from the reversal of the wealth effect and from the necessity of households and corporations to mend balance sheets strained by the enormous accumulation of debt; and, finally, by the decline of the banks' capacity to lend under a mountain of non-performing loans that were the predictable consequence of the collapse of equity and land prices.

Japan in recession, 1991–95

In 1989 and 1990, Japanese authorities sharply raised interest rates in order to rein in the stock market and land bubbles. But in so doing, they sparked off a deepening recession that resulted not only from the bursting of the bubble, but also from the failure of the bubble to have endowed the economy with the capacity to resolve its underlying difficulties of declining competitiveness within a laggardly world economy. Following the cyclical peak of February 1991, there followed a 32-month recession, the second longest of the post-war epoch.

Over-capacity

Above all, corporations across much of the economy found themselves in possession of far more productive capacity than they could use, the legacy of access to nearly costless capital which funded massive investment throughout the years of the bubble. Moreover, with the values of their equities reduced, corporations found it more expensive to raise funds, all the more so since interest rates had risen from 2.5 to 6 per cent in little more than a year. They also faced contracting demand, as households and firms not only cut back on their expenditures, but also slowed their borrowing and increased their savings. To make matters worse, they were chained down by unusually high fixed costs, as a result of the generalized reluctance to lay off workers, as well as their much increased interest payments on the huge debts that they had initially contracted at much lower rates.

As part and parcel of the same development, Japanese banks experienced increasing financial fragility. They thus had to pay the price for their massive lending over the previous half-decade, not only to over-stretched manufacturing firms now facing a profit squeeze, but also to real estate and brokerage firms that had speculated in land and shares and were now rendered insolvent by the implosion of the bubble. When the recession set in, banks thus found themselves holding huge quantities of non-performing loans, which badly impaired their ability to lend, further retarding capital accumulation in the economy as a whole. Between 1991 and 1995, Japan's GDP stumbled along at an average annual rate of just 0.8 per cent.[11]

If the recession's origins can be attributed to the reversal of the wealth effect and, in particular, the over-capacity bequeathed by the bubble, its lengthy persistence was due to the longevity of the same underlying structural problem that had originally threatened depression in the middle 1980s and remained unresolved by the bubble. The economy depended on export growth to counter its in-built tendency to excess capacity resulting from systematic over-investment in manufacturing lines. But export growth was ever more difficult to undertake in the face of the

[11] OECD, *Economic Survey. Japan 1998*, Paris, 1998, pp. 21–35.

tendency of the domestic currency to rise and the international economy's inability to transcend long-term stagnation resulting from system-wide over-capacity and over-production in manufacturing. The problem was rendered all the more difficult to overcome by the wide-ranging system of mutual support, ultimately guaranteed by the government, that protected core industrial and financial corporations from going out of business or even from having to prune redundant plant, equipment, and labour. The economy was thus prevented, to a significant degree, from purging superfluous, high-cost means of production by the standard capitalist methods of bankruptcy, downsizing, and layoffs, with the result that the continued operation of unprofitable, or barely profitable, means of production placed excruciating downward pressure on prices.

From 1991 through 1995, the yen once again took off, the fourth major wave of yen revaluation since 1971. During the last years of the 1980s, encouraged by the exceedingly low interest rates introduced by Japanese authorities, Japanese capitalists had made enormous purchases of US assets, which propped up the dollar and pushed down the yen. But when the recession hit, they were obliged to reduce or cease their overseas buying, liquidate many of their US properties, and bring their money home. Japanese acquisitions of US Treasury instruments, US equities, and other sorts of US assets thus fell sharply. At the same time, with the collapse of demand at home and the earlier recovery from recession in the US, the relative growth of imports as against exports slowed, and the trade surplus again expanded. Meanwhile, despite the Japanese government's reduction of nominal interest rates below those in the US, Japanese real interest rates remained above their US counterparts, because the Japanese recession kept the growth of Japanese prices more than correspondingly lower than those in the US. The relative demand for yen vis-à-vis dollars could not then but mount, with the result that, between 1990 and 1995, the currency's effective exchange rate grew at a punishing average annual rate of 9.5 per cent, even faster than in the previous five years, and its value against the dollar increased by a total of 54 per cent[12] (see above, p. 65, Figure 2.6, and p. 99, Figure 3.3).

[12] Murphy, *Weight of the Yen*, pp. 287–8; OECD, *Economic Survey. Japan 1993*, Paris, 1993, p. 9.

As they had during the early 1970s, the later 1970s, and the second half of the 1980s, Japanese producers sought to compensate for the increase in their costs that resulted from the rising yen by stepping up their productiveness further. By the mid-1990s, they had indeed managed to kick up the technological level of their exports another notch. They had increased the share in total exports of high technology-intensive products – including sophisticated capital goods (such as industrial robots), components (such as liquid crystal displays and other devices for computers and telecommunications equipment), and industrial intermediate materials (such as ceramics) – to 80 per cent, from just 55 per cent in 1985, while trimming back the share of capital-intensive but medium technology products, such as steel, automobiles, and home electronics. They had also hitched up the share of capital goods in total exports to 62 per cent from 48 per cent, while minimizing the share of lower value-added consumer goods correspondingly.[13] But these improvements fell far short of what was required.

Japanese producers could simply no longer raise productivity growth and thereby reduce the growth of costs sufficiently to counteract the increase in their costs that resulted from the fast-rising yen. This was because they could no longer come close to maintaining the very high rates of capital accumulation that were required, since their rate of return could not allow it or justify it. During the second half of the 1980s, they had managed to increase the growth of investment and productivity sufficiently to keep their profit rates from falling only by virtue of the enormous benefits they had derived from the bubble. But, owing to the failure of profitability to have risen much between 1985 and 1991 – and the subsequent onset of over-capacity, declining demand growth, rising fixed costs, and plunging profitability when the stimulus of the bubble collapsed – business and manufacturing investment dropped at the average annual rates of 7 per cent and 14 per cent, respectively, in 1992, 1993, and 1994, after having risen at the average annual rates of 9 per cent and

---

[13] M. Yoshitomi, 'On the Changing International Competitiveness of Japanese Manufacturing Since 1985', *Oxford Review of Economic Policy*, vol. xii, no. 3, 1996; OECD, *Economic Survey. Japan 1996*, Paris, 1996, p. 31.

11 per cent, respectively, in 1990 and 1991. Between 1991 and 1995, investment as a percentage of GDP weakened from 20 per cent to 14 per cent. The average annual increase of the capital stock simultaneously fell off by more than one-third, compared to that for 1985–91.[14]

With capital accumulation diminishing so quickly, producers found it impossible to keep reducing costs in the way they had in the second half of the 1980s. Between 1991 and 1995, the growth of manufacturing productivity declined by 50 per cent, compared to 1985–91. As a result, unit labour costs in national terms, which had actually fallen at close to 1 per cent per annum between 1985 and 1990, increased fairly rapidly (until 1995), more rapidly in fact than did those of their rivals and trading partners. Unit labour costs in international, or trade-weighted, terms thus climbed even faster than the fast-rising effective exchange rate, at the extraordinary annual average rate of 11 per cent, profoundly reducing Japanese export competitiveness.

With their international competitiveness hurtling downward, Japanese manufacturers were able neither to increase export growth, nor to hold off the rapid increase of imports into the Japanese market, nor to prevent a profound erosion of their profit rates. Between 1991 and 1995, Japanese producers managed to increase their exports at roughly the same, very reduced, rate as between 1985 and 1991 – 3.1 per cent – while maintaining their share of world exports (see above, p. 98, Figure 3.2). But they were able to do so only at great cost. To maintain even such modest export growth, they were obliged to stamp down the prices of their exports at an average annual rate of 3.9 per cent. Japanese exporters were thus 'absorbing two-thirds of the currency appreciation' and naturally having to accept an enormous squeeze on their profitability.[15] During the same period, manufacturing import penetration of the Japanese market in *volume terms (constant prices)* almost tripled, from a little less than 3 per cent to a little more than 8 per cent. It is true, by contrast, that in *value terms (current*

---

[14] OECD, *Economic Survey. Japan 1998*, p. 28, Table 3.
[15] For the difficulties of passing through the cost increases resulting from yen revaluation in higher export prices, and consequent downward pressure on profitability, see OECD, *Economic Survey. Japan 1993*, p. 31; OECD, *Economic Survey. Japan 1994*, Paris, 1994, pp. 22, 27 (quotation).

prices) import penetration barely increased. But this is only to say that Japanese manufacturers succeeded in defending their import markets – as they did their export markets – by holding down prices, and very much at the expense of profits.[16]

Given the Japanese institutional set-up and the barriers in the way of the economy's shedding of labour or plant and equipment, the shakeout of high-cost, low-profit means of means of production was able to proceed only slowly even in the face of serious recession, with the result that downward pressure on prices mounted all across the economy. Between 1991 and 1995, the increase in the GDP deflator declined steadily, falling below zero in 1994 and 1995. Over the same four-year period, the growth of product prices in the manufacturing sector averaged −1.5 per cent. Between its 1980s peak, achieved in 1987–88, and its low point during the depths of the recession (1993–94), the profitability for the Japanese business sector as a whole fell by more then 40 per cent. Simultaneously, the manufacturing profit rate disintegrated by fully two-thirds (see above p. 39, Figure 1.3, and p. 97, Figure 3.1).[17]

Reorientation to East Asia

From the time of the Plaza Accord of 1985, Japanese manufacturers had sought to respond to the squeeze on their competitiveness that resulted from the rising yen in part by reorienting production, trade, and finance to East Asia. When, following the bursting of the bubble in 1990–91, domestic investment prospects dimmed while the yen's exchange rate continued to rise, they redoubled their efforts in this direction. The idea was to focus domestic production in Japan ever more exclusively on the highest technology lines by relying on the country's highly skilled but expensive labour force, while sloughing off less advanced production to East Asia, to be combined with local cheap labour that had been made significantly less costly by the appreciation of the yen vis-à-vis local currencies that were mostly tied to the dollar.

[16] OECD, *Economic Survey. Japan 1995*, Paris, 1995, pp. 24–5, especially Figure 14B.
[17] OECD, *Economic Survey. Japan 1996*, p. 18, Figure 4.

At the heart of this initiative was the large-scale establishment of subsidiaries of Japanese multinationals in East Asia, supported by the relocation there of firms within their supplier networks. This enabled Japanese corporations to penetrate indirectly a US market that had become ever more difficult for them to enter directly, as protectionist barriers had risen and the yen had soared. It also provided them better access to the fast-growing markets of Asia itself. In addition it stimulated East Asian demand for Japanese high-technology capital and intermediate goods exports. Playing a major role, along with the state, in orchestrating the whole process, Japanese banks supplied huge loans to Japanese corporations initiating operations in East Asia, as well as to East Asian corporations, and came to constitute the largest external source of bank loans to every country in the region except for Taiwan and the Philippines.[18]

During the first half of the 1990s, manufacturing investment in East Asia recorded an average profit to sales ratio that almost *tripled* that in Japan. Subsidiaries in the labour-intensive textile industry were particularly profitable as a result of much lower East Asian labour costs. Understandably, the transformation was carried out with all deliberate speed. By 1996, East Asia was absorbing more than 40 per cent of Japan's exports and about the same percentage of its foreign direct investment in manufacturing, up from about 30 and 20 per cent, respectively, six years earlier. Japan's banks were responsible, moreover, for between 30 and 40 per cent of East Asia's outstanding loans from the advanced capitalist economies.[19]

[18] For this, and the previous, paragraph, see W. Hatch and K. Yamamura, *Asia in Japan's Embrace. Building a Regional Production Alliance*, Cambridge, Cambridge University Press, 1996; M. Bernard and J. Ravenhill, 'Beyond Product Cycles and Flying Geese: Regionalization, Hierarchy, and the Industrialization of East Asia', *World Politics*, vol. xlvii, January 1995; R. Bevacqua, 'Whither the Japanese Model? The Asian Economic Crisis and the Continuation of Cold War Politics in the Pacific Rim', *Review of International Political Economy*, vol. v, Autumn, 1998.

[19] Bevacqua, 'Whither the Japanese Model?', pp. 414–15; OECD, *Economic Survey. Japan 1995*, pp. 26, 154.

No exit from the downturn

During the course of 1994, the Japanese economy seemed finally to be emerging from its recession. But its revival was once again interrupted, by a new, vertiginous rise of the yen. Having been burned so often before by dollar devaluation, Japanese private investors now showed themselves far less willing than in the past to buy US assets. When the Mexican peso crisis hit in late 1994 and early 1995, there was a new run on the dollar, and by April 1995 the yen had reach its highest level in history, at 79/$. In 1994–95 manufacturing investment to East Asia surged in response to yen appreciation, almost doubling in those two years, after having increased by less than 50 per cent in the previous two. At this point, for the first time ever, the growth of overseas production began to have a net negative effect on domestic production and employment, as the gains from increased exports of capital and component parts to Japanese subsidiaries abroad were more than counterbalanced by the losses due to the substitution of production abroad for Japanese exports, as well as the increase in imports from foreign subsidiaries. Import growth simultaneously sharply accelerated and became a major drag on the growth of GDP.[20] In 1994 and 1995, manufacturing product prices fell at the average annual rate of 3 per cent – the greatest two-year decline by far during the post-war epoch.[21] During the first part of 1995, the Japanese manufacturing economy once again began to freeze up, threatening a new recession at home – and a flight of Japanese capital from the US.

GERMANY

From very early on in the post-war period, the German economy suffered from a pattern of self-undermining export expansion somewhat analogous

[20] OECD, *Economic Survey. Japan 1994*, p. 39; OECD, *Economic Survey. Japan 1995*, p. 25; OECD, *Economic Survey. Japan 1998*, pp. 27, 30–2; G. Baker, 'A Powerful Pull on the World', *Financial Times*, 31 July 1995.
[21] In the previous two years, 1992 and 1993, when Japan was formally in recession, manufacturing prices had managed to remain flat.

to that of the Japanese. From the end of the 1940s to the end of the 1960s, and especially during the 1950s, it achieved impressive growth primarily by means of the very rapid growth of manufacturing sales abroad, and it did so not only through exploiting the extraordinary expansion of the world market that took place during the long post-war boom, but also by taking an ever-increasing share of that market. But this mode of development was plagued by a fundamental contradiction. German authorities sought to maintain the conditions for export-led growth through restrictive fiscal and monetary policies that repressed the growth of domestic demand, keeping down the increase of domestic costs and prices. Their efforts did help speed up exports through facilitating the slower growth of export prices, but they simultaneously slowed imports, with the result that (manufacturing) trade surpluses became chronic and made for forceful upward pressure on the German currency. Tight money making for relatively high interest rates in international terms conduced to the same effect. It proved, in both the medium and long run, impossible to transcend this syndrome, especially because a broader intensification of international competition throughout the advanced capitalist world – and beyond – was simultaneously making for system-wide manufacturing over-capacity and over-production.

Already in 1961, German authorities were forced to revalue the mark by 5 per cent. Their move came in the wake not only of rising trade surpluses, but also of the beginning of substantial competition, not only from surging manufacturing economies within Europe, notably France and Italy, but from the US and Japan as well. It therefore ended up coinciding with the end of the super-fast export-led growth of the 1950s.

After 1965, as the US economy and its market expanded rapidly in response to record federal deficits arising from the Vietnam War and as US competitiveness once again fell back, German, as well as Japanese, exports to the US grew correspondingly, leading to enormous US trade and current account deficits and parallel German, and Japanese, trade and current account surpluses. In this context, as has been seen, US manufacturing profitability fell steeply, manifesting not only declining US competitiveness, but also system-wide over-capacity, registered in the 25 per cent decline in aggregate G-7 manufacturing profitability between

1965 and 1973. But the dollar also had to fall, and as the mark rose by 32 per cent against the dollar between 1969 and 1973, German manufacturers saw their profitability fall by 30 per cent. All told, profitability in German manufacturing had by 1973 sunk by a total of 53 per cent from its very elevated peak of 1955, and Germany entered the long downturn, along with the rest of the world economy (see above, p. 19, Figure 1.1).

Nor was the syndrome transcended in the 1970s. The US economy, under the stimulus of rising Federal deficits, pulled the German economy from the deep oil-crisis recession of 1974–75, but not before the accompanying deep fall-off of world trade had forced a German manufacturing sector, suffering from a secular decline in competitiveness, to shed almost a fifth of its labour force. The German authorities sought to revive growth on an export-led basis by repressing domestic costs through adopting, once again, a highly restrictive macroeconomic policy stance. But the German trade surpluses that ensued, which were paralleled of course by runaway US trade and current account deficits, ensured a new rise of the mark, which accompanied the further decline of the dollar. German costs could not be slimmed down sufficiently to compensate for the rising currency, and German manufacturing profitability fell somewhat further, precipitating a huge dip in the growth of the capital stock over the course of the 1970s (see above, p. 19, Figure 1.1).[22]

The 1980s: the impasse of export-led manufacturing

A combination of runaway oil prices and a coordinated international turn to tight money by governments throughout the advanced capitalist world precipitated, as almost everywhere else, a very major recession for the German economy at the end of the 1970s. During the three years 1980, 1981, and 1982, the average annual growth of GDP fell to 0 per cent, and the rate of profit in manufacturing, though not outside it, dropped to

[22] For the previous two paragraphs, see R. Brenner, 'The Economics of Global Turbulence', pp. 70–6, 124–8, 173–8; H. Giersch, K.-H. Paqué, and H. Schmeiding, *The Fading Miracle. Four Decades of Market-Economy in Germany*, Cambridge, Cambridge University Press, 1992, especially pp. 197–8.

very low levels, on average 50 per cent below its level of 1979. But the cyclical downturn did not shake the resolve of the German governing authorities. In the wake of what they deemed to be a highly unsatisfactory experiment with Keynesian deficits at the very end of the 1970s, forced upon them by the Carter administration, they were bent on taking 'sound finance' even further than ever before.

This policy of seeking economic contraction in the interests of greater cost-effectiveness had, of course, a certain logic, since major sections of Germany's manufacturing plant and equipment had, in the face of the irrepressible mark and the further intensification of international competition, become redundant in international terms, requiring trimming, rationalization, upgrading, and supersession. The German authorities thus intended to leave it to the market to pressure the economy for change, and to Germany's capitalist institutions, and particularly its unmatched labour force, to fabricate the required transformation. Yet, to pose such a challenge to the German economy was hardly to ensure a successful response, especially since the deep roots of the problem were not by any means merely German, but lay also in the over-capacity and over-production that dogged international manufacturing.

The German authorities refused to significantly loosen the supply of credit until 1987. They also reduced the budget deficit as a proportion of GDP from 3.1 per cent in 1980 to 1.1 per cent in 1985. With the cost of borrowing in the US simultaneously skyrocketing, the German economy saw its real interest rates rise from an average of about 2.5 per cent during the 1970s to an average of 5.1 per cent between 1979 and 1984 and 4.1 per cent between 1984 and 1989.[23]

Under such severe deflationary pressure, the German economy had little difficulty in sharply reducing the growth of costs. Between 1980 and 1986, manufacturing output failed to rise as high as 2 per cent in any year. The manufacturing labour force meanwhile fell precipitously, by a further one-tenth in terms of hours. Manufacturers were therefore able to cut the growth of real wages in half, compared to the years between 1973

---

[23] For this and the previous two paragraphs, see Brenner, 'The Economics of Global Turbulence', pp. 226–7; Giersch et al., *Fading Miracle*, pp. 192–5, 212.

and 1979, and to secure a certain increase in productivity merely through rationalization and downsizing. They thereby pretty much succeeded in bringing inflation under control, as the annual increase of the consumer price index fell from 6.2 per cent in 1981 to 0.6 per cent in 1987. Between 1982 and 1990, the average annual growth of unit labour costs in German manufacturing fell by more than half, to 2.1 per cent, from 4.8 per cent between 1973 and 1979.

In this context, the growth of overseas sales did succeed in bringing about a new cyclical upturn. Especially as the stimulus from Ronald Reagan's military Keynesianism reached its culmination and the dollar rose sharply against the mark, export growth in Germany, as in Japan, bounced back, averaging close to 8 per cent for 1984–85. Nevertheless, based as it was on a combination of US deficits and a high dollar, export-led growth could not really take hold, and turned out once more to be self-limiting.

With imports held down and exports rising, German trade and current account surpluses increased rapidly, placing ever greater upward pressure on the currency. Once the Plaza Accord was agreed in 1985, the mark appreciated sharply, its effective exchange rate increasing at an average annual rate of 4.6 per cent during the next five years (see above, p. 99, Figure 3.3). German producers were obliged to absorb virtually all of the cost increase entailed by this revaluation, manufacturing unit labour costs in international terms growing at an average annual rate of 4.2 per cent in those years. German producers, like their Japanese counterparts, went out of their way to keep their export prices down so as to keep export growth and market shares up, and export prices expressed in terms of the national currency fell at an average annual rate of 1.1 per cent between 1985 and 1989. But, in so doing, they inevitably had to sacrifice profitability. Even by the end of the decade, the manufacturing rate of profit was no higher than it had been at the end of the 1970s, at which point it was 10 per cent lower than it had been in 1973, 36 per cent lower than in 1969, and 65 per cent lower than it had been in 1955 (see above, p. 19, Figure 1.1).

Because manufacturing profitability failed to recover, the revival of manufacturing capital accumulation was also stalled. The growth of the manufacturing capital stock, already sharply reduced in the 1970s, fell significantly further, to an average annual rate of just 1.4 per cent between 1979 and 1990, from an already low 2 per cent between 1973 and 1979. As a result, manufacturing labour productivity growth declined, too, increasing at an average annual rate of less than 2 per cent between 1979 and 1990, compared to 3.45 per cent between 1973 and 1979. During this period, Germany had the lowest rate of manufacturing labour productivity increase among the G-7 economies, except for Canada.[24]

As in the case of Japan, the counterpart of stagnating investment at home was the explosion of investment overseas. Until 1985, German foreign direct investment had been stable at around DM 10 billion per year, and largely offset by an influx of foreign investment into Germany. But, between 1985 and 1990, as the mark rocketed skyward, German direct investment overseas tripled to DM 30 billion per year, while foreign direct investment in Germany failed to rise.[25]

The problem thus confronting German manufacturing was easy to discern. In the face of its own declining competitiveness, which resulted especially from the secularly rising mark, export prospects, within the context of system-wide manufacturing over-capacity and over-production, were insufficient to elicit enough investment to bring down costs to a level liable to raise profitability. It is therefore understandable that, over the course of the decade, although the economy returned to full capacity, manufacturing stagnation issued, for the first time in the post-war epoch, in what can only be called mass unemployment. During the second half of the 1980s, the German unemployment rate averaged over 7 per cent.

The structural difficulties that haunted the German manufacturing sector were concealed by a brief boom at the end of the 1980s and the beginning of the 1990s. In response to the stock market crash of October 1987, macro-policy loosened both at home and across the advanced capitalist economies, and the German economy in general, and German exports in particular, enjoyed stepped-up growth. Then, in the wake of

[24] For this and the previous two paragraphs, see Brenner, 'The Economics of Global Turbulence', pp. 228–31.
[25] P. Norman, 'Savage German Shake-Out as Industrial Jobs Go Abroad', *Financial Times*, 7 February 1997.

unification, the German government unleashed a massive programme of subsidies aimed at reconstructing the economy of eastern Germany. The ensuing transfer of funds from western to eastern Germany provided a major shot in the arm to western German firms, pumping up the demand for their goods from the east.

Nevertheless, the record-breaking government deficits that financed reconstruction in eastern Germany could not be sustained indefinitely. They soon issued in a major flare-up of inflation, quite intolerable to the German authorities, who moved with alacrity to rein in the macroeconomic stimulus that had been driving the boom, opening the way to a new recession. Deprived of the subsidies to demand upon which it had been depending, the German economy could not avoid sinking into recession.[26]

Germany in recession, 1991–95

In 1991, to counteract the inflationary effects of the major state deficits that had financed the subsidies to East Germany, the German authorities cut spending and raised taxes. They also initiated an extended period of high interest rates to ensure long-term stability. Thus, almost like clockwork, the German authorities turned, on yet one more occasion, to macroeconomic probity to keep costs down in the interest of stability and cheaper exports. Nevertheless, as before, they not only decimated the domestic market, but also ended up undercutting Germany's international competitiveness by precipitating a new explosion upward of the mark. Matters were made very much worse when the US government refused to assume its accustomed role of sustaining increased federal deficits to keep the world economy turning over. The German economy once again came face to face with the problem of relatively high costs in international terms, under conditions of system-wide manufacturing over-capacity and over-production, and, like Japan, entered its worst and

---

[26] OECD, *Economic Survey. Germany 1990–91*, Paris, 1991, pp. 15, 19–20.

longest recession since 1950. Between 1991 and 1995, GDP grew at an average annual rate of just 0.9 per cent.

With the return to austerity at home, the German economy was, from 1991, thrust back into its standard dependence upon exports to mitigate recession and to secure its recovery under even more difficult conditions than previously. But, largely as an effect of the elevated interest rates that had been imposed to keep domestic costs down, the effective exchange rate of the mark rose at an average annual pace of 4 per cent (see above, p. 99, Figure 3.3). Those same elevated interest rates, as well as reduced German import growth, transmitted the German cyclical downturn to the rest of Europe, and this made it even harder for German manufacturers to sell abroad. Under these deteriorating cost and demand conditions, it is not surprising that manufacturers were disinclined to invest or expand. For 1992 and 1993 (the last years for which such data are available) the growth of manufacturing capital stock in western Germany averaged a mere 0.4 per cent, while manufacturing investment fell by 7.75 per cent and 23.7 per cent, respectively. Manufacturing productivity growth could not but languish, increasing at an average annual rate of only 1.5 per cent between 1991 and 1995.

The German manufacturing sector thus proved incapable of increasing investment to raise productivity growth so as to reduce costs to compensate for the rise of the currency. In fact, as in Japan in the same period, relative unit labour costs grew even faster than did the exchange rate, at an average annual rate of 5.35 per cent between 1991 and 1995. This meant that, even leaving aside the appreciation of the mark, German competitiveness was declining. West German manufacturers, as usual, sought to keep up overseas sales by keeping down the growth of prices, which increased at an average annual rate of just 1.5 per cent between 1991 and 1995, far below the growth of costs.[27] But, even so, they were unable to defend export growth, while naturally sacrificing profitability. Exports fell by 0.3 per cent in 1992, then fell again by 4.7 per cent in 1993; as a result, even by 1995, when a cyclical recovery had already begun, exports were only 6 per cent above their level of 1991. In 1995,

---

[27] OECD, *Economic Survey. Germany 1995–96*, Paris, 1996, p. 9.

the German share of world exports was down to 10.4 per cent, from 12.1 per cent as recently as 1990 and 12.4 per cent in 1987.

Faced with rising costs, huge downward pressure on prices from the world market, and the inability to increase exports, manufacturers could not avoid the deepest fall in their profitability of the post-war epoch. Between 1990 and 1993, the manufacturing rate of profit fell by three-quarters. By 1995, it had come back to no more than 50 or 60 per cent of its 1990 level (see above, p. 97, Figure 3.1).[28]

The combination of domestic austerity and export crisis brought a day of reckoning to the West German manufacturing sector, the third in the series of major shakeouts that marked its evolution through the length of the long downturn. Right up to 1970, the German economy had, by virtue of its export success, maintained an extraordinarily large manufacturing sector, constituting close to 40 per cent of both output and the labour force. It had done so partly on the basis of its strong manufacturing competitiveness in a period of rising demand for the goods in which it specialized, partly on the basis of the increasing under-valuation of its currency. But with the incessant rise of German relative costs, driven by the unrelenting rise of the mark under the impact of irrepressible trade and current account surpluses, the viability of an ever greater portion of this sector's productive power was progressively undercut from as early as 1961. In the crisis years culminating in the oil embargo of the early to mid-1970s and, then again, in the crisis years of 1979–85, the German manufacturing sector had lost 18.4 per cent and 10.25 per cent, respectively, of its labour force (in terms of hours). The deep recession of the 1990s brought still another phase in this trimming-down and weeding-out process. By 1995, the level of manufacturing output was 10 per cent below that of 1991, and, in the intervening years, the manufacturing labour force had fallen by 16 per cent.

---

[28] Ibid., p. 15, Figure 6.

CHANGING PLACES IN A STAGNANT WORLD ECONOMY

The recovery of profitability and economic dynamism in US manufacturing between 1986 and 1995 – based heavily on stepped-up export growth and rising competitiveness, rooted in a falling dollar and the holding down of wage growth, and only late in the day on increased investment growth and productivity growth – had quite clearly put great pressure on the manufacturing and export-oriented economies of Japan and Germany, with major consequences for western Europe as a whole. The deep recessions and large-scale manufacturing shakeouts experienced by Japan, Germany, and western Europe during the first half of the 1990s, in the presence of high currencies and in the wake of financial expansions, may thus fruitfully be considered as analogous to the crisis experienced by US manufacturing in the first half of the 1980s, following the Volcker shock, the take-off of the dollar, and the Reagan–Regan lurch toward finance.

The fact remains that, while the US economic revival took place largely at the expense of its leading rivals, that it had to do so was ultimately at the cost of the US economy itself. The US recovery of the early 1990s was thus itself limited by the ever slower growth of world demand, and in particular the related intensification of international competition in manufacturing, which placed intense downward pressure on prices throughout the world economy. Perhaps most directly to the point, in an interdependent world economy, the US economy could not easily sustain a truly serious crisis of its leading partners and rivals. Just as Japan and Germany had had to accede to the Plaza Accord and a falling dollar to rescue US manufacturing from its crisis of the first half of the 1980s, at great cost to themselves, so the US would soon be obliged to accept a quite similar bailout of Japan's crisis-bound manufacturing sector – again with epoch-making results.

CHAPTER 4

TURNING POINT: THE REVERSE PLAZA ACCORD

Even by the mid-1990s, the world economy showed little sign of awakening from its long period of dormancy. Growth was significantly slower in the advanced capitalist economies between 1990 and 1995 than in any other comparable period back to 1950. This was true not only of the Japanese and European economies, buried in their deepest recessions since 1950, but also of the US economy itself (see above, p.47, Table 1.10). The US economy expanded even more slowly in this half decade than it had during the 1970s and 1980s, although it must be acknowledged that slow growth in the US during the first half of the 1990s was, in key respects, the intended result of government policy, notably the Clinton administration's shift to balancing the budget and the Fed's hawkishness on the inflation/unemployment trade-off.

The Clinton administration's entire programme was, as has been seen, fixated on reducing the growth of wages and prices, and what could be better to attain that end than sluggish demand? The brake on wages and prices was essential for continuing the revival of manufacturing competitiveness and profitability and maintaining investment-driven, export-oriented growth in the face of withering international competition, as well as the decline of government subsidies to demand. It was also indispensable for maintaining profitability outside manufacturing, where productivity growth had maintained a snail-like pace since the later 1970s. Last but not least, the financial sector, which was increasingly occupying centre-stage, along with rentier interests more generally, required anti-inflation policies both to maintain the value of its loans and to profit from rising equity prices.

The fact remains that, although the US economic expansion of the 1990s was notoriously slow to accelerate, from the last quarter of 1993 the economy as a whole did finally begin to expand vigorously, drawing its strength in particular from the ongoing revival of the manufacturing sector. The economy had only just begun to pick up steam when it was slowed temporarily to a crawl in 1995 as a consequence of the Fed's brutal raising of interest rates throughout the previous year. But, following the Fed's return to ease in the middle of 1995, the economy eventually regained its momentum. During 1996 and especially 1997, the growth of every major economic variable increased sharply, with the notable exception of real wages.

Clearly, the recovery of corporate profitability and financial solidity, especially in the manufacturing sector, based heavily on dollar devaluation, wage repression, and corporate tax relief – and amplified from 1993–94 by the new boom in investment and resulting up-tick in productivity growth – was paying dividends all across the economy. The non-manufacturing sector had, from the start of the 1980s, when the manufacturing sector had entered into crisis, lost some of its vitality, but, responding in part to the new acceleration of manufacturing output and demand, it was once again moving forward rapidly (see above, pp. 78–81). In 1997, as real exports grew by 14 per cent, the US economy flourished as it had not for several decades, and it began to appear that it might finally lead the world economy out of its long stagnation. The expansion of the US domestic economy was, as usual, stimulating export-led growth among US producers' trading partners and rivals across the world economy. But, the US economy was itself no longer being driven, as it had long had to be, by growing government deficits, but rather, to an important degree, by rising capital investment, founded upon rising profit rates. Could a new world division of labour, emerging from the major crises and shakeouts of the early 1980s and early 1990s and based on a new world order of fully liberated commodity and capital markets, finally be overcoming two decades of international over-capacity and over-production in manufacturing, in which competition had over-ridden complementarity and redundant production had prevailed over mutually beneficial specialization?

In fact, by the time that growth once again began to pick up at the end of 1995 from where it had left off at the end of 1994, its very foundations were beginning to be corroded – and also dramatically transformed. In 1996 the US manufacturing sector thus experienced the sudden termination of the long-term rise in its profit rate and, from 1998, the exhaustion of its competitiveness- and export-based revival, opening the way to a sharply falling manufacturing profit rate. Simultaneously, the US stock market took off on the greatest ascent in its history, leaving underlying profits in the dust. Finally, by making possible the explosive growth of household and corporate indebtedness, the expanding equity price bubble facilitated an eventual decisive shift in the engine driving the US economic expansion – from the recovery of US manufacturing in the world market toward the growth of US domestic consumption, as well as investment aimed at the home market. It thereby maintained, and even accelerated, the US boom while ultimately rendering it unsustainable.

The turning point in the germination of all of these developments, and indeed the evolution of the world economy during the second half of the 1990s, was the agreement forged by the US, Japan, and Germany that would come to be called the 'reverse Plaza Accord'. During the first part of 1995, in the wake of the Mexican peso crisis and the subsequent US rescue of the Mexican economy, there was a new run on the dollar, sharply accentuating its long-term downward trend during the previous half decade and decade. But since US authorities had for so long been encouraging the devaluation of the dollar as an indispensable basis for the recovery of US competitiveness, and achieving such great success in so doing, the Clinton administration saw no reason to stand in the way of the currency's further decline. Indeed, it sought to exploit the mounting pressure that the Japanese were experiencing as a result of the rising yen, by threatening to close off the US market for Japanese cars, if the Japanese did not agree to open up their market to US auto parts.

By April 1995, however, the yen had reached an all-time high of 79 to the dollar, its effective, or trade-weighted, exchange rate having sprouted by 60 per cent over its level at the start of 1991 and by 30 per cent above its level at the beginning of 1994. With the currency at such a pinnacle, Japanese producers could not even cover their variable costs, and, as has been seen, the Japanese growth machine appeared to be grinding to a halt (see above, p. 118; also above, p. 99, Figure 3.3). US authorities were in no position to regard this development with equanimity, despite what had been, up to this juncture, their almost obsessive concern with US manufacturing competitiveness. They had just been shocked by the Mexican collapse, which, out of the blue, had rocked the international financial system. A Japanese version would obviously be much more dangerous. Even if a Japanese crisis could be contained, it would probably entail the large-scale liquidation of Japan's enormous holdings of US assets, especially Treasury Bonds. Such a development would chase up interest rates, frighten the money markets, and possibly engender a recession at the very moment that the US economy appeared finally ready to right itself. The upcoming 1996 presidential election was, moreover, beginning to loom in the background.

Led by Treasury Secretary Robert Rubin, during spring and summer 1995 the US thus summarily dropped its campaign to force open the Japanese auto parts market. It entered, moreover, into an arrangement with the Japanese and German governments to take joint action to force down the yen (and the mark) and elbow the dollar upwards, turning upside down what had appeared, up to that very moment, to be the cornerstone of a competitiveness- and export-oriented US foreign economic policy. This shift was to be accomplished in part by lowering Japanese interest rates with respect to those in the US, but also by substantially enlarging Japanese purchases of dollar-denominated instruments such as Treasury bonds, as well as purchases of dollars by Germany and the US government itself.[1]

It was an agreement to conjure with, representing a stunning – and entirely unexpected – about-face in the policy stance of both the US and its main allies and rivals, in much the same way as had the original Plaza Accord of 1985. In the mid-1980s, it had become necessary for the Japanese and Germans to rescue a crisis-bound US manufacturing econ-

---

[1] For this and the previous paragraph, R.T. Murphy, *The Weight of the Yen*, New York, Norton, 1996, pp. 292–5; J.B. Judis, 'Dollar Foolish', *The New Republic*, 9 December 1996; OECD, *Economic Survey. United States 1995*, Paris, 1995, pp. 54–8.

omy that was being brought down by a fast-rising dollar in the context of international over-capacity and over-production. In the mid-1990s, it had become similarly necessary for the US to rescue a crisis-bound Japanese manufacturing economy that was being brought down by a fast-rising yen in analogous circumstances. The US economy relinquished the decisive competitive advantage that its cheapening currency had been providing for its reviving manufacturing sector for almost a decade. But it gained in exchange the prospect of both a huge inflow of investment funds from overseas and a flood of cheap imports. The former could be expected not only to help cover the economy's rising current account deficit, but also to lower interest rates and drive up equity prices. The latter could be counted on to press down on domestic prices, doing some of the Fed's job of containing inflation.

In a sense, the Clinton administration was favouring suppliers of non-tradable goods, lenders, and stock market speculators at the expense of manufacturers, in much the same way as had the Reagan administration during the first half of the 1980s. It may have believed that a slimmed-down, increasingly competitive US manufacturing sector could now successfully withstand a new rise of the dollar. It may also have felt that increasing profitability and economic dynamism in the non-manufacturing sector and growing domestic consumption of manufacturing output would make up for the increasing pressure on the manufacturing sector that would result from rising relative costs in international terms and declining export growth. Still, whatever the calculations that drove it, the striking turnaround in the approach to international economic policy had to be something of a gamble, if a largely unavoidable one.

The titanic reverberations from the reverse Plaza Accord were felt immediately – and ever increasingly – throughout the world system, replicating in inverse fashion the dramatic impact of the original Plaza Accord. From 1985, a plummeting dollar had not only set off the US manufacturing recovery, but had also vastly amplified the manufacturing- and export-based East Asian 'miracle' because the East Asian currencies were by and large tied to the declining dollar. It had, however, at the same time, not only plunged the Japanese manufacturing sector into a secular crisis of competitiveness and profitability, but also opened the way for a Japanese asset price bubble that, in defiance of the underlying stagnation of profitability, prolonged, and vastly magnified, the Japanese expansion of the 1980s, until the growing gap between paper wealth and real income brought the inevitable crash.

From 1995, the roles were reversed. A rising dollar now began to squeeze profits and weigh down US (instead of Japanese and German) manufacturing; the Japanese and German manufacturing sectors (rather than that of the US) initiated (short-lived) recoveries; and East Asia slid from record boom, prompted by the Plaza Accord, to export impasse, speculative bubble, and regional depression, occasioned by a currency revaluation ignited by the reverse Plaza Accord. Meanwhile, an historic equity price bubble inflated in the US, and enabled the economic expansion to accelerate – even as the manufacturing sector lost some steam – on the basis of leaping stock prices, increasing debt, cheap capital, and the runaway growth of consumption – only to be profoundly imperilled in 1998 as the East Asian crisis became a world crisis.

CHAPTER 5

THE ONSET OF THE BUBBLE

It took little time for the forces unleashed by the reverse Plaza Accord of 1995 to register their effects. The processes driving up the dollar thus issued, almost instantaneously, in the end of the long ascent of the manufacturing profit rate, an historic take-off of equity prices, an ever-expanding gap between those runaway equity prices and underlying corporate profits, and the acceleration of investment and consumption growth under the impact of the 'wealth effect' of the rising stock market. They also set in motion, immediately, a slowly maturing international crisis that would, by 1997–98, be engulfing first East Asia, then Japan, and ultimately the US itself.

MANUFACTURING EXPANSION CONTINUES, PROFIT RATE RISE ENDS

In 1996 and 1997, the manufacturing revival that had originated at the end of 1993 regained, and even increased its momentum after faltering in 1995 following the Fed's interest rate tightening the previous year. Manufacturing output grew reasonably rapidly, at 3.5 per cent per year, stimulated by fast-rising manufacturing exports. Investment also forged ahead, at 9.5 per cent per year, paving the way for major improvements in the productiveness of both capital and labour. Real wages, meanwhile, actually fell. The growth of manufacturing labour productivity for these two years averaged 3.2 per cent, that of capital productivity (the real output–capital ratio) 1.2 per cent. With real compensation growth averaging −0.8 per cent, the growth of unit labour costs averaged −1.5 per cent. But, despite this impressive cost performance, the manufacturing sector saw the long-term rise of its rate of profit come to a conclusion, because the decade-long fall of the dollar that had been so crucial in underpinning it had summarily reversed itself, opening the way to intensifying downward pressure on prices.

In the wake of the reverse Plaza Accord of mid-1995, the effective, i.e. trade-weighted, exchange rate of the dollar rose at the rapid average annual rate of 6 per cent in 1996 and 1997 (see above, p. 99, Figure 3.3). Because the manufacturing sector was, in the same period, able to hold down unit labour costs in national terms so very well, the manufacturing sector was able to hold down unit labour costs in relative international terms to an average annual rate of just 2.5 per cent. This indicates that the US manufacturing sector was thus, in national terms, raising productivity growth vis-à-vis wages more effectively, on average, than its international competitors. But it was not doing so quite fast enough to fully compensate for the rise of the dollar. Owing to the big rise in the dollar's exchange rate – and also, as shall be seen, a serious worsening of over-capacity in international manufacturing at this point – US manufacturing had lost competitiveness and was seeing its profitability squeezed.

So as to cope with the ascending dollar, US companies were thus obliged to reduce their export prices at the average annual rate of 2.6 per cent in 1996 and 1997, after having been able to increase them at the average annual rate of 1.2 per cent between 1986 and 1995. US manufacturers were, by the same token, compelled to bring down product prices at an average annual rate of 0.5 per cent, after having been able to increase them at an average annual rate of 1.2 between 1986 and 1995. As a consequence, despite their success in holding down costs, manufacturers saw their profit rates remain flat in both 1996 and 1997, after having risen by more than 60 per cent between 1986 and 1995 (see Figure 5.1).

The role of the rising dollar in flattening the trajectory of the profit rate in the manufacturing sector after 1995 can be directly confirmed by reference to the parallel trends in costs and profitability in the same period in the non-manufacturing sector. Simply put, non-manufacturers

Figure 5.1 Growth of US manufacturing product prices and goods export prices, 1978–99

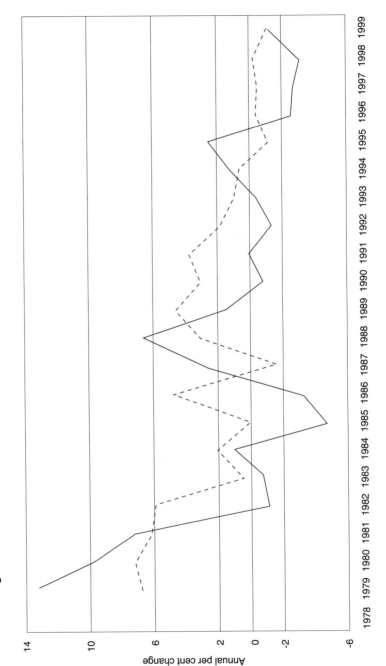

Annual per cent change

1978 1979 1980 1981 1982 1983 1984 1985 1986 1987 1988 1989 1990 1991 1992 1993 1994 1995 1996 1997 1998 1999

——— Goods export prices   – – – Manufacturing product prices

saw their costs grow significantly faster than did their counterparts in manufacturing, but, because they were largely immune from international competition, they were able to raise their prices even more rapidly and, in that way, achieve a significant increase in their profit rates, while manufacturing profitability stagnated. In 1996 and 1997, then, in non-manufacturing, the average annual growth of labour productivity, at 2.35 per cent, was lower than in manufacturing (3.2 per cent); that of nominal wages, at 3.2 per cent, higher than in manufacturing (1.7 per cent), and that of unit labour costs, at 0.85 per cent, higher than in manufacturing (−1.5 per cent). Nevertheless, because non-manufacturers were unfettered by the downward stress on prices resulting from rise of the dollar – in fact just the opposite – they were able to raise prices at an average annual rate of 1.85 per cent, compared to −0.5 per cent in manufacturing. As a result, they succeeded in increasing their profit rates by 17 per cent between 1995 and 1997, while their counterparts in manufacturing had to settle for their existing rates of return.[1]

Between 1995 and 1997, the US manufacturing sector was thus having to run ever harder just in order to stay in place. Had it not been for the extraordinary repression of wages, which was bound to be reversed as the economic expansion lengthened, its profit rate would have fallen, despite its outstanding performance in terms of investment and productivity. It therefore had decreasing room to manoeuvre in the face of intensifying international competition, and could offer therefore a decreasingly reliable foundation for the US economic boom. It would be increasingly vulnerable to shocks – of the sort that would inexorably come in 1997–8 from the direction of East Asia, as a result of the same rising dollar that was the original source of its own increasing stress.

---

[1] The manufacturing profit rate in 1997 was 3.6 per cent higher than in 1995. 'After a rapid rise from 1992 to the middle of 1997, corporate profits have weakened recently, and their share of the national income has begun to drop.' OECD, *Economic Survey. United States 1999*, Paris, 1999, p. 32, and also Figure 7.

THE STOCK MARKET GOES INTO ORBIT

As the manufacturing profit rate flattened, equity prices took flight, leaving corporate profits lagging behind to a degree unprecedented in US economic history. By 1995, the US stock market had already been enjoying an historic ascent, which originated at the time of the Volcker recession at the start of the 1980s. This had been brutally interrupted by the stock market crash of 1987. But, when not only the US Fed, but also Japanese financial authorities, took decisive action to counter the collapse of equity prices, many investors began to believe that the stock market would never be allowed to fall too far, and the bull run was enabled to continue. There was a further mini-crash in 1990, but, between 1990 and 1993, the Federal Reserve brought about the reduction of real short-term real interest rates from above 5 per cent to near-zero in order to rescue debt-burdened corporations and failing banks. The groundwork was thus laid for a huge expansion of liquidity. Opportunities to profit were still relatively limited in a US real economy only very slowly recovering from recession. A significant part of the resulting inundation of extra-cheap money was thus allowed to flow into East Asia and Latin America, the founding moment of the so-called 'emerging markets'. But a major portion of the newly available funds also poured into the US stock market, setting off a new big upturn in equity prices during these years.

The fact remains that by the end of 1995, even after increasing rapidly for the better part of a dozen years, share prices had not outdistanced the growth of corporate profits. It could indeed be said without exaggeration that the dramatic increase of the stock market up to that point basically reflected the dramatic recovery of profitability in the US economy from its depressed state in the recession at the start of the 1980s. Between 1980 and 1995, the index of equity prices of the New York Stock Exchange had risen by a factor of 4.275, while after-tax corporate profits had increased by a factor of 4.67. At the end of 1995, the price–earnings ratio for the S&P 500 was 15.35, roughly its average for the years 1985–90 and indeed for the post-war epoch as a whole. But from this point onwards, share prices disengaged themselves from underlying corporate profits, and a major stock market bubble began to blow up (see Figure 5.2).

The profit rate recovery that had begun a decade previously, and the high levels of investor confidence that this had created, constituted without question the necessary conditions for the historic surge of equity prices that took place from 1995 onwards. The forces that actually set off that surge are, however, less easy to specify. Still, it is hard to resist the conclusion that the dramatic transformations in financial conditions and international financial flows that took place over the course of the year 1995 (and immediately thereafter) were largely responsible.

In March 1995, following the US bailout of the Mexican economy (and holders of Mexican bonds), the Fed was obliged, in the interest of both domestic and international economic stability, to end its credit tightening campaign begun about a year earlier and, starting in July 1995, it quickly lowered rates by three-quarters of a percentage point. It would end up waiting more than two years before implementing another interest rate increase, and two years more before imposing a further one. But probably even more significant were the measures taken to implement the 'reverse Plaza Accord'. They not only began to bump the dollar upwards, thereby amplifying increases in the value of US assets (including equities) for internationally oriented investors. They also unleashed a torrent of cash from Japan, East Asia, and overseas more generally into US financial markets, which sharply eased interest rates and opened the way for a mighty increase in corporate borrowing to finance the purchase of shares on the stock market.

In April 1995, the Bank of Japan cut the official discount rate, already a very low 1.75 per cent, to 1 per cent and the following September slashed it further to 0.5 per cent. This did help bring down the yen's value, immediately reviving exports, competitiveness, and the economy more generally. But Japan's ultra-low interest rates also had the effect of pumping up the global supply of credit as a major portion of the increase of Japanese liquidity leaked out of Japan. US investors in particular fabricated a very profitable 'carry trade', borrowing yen in Japan at a low rate of interest, converting them into dollars, and using the latter to invest

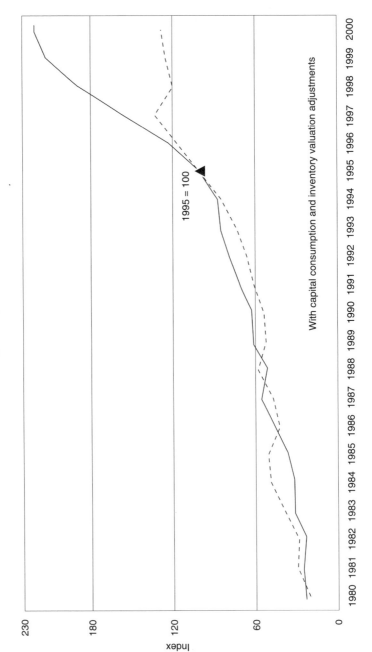

Figure 5.2 Index of corporate profits after tax net of interest versus New York Stock Exchange Composite Index, 1980–2000

around the world. Much of the proceeds found their way into the US stock market.[2]

Meanwhile, Japanese authorities were pumping money into US government securities and US currency, and encouraging Japanese insurance companies to follow suit, while loosening regulations on overseas investment to make this possible. Governments from East Asia, aiming to hold down the value of local currencies so as to sustain export growth, did the same, and were followed by private investors, especially hedge funds, from all over the world. In 1995, the rest of the world thus bought US government securities worth $197.2 billion, two and a half times the average for the previous four years, and followed up with purchases of $312 billion in 1996 and $189.6 billion in 1997, a total sum of $0.7 trillion. Of these purchases, by far the greater part were Treasury instruments – $168.5 billion in 1995, $270.7 billion in 1996, and $139.7 billion in 1997. The balance of more than half a trillion dollars of US Treasury instruments purchased by foreigners in these three years covered not only the total new debt issued by the US Treasury in this period, but also a further $266.2 billion of US government debt previously held by, and now bought from, US citizens.[3]

Such enormous purchases could not but dramatically loosen the chains on US money markets, chasing down interest rates and freeing a cascade of liquidity to purchase US equities. Between January 1995, when it hit its peak in the wake of the bond market crunch of 1994, and January 1996, the interest rate on thirty-year Treasury bonds bombed from 7.85 per cent to 6.05 per cent. This near 23 per cent reduction in the cost of long-

---

[2] R.T. Murphy, 'Japan's Economic Crisis', *New Left Review*, new series, No. 1, January–February 2000, pp. 42–3; R. Bevacqua, 'Whither the Japanese Model? The Asian Economic Crisis and the Continuation of Cold War Politics in the Pacific Rim', *Review of International Political Economy*, vol. v, Autumn 1998, p. 415.

[3] Board of Governors of the Federal Reserve System, *Flow of Funds Accounts of the United States. Flows and Outstandings* [henceforth FRB, *Flow of Funds*], Table F.107, Rest of World (flows), and Table F.209, Treasury Securities (flows); OECD, *Economic Survey. United States 1995*, Paris, 1995, pp. 55–8; OECD, *Economic Survey. United States 1996*, Paris, 1996, pp. 49–51; OECD, *Economic Survey. United States 1997*, Paris, 1997, pp. 73–5, The difference between total government securities and total Treasury instruments purchased by the rest of the world in these years was made up of purchases by the rest of the world of government agency securities issued by US Government Sponsored Enterprises, such as FNMA, FHA, and so on.

term borrowing over the course of 1995 had to have been a major factor in fomenting the stock market run-up, especially as it detonated a sharp, parallel acceleration in the growth of the money supply, which grew four times faster in 1995 than it had in 1994 (see Figure 5.3). So, too, did the new take-off of the dollar itself, which was initially spurred by dramatic, coordinated dollar purchases by US authorities, along with their Japanese and German counterparts, in May and August of 1995, and which was subsequently propelled by the deluge of foreign purchases of US government securities. The dollar's effective exchange rate would thus increase by 20 per cent in the short period between April 1995 and the end of 1996 and magnify to the same extent the rise in the value of US shares in international terms.[4]

The take-off of the stock market run-up is routinely linked to the stunning returns to Netscape's initial public offering at the start of August 1995, which was taken to be indicative of the enormous promise of the New Economy in general, and information technology in particular. But it is probably more validly attributed to the sudden easing of financial conditions and run-up of the dollar, which occurred at almost precisely the same time, in the wake of the reverse Plaza Accord. Hitherto the growth of equity prices was basically driven by the growth of profits. Henceforth, it would take on a life of its own.

The Fed nurtures the bubble

With the cost of borrowing falling so sharply and the dollar rising so rapidly, the stock market was bound to take flight. After having dipped slightly over the course of 1994, the NYSE and S&P 500 indexes soared upwards by 31.3 per cent and 34 per cent, respectively, during 1995, by far their fastest rates of increase since 1987, when the rapid run-up of equities had ended in the October crash. During 1996, they sprouted a further 20 per cent. By December of that year Alan Greenspan was moved

---

[4] *Economic Report of the President 2000*, Washington, DC, 2000, p. 391, Table B–71; OECD, *Economic Survey. United States 1997*, pp. 71–3.

Figure 5.3 Growth of the US money supply (M3), 1985–2000

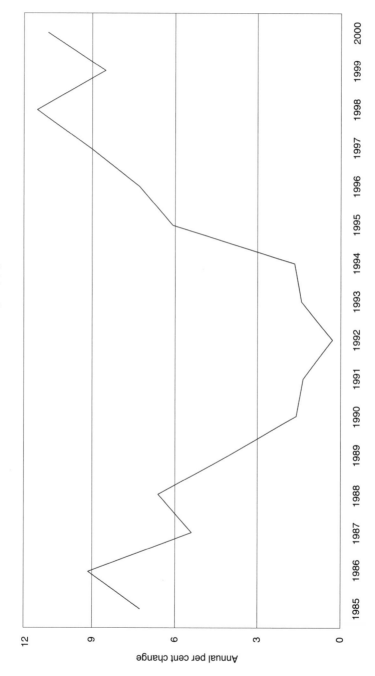

to make his famous warning about the stock market's 'irrational exuberance'. In February and March 1997, he followed up that admonition before the Senate Banking Committee, asserting that '[t]he sharp rise in equity prices during the last two years . . . have obviously raised questions of sustainability.'[5]

Nevertheless, the stock market ignored Greenspan. In 1997 the S&P 500 rushed upwards another 30 per cent, the NYSE by an additional 27 per cent, and these indexes would continue to rise for at least another two years. All told, between 1994 and 1997, after-tax corporate profits (net of interest) grew by 57 per cent, while corporate earnings of S&P 500 companies expanded by 38.6 per cent. But these gains in earnings were dwarfed by the rise of equity prices, the NYSE index galloping ahead by 80 per cent and the S&P 500 index doubling during the same period.

Why purchasers of shares paid little heed to Greenspan's warning is not hard to understand. He did nothing to indicate by his actions any serious worry about orbiting equity prices. Just the reverse was the case. Between 1989 and 1994, the annual growth of the money supply (M3) had averaged just 1.3 per cent (1.7 per cent in 1994) (see above, p. 143, Figure 5.3). But thanks to the transformation of financial conditions that took place in 1995, not least the Fed's lowering of short-term interest rates, it surged to 6.1 per cent in 1995, and continued to accelerate for the remainder of the decade, averaging 8.6 per cent between 1994 and the first half of 2000.

The hypertrophy of borrowing represented by this stepped-up availability of money could hardly have been more relevant to the breathtaking stock market run-up. For what it represented, in large part, was the escalating assumption of debt by US corporations for the express purpose of buying back their own stocks in ever greater quantities so as to directly push up their value. By way of a borrowing binge of historic proportions, US non-financial corporations were in the process of becoming the leading net purchasers on the US equity market, and reaping the benefits of the unprecedented revaluation of their assets that was resulting, not

[5] Quoted in B. Woodward, *Greenspan's Fed and the American Boom*, New York, Simon and Schuster, 2000, p. 182.

the least of which were to be able to borrow more, buy more shares, and benefit more.

Yet, despite his professed concern about a bubble in the equity markets, Alan Greenspan did nothing to cool those markets down. He did not raise interest rates significantly or impose greater reserve requirements on banks. Nor did he, as was well within his power, implement Regulation T, which provides for raising margin requirements on the purchases of equities.[6] Greenspan's initial refusal to raise rates through 1996 almost certainly derived from his uncertainty about an economy, now under pressure from a rising dollar, that had not clearly transcended its slowdown of the previous year, and which accelerated and decelerated quarter-by-quarter thoughout the year. By March 1997, with the expansion seemingly assured – and being magnified by the expanding wealth effect of rising equity prices on both corporate investment and household consumption – the Fed did begin a new round of the traditional sort of 'anti-inflationary' credit tightening, but by now it was too late. This same increase in interest rates, with the promise of more to come, rattled nervous investors in Thailand, setting off the flight of capital away from East Asia. By August and September, as the crisis in their region deepened, East Asian governments launched a major sell-off of Treasury instruments as they sought to defend their embattled currencies, setting off a sharp tumble in US share prices. In response, the Fed, facing little threat of inflation and unwilling to test the impact of a major stock market correction on a real economy that was now facing deepening international instability, sought to reassure the markets by calling off its plans to raise rates and thereby stoked up still another run-up of the share prices. The Fed would make much more dramatic interventions to similar ends in autumn 1998 and autumn 1999, with even greater inflationary effects on equity values. Indeed, as it turned out, aside from the solitary March 1997 increase of 0.25 per cent in the Federal Funds Rate, the Fed would go more than four years, from February 1995 through May 1999, without raising interest rates – and would actually temporarily lower them in both

---

[6] J.B. Judis, 'Method Acting', *New Republic*, 22 January 2001. Cf. H.S. Reuss, 'Blunderbuss or Rifle Shot?' *FOMC Alert*, vol. iii, 24 August 1999.

late 1998 and late 1999 – even as the equity markets experienced the greatest bubble in US history, with momentous effects on the real economy.

By his inaction, Greenspan was widely interpreted as giving the over-heated stock market his implicit sanction. In fact, he would soon go much further. By spring 1998, he would be explicitly rationalizing tearaway equity prices in terms of 'New Economy' productivity gains that he saw as at once keeping down inflation and giving credence to investors' expec-tations of the 'extraordinary growth of profits into the distant future'. He would also be expressing his warm appreciation of the stepped-up corpor-ate investment and household consumption that flowed from the wealth effect of exploding asset values, and which strengthened the boom. The fact that inflation was being held down by the same rising dollar that was both urging equity prices upward and forcing profit rates downward did not seem to exercise Greenspan. That the equity price ascent was matched by the rise in *expectations of profits*, but emphatically *not* in *actually realized profits*, also failed to concern him. Equity speculators could hardly be faulted if they drew the conclusion that the Fed Chairman, despite his professed caution, found their exuberance not just not irrational, but also sensible and beneficial (see below, pp. 177–9).

Corporate share purchases drive up equity prices

If conditions for the expansion of the equity market bubble were prepared by the transformation of domestic and international financial conditions in 1995 and were perpetuated by the Fed during the next four years through its easy credit regime, equity prices were themselves directly, and con-sciously, pushed up by corporations. Thanks to the relaxed conditions on the financial markets maintained by the Fed – as well as to the augmenta-tion in the value of their assets that resulted from the rise in their equity prices – non-financial corporations were enabled to vastly ratchet up their borrowing for the purpose of buying shares in colossal quantities – either to accomplish mergers and acquisitions or to simply re-purchase (retire) their own outstanding equities. In the process, corporations became far and away the leading net purchasers of equities and the main active force dilating the stock market bubble during the second half of the 1990s.[7]

Until the 1980s, corporate purchases of shares had been fairly minimal during the post-war epoch. But, in the course of the leveraged buyout craze, firms began to make such purchases on a huge scale in the course of mergers and to pay for them largely through the ever-increasing assumption of debt, encouraged to do so by US tax law, which provides for lower tax rates on capital gains than dividends (for stockholders) and allows corporations to write off interest payments entirely. They also began to re-purchase their outstanding shares in a big way, largely, it seems, to help push up their price. The remarkable outcome was that non-financial corporations' purchases accounted for no less than 72.5 per cent of the value of total US net equity purchases between 1983 and 1990, becoming the main instigators of the accompanying run-up of equity prices during that era. Corporate cash flow (after-tax profits net of interest minus dividends plus depreciation) was able to cover almost, but not quite, all of non-financial corporations' (rather limited) capital expenditures in this period. Thus *all* of the net stock purchases made by corporations in these years were financed by increased borrowing. Their net purchases of equities absorbed 50 per cent of all funds borrowed by non-financial corporations in these years, and they amounted to 125 per cent of non-financial corporations' retained earnings (after-tax profits net of interest minus dividends) and 25 per cent of their cash flow.[8]

During the first three years of the 1990s, in the wake of the corporate debt crisis, corporations largely ceased to buy stocks or to borrow (adding to their debt at a mere $15 billion per year on average between 1990 and 1993). But, beginning in 1994, taking up where they had left off during the leveraged mergers and acquisitions movement of the 1980s, they once again began to buy equities on a large scale, and, as before, buried

---

[7] Net equity purchases by non-financial corporations is defined simply as gross share retirements minus gross share issuances. Gross retirements is itself constituted by share purchases in the course of mergers (made in cash) plus share re-purchases, i.e. corporate buybacks of their own outstanding shares.

[8] FRB, *Flow of Funds*, Table F.102, Nonfarm Nonfinancial Corporate Business (flows); Table F.213, Corporate Equities (flows).

themselves ever more deeply in debt to pay for these purchases, which again had to be financed *entirely* by means of borrowing. As in the 1980s, a step-up in mergers and acquisitions accounted for a significant part of this purchasing. But, as the 1990s progressed, mounting corporate equity retirements were motivated to an even greater extent simply by the desire of corporate executives to push up their company's equity prices.

Thus, between 1994 and 1998, the annual value of gross equity retirements of non-financial corporations – including both corporate purchases that resulted from mergers and those that resulted simply from corporations' re-purchases of their own shares – tripled and in 1997, 1998, 1999, and 2000 reached the hitherto unheard of figures of $220.2 billion, $299.5 billion, $261.3 billion, and $246.4 billion, respectively. But the trajectory of corporations' re-purchases of their own shares was inclined even more sharply upward. Between 1994 and 1998, their annual value quadrupled, reaching $134.3 billion in 1997, $169.1 billion in 1998, and $145.5 billion in 1999 and constituting close to 60 per cent of total gross retirements in these three years. Before the 1990s, the highest annual total ever recorded for stock re-purchases had been $51.4 billion in 1989 (see Figure 5.4).[9]

Since equity prices were rising rapidly, making it ever cheaper for corporations to raise funds through the issue of shares, it would have been reasonable to expect that, all else being equal, corporations would turn much more to selling shares in order to finance themselves than to buying shares by means of borrowing. Direct finance through the issue of shares was thus decreasingly expensive compared to debt finance. That US non-financial corporations, taken in aggregate, chose to such a great extent a more costly form of raising money than issuing shares precisely in order to be able to buy back equities confirms the fact that corporate executives were less and less seeking to maximize income in the old-fashioned manner of investing, reducing costs, and meeting demand, and were rather seeking to maximize shareholder value by directly fattening up share prices.[10]

---

[9] Unpublished Federal Reserve Board times series. I wish to thank Nellie Liang for kindly having these forwarded to me.
[10] A. Smithers and S. Wright, *Valuing Wall Street. Protecting Wealth in Turbulent Markets*, New York, McGraw Hill, 2000, pp. 152–3, where the calculation of the relatively greater

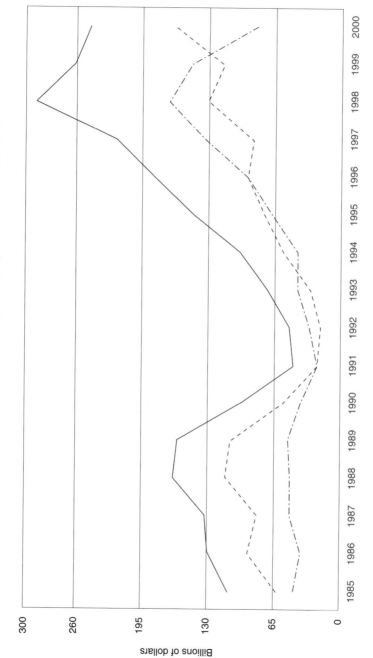

Figure 5.4 US non-financial corporate gross equity retirements, 1985–2000

——— 1. Total retirements/purchases (=2+3)   – – – 2. Retirements via domestic mergers and acquisitions   —·—· 3. Share buybacks/re-purchases

Corporations' desire to take this tack derived generally of course from the relentless pressure on management to produce the highest possible returns for stockholders in the shortest feasible time. But it expressed, more specifically, the interests of top corporate executives who received an ever larger portion of their salaries in the form of stock options as share prices rose, as well as of employees, who in growing numbers, especially in the information technology sector, received some of their compensation in stock options. Since holders of options were generally debarred from receiving dividends, they had all the more reason for wishing to see corporate earnings spent on share buybacks and held back from direct distribution to shareholders.

Corporations were given further incentives to compensate executives and employees by means of stock options by US accounting regulations, which free them from the obligation to report the cost of stock options in their reports to shareholders, and also by US tax regulations, which allow corporations to deduct these same costs from company income. The treatment of stock options by US law thus encourages corporations to exaggerate their earnings in public for the benefit of their stockholders, while deflating them in private for the benefit of the Internal Revenue Service.[11] As the 1990s progressed, and corporations failed to report the ever greater expenditures they had to make to cover the cost of their executives' and employees' stock options, they increasingly overstated their earnings – the estimates of the degree of inflation running anywhere from 5 per cent to 30 per cent for the last several years of the decade.[12]

---

cost of debt compared to equity financing is presented. It needs to be stressed that the huge rise in net purchases is for the non-financial corporate sector as a whole. It is compatible with the fact that certain sections and certain firms within that sector were major net issuers.

[11] G. Morgenson, 'Stock Options Are Not a Free Lunch', *Forbes*, 18 May 1998; G. Morgenson, 'The Consequences of Corporate America's Growing Addiction to Stock Options', *New York Times*, 13 June 2000; G. Morgenson, 'Investors May Now Eye Costs of Stock Options', *New York Times*, 29 August 2000; R. McGough, 'Stock Options Pad Cash Flow of Soaring Technology Issues', *Wall Street Journal*, 17 July 2000; S.J. Weisbenner, 'Corporate Share Repurchases in the 1990s: What Role Do Stock Options Play?' Federal Reserve Board Working Papers, Finance and Economic Discussion Series, April 2000, FRB website.

[12] Morgenson, 'Investors May Now Eye Costs of Stock Options'. According to a comprehensive Bear, Stearns study of all of the S&P 500 companies, net income for 1999 would have been 6 per cent lower, on average, had stock options been accounted as an expense.

At the same time, corporations evidently derived growing benefits from tax deductions justified by the cost of stock options – deductions that became so large as to enable a number of leading companies to avoid paying any taxes at all in some years, prominent among them Cisco and Microsoft in the fiscal year 2000.[13]

Between 1994 and 1998, non-financial corporations spent $509.2 billion, in net terms, on share purchases – i.e. on share retirements accomplished in the course of mergers and on re-purchases of their own outstanding stock minus new equity issues. To make this possible, corporations were obliged to enter into the greatest wave of accumulation of debt in their history, an explosion of borrowing that would raise annual borrowing by non-financial corporations as a percentage of the growth of non-financial corporate GDP to its highest levels ever, even as non-financial corporate GDP rose unusually rapidly. Thus, the $509.2 billion that non-financial corporations devoted to net share purchases absorbed a full 50 per cent of the total of $1.035 trillion they borrowed in these years.[14] Since that figure also constituted 37 per cent of the total value of net purchases of US equities in these years – rising to a stunning 58 per cent in 1998 – it could not be more evident that corporate share retirements played a fundamental role in manufacturing the stock market bubble.

In sum, the Federal Reserve continued to make credit easily available, even though this was paving the way for non-financial corporations to engage in the most blatant financial manipulation. Non-financial corporations were enabled to engorge their borrowing facilities so that they might buy back their own shares, as well as purchase those of other

---

Earnings at 122 of these companies – almost one quarter of the stocks in the index – would have been reduced by more than 10 per cent. Perhaps most spectacular, earnings at such companies as Yahoo, Broadcom, JDS Uniphase and a dozen other leading high-tech firms would have been entirely wiped out, and in many cases gone deeply into the negative, had they been forced to report their stock options as costs.

[13] Morgenson, 'The Consequences of Corporate America's Growing Addiction to Stock Options'.

[14] FRB, *Flow of Funds*, Table F.102, Nonfarm Nonfinancial Corporate Business (flows); Table F.213, Corporate Equities (flows). To convey a further idea of the magnitude of these purchases, they amounted to 83 per cent of the retained earnings and 20 per cent of the cash flow of non-financial corporations in these years.

corporations, and thus goad the headlong rush of equity prices. Since rising equity prices, by providing growing paper assets and thereby increased collateral, facilitated still further borrowing, the bubble was enabled to sustain itself, as well as to fuel the strong cyclical upturn already in progress.

THE BUBBLE AMPLIFIES THE BOOM

The expansion of the US equity price bubble beginning in 1995 was thus soon amplifying the accelerating economic expansion. Major sales of shares (in net terms) by households to non-financial corporations that financed their buybacks through debt added substantially to households' purchasing power through the accrual of capital gains. At the same time, the inflation of asset values resulting from the rise in stock prices appeared to endow households with such magnified wealth as to justify an historic erosion of household savings, as well as a big boost in household borrowing, both of which further prompted consumer spending. Significant numbers of households appear, finally, to have taken the rise in stock prices to be an indication of the economy's generally good health, and, feeling economically more secure, were less constrained to save and freer to consume.[15] The resulting increase in the growth of consumption demand gave a major kick to what already appeared to be an increasingly powerful boom that had initially been dynamized by the recovery of profitability, competitiveness, and exports in the manufacturing sector. That boom was further augmented, as non-financial corporations, their paper value hugely increased by the rise in the prices of their shares – which had of course been amplified by their huge debt-financed equity retirements – were able both to expand their borrowing yet more and to raise greater funds through issuing stocks at ever more inflated prices,

---

[15] J.M. Poterba, 'Stock Market Wealth and Consumption', *Journal of Economic Perspectives*, vol. xiv, Spring 2000, pp. 116–17; M.W. Otoo, 'Consumer Sentiment and the Stock Market', Federal Reserve Board Working Papers, Finance and Economics Discussion Series, November 1999, FRB website.

both of which facilitated the amplification of their already stepped-up investment growth.

With the manufacturing sector still growing rapidly and the non-manufacturing sector enjoying increased profitability, it appeared in 1996 and 1997 that the US economy was finally firing on all cylinders. It was, moreover, driving the other advanced capitalist economies from the doldrums, extricating them from their recessions of the first half of the decade. In the new international cyclical upturn that ensued, 1997 represented a definite peak.

Nevertheless, by the latter part of 1997, the initial, and fundamental, source of the US economic revival – the rise in manufacturing competitiveness, exports, and profitability over the previous decade – was fast drying up. The same rising dollar that was helping to push up US equity markets, thereby stimulating consumption and investment through the wealth effect, was simultaneously undercutting manufacturing profitability and the manufacturing-led expansion. It was thereby rendering the US economy vulnerable to the looming international economic crisis that it itself had detonated in East Asia, beginning in 1995.

CHAPTER 6

A CHAIN REACTION OF CRISIS

The Japanese economy, it will be recalled, had begun in 1994 to emerge from its long, deep cyclical downturn, but had been thrust back toward recession during the first half of 1995 by a dramatic new rise of the yen (see above, p. 118). Following the reverse Plaza Accord, however, the yen fell dramatically, just as policy-makers intended. Starting from the second half of 1995, moreover, the Japanese economy did begin to emerge strongly from its downturn. Japanese exports spurted immediately and profit rates and investment growth followed suit. Over the next two years, the Japanese economy gave the appearance of resuming its trajectory of the years through 1985, before the decade-long run-up of the yen had brought it to a standstill. The German economy, benefiting like the Japanese from a plummeting currency, simultaneously experienced an analogous trend, and so did much of western Europe. In fact, in 1997, the advanced capitalist economies taken together – exploiting the huge stimulus to world demand emanating from the US, as well as reduced exchange rates vis-à-vis the dollar – achieved their best performance of the entire decade.

But the process did not end there. The very debilitation of the yen with respect to the dollar that impelled the Japanese economy forward soon proved disastrous for the fast-developing economies of East Asia. Most of these economies had pegged their exchange rate to the dollar. The yen's steady rise between 1985 and 1995 had thus made them ever more competitive, very much helping them to flourish. But when the yen fell sharply between 1995 and 1997, they found themselves stopped in their tracks as their own currencies rose precipitously along with the ascending dollar. Their export booms came to a halt, and were replaced by equity, land, and construction bubbles that were driven by the same rising currencies that were undercutting their exports. But when their bubbles proved unsustainable in the face of their export downturns and the end of their manufacturing booms, they were brought down by what became the most serious international economic crisis of the post-war period.

Nor was the developing chain reaction soon contained. The Japanese economy had sought to counter the persistence of the high yen in part through relocating low-end production to East Asia, with the result that Japanese direct investment, exports, and bank finance to the region had all increased spectacularly during the 1990s. It therefore soon found its attempt to escape recession from 1995 through the reverse Plaza Accord boomeranging disastrously. The low yen, revived Japanese exports, and declining Japanese imports laid East Asia low, with the result that the Japanese economy was deprived of its best markets for foreign direct investment, exports, and bank loans, and was itself thrown back into recession.

Even the US economy was ultimately engulfed. As the dollar rose vertiginously from 1995, the newly revived US manufacturing sector continued to expand impressively. But during 1996 and 1997, as has been seen, the gravity-defying dollar began to corrode the foundations of US manufacturing dynamism by putting an end to the long ascent of manufacturing competitiveness and profitability, which had originated a decade before. When, in 1998, the US economy was faced simultaneously with imploding East Asian markets and exploding East Asian exports, it, too, faced its most serious threat of the post-war epoch.

FROM BOOM TO CRISIS IN EAST ASIA

East Asia had been the only part of the world to enjoy truly dynamic economic growth during the decade 1985–95. The powerful expansion of manufacturing, and especially manufacturing exports, spurred the East Asian economies forward, although it is necessary to distinguish the extraordinary growth trajectories of Korea and Taiwan, both of which dated back at least a quarter century and were rooted in their successful adoption of versions of the Japanese model, from those of the ASEAN economies, which gathered force from 1985 and especially 1991 and were more driven by the Japanese economy than emulative of it. Nevertheless, what made for the truly unprecedented economic leap forward achieved by the region as a whole in this decade was the confluence of a number of conditions that turned out to be temporary, the most important of which was the supersonic upward thrust of the yen.[1]

From the time of the Plaza Accord in 1985, Japanese manufacturers had, as has been emphasized, responded to the runaway yen in part by relocating production in East Asia, where not only were wages much lower compared to skill, but also currencies were tied to the dollar and thus tended to fall as the yen rose. When at the start of the 1990s the Japanese economy fell into recession and the yen ascended further, they accelerated their thrust in this direction, channelling foreign direct investment to the region at an historically unprecedented pace through their overseas subsidiaries and the constellation of suppliers that had relocated with them. Between 1991 and 1995, annual Japanese manufacturing direct investment in East Asia almost tripled from $2.9 billion to $8.1 billion, and Japanese exporters supplied the region with vastly stepped-up quantities of capital and intermediate goods as they raised the share of Japanese exports going to East Asia by 40–50 per cent in the same short period. Japanese consumer goods imports from the region simultaneously rose almost as rapidly. Massive Japanese bank lending to East Asia, both to Japanese multinationals and locally owned firms, lubricated an already tumultuous process of development.[2]

---

[1] In the section that follows, I am especially indebted to R. Bevacqua, 'Whither the Japanese Model? The Asian Economic Crisis and the Continuation of Cold War Politics in the Pacific Rim', *Review of International Political Economy*, vol. v, Autumn 1998.

[2] W. Hatch and K. Yamamura, *Asia in Japan's Embrace. Building a Regional Production Alliance*, Cambridge, Cambridge University Press, 1996; M. Bernard and J. Ravenhill, 'Beyond Product Cycles and Flying Geese: Regionalization, Hierarchy, and the Industrialization of East Asia', *World Politics*, vol. xlvii, January 1995; OECD, *Economic Survey, Japan 1996*, Paris, 1996, p. 19, Table 3; pp. 30, 32; p. 185 n. 3; p. 229; OECD, *Economic Survey. Japan 1995*, Paris, 1995, pp. 23–5.

For their part, the East Asian economies, with the notable exceptions of Taiwan and Singapore (and China), had from the end of the 1980s deregulated their financial markets so as to ease not only the inflow but also the outflow of capital, and affirmed the peg of their currencies to the dollar to make for exchange rate stability. The goal was to attract bank loans and portfolio capital to the region. The ASEAN economies had pioneered this path but South Korea had soon followed suit, partly to meet incessant US demands for financial market opening, but also to respond to domestic imperatives, specifically the government's drive to simultaneously reduce state intervention and meet the requirements of the great *chaebol* (conglomerates). The latter were finding themselves increasingly squeezed at this juncture by low-end competitors from Southeast Asia and China (and perhaps Mexico) and high-end producers from Japan and the US. They thus longed for free access to world financial markets, where short-term loans could be secured more cheaply, in greater amounts, and with fewer strings attached than at home or by way of state-supervised access to international lenders.[3]

Abundant short-term capital flows to the region did materialize, very much swelled by the great expansion of international liquidity during the period. The availability of cash on a world scale was sharply increased at the start of the 1990s when the US Federal Reserve introduced deep reductions in short-term interest rates to cope with recession and the financial fragility of banks and corporations. Since relatively little of the money thereby made available was demanded for investment in the still recession-bound US productive economy, much of it was free to funnel its way to East Asia, as well as to US equity markets. The growth of liquidity was further increased when the Japanese government sought to reflate the domestic economy following the bursting of the bubble. As earlier in the US, much of the resulting river of cheap money bypassed the domestic

[3] W. Bello, 'East Asia: On the Eve of the Great Transformation,' *Review of International Political Economy*, vol. v, Autumn 1998, pp. 427–8; W. Bello, 'The Rise and Fall of South-east Asia's Economy', *The Ecologist*, vol. xxviii, January–February 1998, pp. 10–11; S. Kim and B. Cho, 'The South Korean Economic Crisis: Contrasting Interpretations and an Alternative for Economic Reform', *Studies in Political Economy*, no. 60, Autumn 1999; M. Bernard, 'East Asia's Tumbling Dominoes: Financial Crises and the Myth of the Regional Model', in L. Panitch and C. Leys, eds, *The Socialist Register 1999*, New York, Monthly Review, 1999, pp. 197–8.

economy and was re-channelled, via the 'carry trade', to East Asia or the US itself. The first half of the 1990s is the originating moment of the 'emerging markets' craze. According to the IMF, portfolio capital flows to the LDCs totalled $350 billion between 1990 and 1995; of this amount, a stunning $261 billion, or 74.5 per cent, went to East Asia.[4]

An astounding manufacturing export expansion ensued, which made for booming economies throughout the region. In 1990, the shares of the world market in exports held by the US and by Asia (excluding Japan), respectively, were roughly similar, at 11.2 per cent and about 11.7 per cent. But by 1995, the US share had declined slightly to 11 per cent, while the Asian share had zoomed up by almost one half to around 16.4 per cent. By 1996, total capital formation (the sum of corporate, government, and housing investment) in East Asia (excluding Japan) had grown by nearly 300 per cent over its level of 1990, compared to slightly over 40 per cent in Japan and the US and just 10 percent in Europe. In that year, investment in East Asia accounted for more than 18 per cent of the investment in these four regions combined, three times its share just six years earlier.[5] But, by this time, the foundations of the East Asian boom were deteriorating as a result of the worsening state of international over-capacity and over-production in manufacturing during the first half of the 1990s (to which East Asia had made a signal contribution), as well as of the rapid appreciation of the region's currencies in association with the rising dollar.

Between April 1995 and April 1997, the yen fell by 60 per cent (27 per cent on a yearly basis between 1995 and 1997) with respect to the dollar. The yen's steep fall came hard on the heels of the Chinese government's devaluation of the yuan in 1994 by 50 per cent. Meanwhile, in the wake of Mexico's severe financial and economic crisis, the peso's exchange rate against the dollar dropped by 57 per cent between 1994

---

[4] S. Griffith-Jones, *Global Capital Flows. Should They be Regulated?* New York, St Martin's Press, 1998, p. 29, Table 2.2. The flow of foreign direct investment to East Asia was significantly slower, although of the total of $203.3 billion going to all of the LDCs in the same five-year period, the East Asia region still accounted for $79.6 billion, or 39 per cent.

[5] OECD, *Economic Outlook*, no. 66, Paris, December 1999, Table A46; Bevacqua, 'Whither the Japanese Model?' p. 414.

and 1996. The East Asian economies, their currencies for the most part pegged to the dollar, were now caught in a pincer, pressed by Mexican and Chinese competition for low-end and medium-tech goods and Japanese competition for high-end products. The East Asian authorities had the option, of course, of immediately detaching themselves from the dollar peg in the interest of maintaining manufacturing competitiveness. But, apparently addicted to what appeared to be a never-ending bounty of cheap short-term loans, they balked at this, and their currencies rose with the dollar. Under the stress of the region's appreciating currencies, as well as mounting over-capacity in manufacturing on a world scale, the enormous accretions made to the region's plant and equipment over the previous years, which had hitherto proved generally profitable, thus suddenly turned out to manifest large-scale over-accumulation. The struggle for markets in a global manufacturing sector that remained haunted by over-supply continued to take the form of a zero-sum struggle, with winners and losers determined heavily by the movement of exchange rates.

Most of East Asia sought to respond to the challenge of intensifying international competition by pushing overseas sales. This might appear paradoxical, but, in view of the impossibility of a profitable reorientation to the home market in the short term, manufacturers in the region had little choice but to try to export their way out of their problems. In 1996 export *volumes* for most of the East Asian economies thus continued to grow rapidly, if no longer at their previous breathless pace, but export *values* buckled under the dual stress of international over-capacity and rising currencies, which together brought terrific downward pressure on prices. World exports in value terms (measured in dollars) had risen at an average annual rate of 17 per cent in 1994 and 1995, but, in 1996, reflecting in part both the continuing rise of East Asian export volumes and the unusually slow growth of imports in that year from an increasingly competitive US economy, they crawled up by just 4 per cent. The reason was that, after having increased at an average annual rate of 6.6 per cent in 1994–95, world manufacturing prices in dollar terms fell by 2.7 per cent in 1996, and a further 7.3 per cent in 1997 (see Figure 6.1). In parallel manner, the growth of exports in value terms throughout East

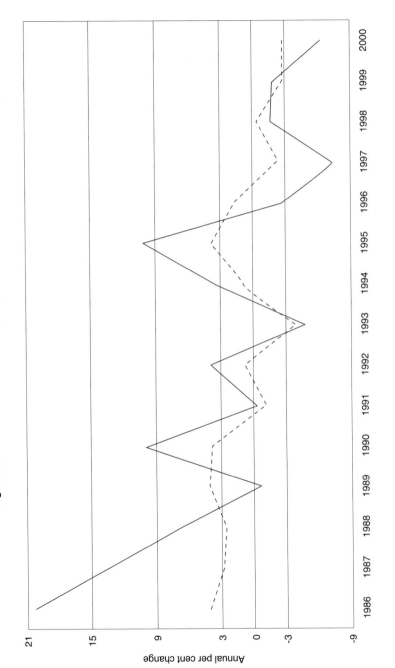

Figure 6.1 World manufacturing export prices, 1986–2000

Source: Courtesy IMF

Asia (excluding Japan) plunged from a top annual rate of more than 30 per cent in early 1995 to zero by mid-1996.[6]

The strong gravitational forces being exerted on prices was clearly placing excruciating pressure on profitability. Between 1992 and 1995, as its currency fell (along with the dollar) by almost 25 per cent against the yen, Korea, the region's leading economy, had seen its annual exports rocket upwards by some two-thirds in value terms, 53 per cent in volume terms. But, in 1996, as the won rose by about 15 per cent against the yen, export values slid by 10 per cent, even as export volumes increased by 20 per cent; in 1997, while export volumes increased by another 25 per cent, export values dipped by 1 per cent. In 1994–95, the Korean manufacturing profit rate (profits over total assets) rose to its highest point since 1988, an average that was twice that for 1991–93. But in 1996 it fell suddenly and precipitously by 75 per cent and plummeted deep into negative territory in 1997 and 1998 (see Figure 6.2).[7]

Even as returns from East Asian exports were contracting, speculative flows into East Asia continued to mount, driven especially by the appreciation of the region's currencies. The same 1995 loosening of credit by Japanese authorities that had knocked down the value of the yen and reduced East Asia's export prospects had simultaneously let loose a flood of money into the region, much of it from Japan itself, to take advantage of the upward flotation of the local currencies. The resulting overheating was only made worse when local authorities unleashed credit after 1995 to restrain the further revaluation of local currencies under the impact of those inflows. Huge stock market, land, and construction manias were the unavoidable result. The Japanese bubble had, in effect – with the help of

---

[6] S. Radelet and J.D. Sachs, 'The East Asian Financial Crisis: Diagnosis, Remedies, Prospects', *Brookings Papers on Economic Activity*, no.1, 1998, pp. 31–5; Bevacqua, 'Whither the Japanese Model?'; Time series on world manufacturing prices courtesy of IMF. I wish to thank Cathy Wright for forwarding this material to me. According to Ms Wright, these figures reflect, for the most part, price trends in the advanced capitalist economies.

[7] This profit rate series was derived by Professor Soohaeng Kim of Seoul National University from Bank of Korea data, and I wish to express my gratitude to him for forwarding it to me. As he emphasizes, it must be taken with a grain of salt. For a quite parallel series for the manufacturing profit rate (expressed as net value-added/total assets), which follows rather closely, and thus seems to confirm, the same general trend, see OECD, *Economic Survey. Korea 1999*, Paris, 1999, p. 28, Figure 3B.

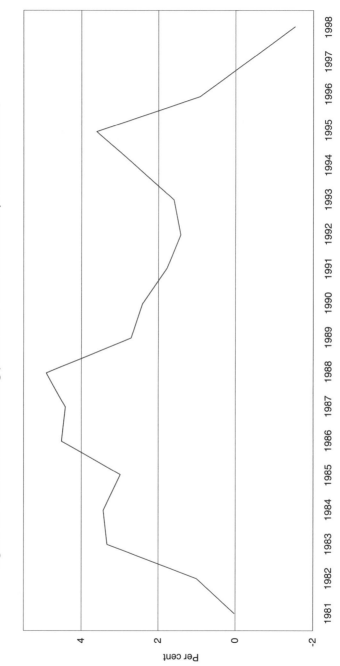

Figure 6.2 Korean manufacturing profit rate, 1981–98 (current profits/total assets)

'emerging market' investors from around the world – been resurrected in East Asia during the middle years of the decade. As the US equity price bubble took off from 1995, an East Asian bubble blew up right alongside it, even as the manufacturing export foundations of the East Asian regional economy – and indeed that of the US – were being undermined by the dramatic reversal of exchange rates.[8]

As remittances from exports fell sharply, East Asian producers found it ever more difficult to repay loans, and growth prospects in the region palpably weakened. From the beginning of 1997, a long succession of Korea's leading *chaebol* went bankrupt, evidencing the extremity of the situation. As loan defaults began to pile up, funds started to quit the region – far more rapidly than they had entered. According to the Bank for International Settlements, foreign banks had already withdrawn 30 per cent of all their loans to the region in the three months between April and June 1997. Equity prices now began to crumble, accelerating the outflow and making for downward pressure, and soon speculation, on local currencies. Central banks raised short-term rates to stem the exodus of capital and prevent their currencies from collapsing, but this caused financial institutions to go bankrupt, leading to a further collapse of asset prices and stock markets and thus more capital flight. Over the course of 1997, East Asia suffered a net decline in capital inflows of $105 billion (from $93 billion inflow to $12 billion outflow).[9]

East Asia thus found itself suffering from the same sort of downward spiral that is experienced in a stock market panic. Each foreign lender feared that all the others might withdraw their money, and tried to get out as quickly as possible. The result was the self-fulfilling disappearance from the economy of the region of the overseas credit that had made it possible for producers, used to routinely rolling over their loans, to honour their commitments. The situation was made very much worse for Asian borrowers by the fact that they were having to repay their foreign

---

[8] Bevacqua, 'Whither the Japanese Model?'
[9] Ibid., pp. 416–18; Kim and Cho, 'The South Korean Economic Crisis', pp. 15–16; Radelet and Sachs, 'The East Asian Financial Crisis', p. 2.

loans with currencies that had lost much of their value and that exceedingly high debt–equity ratios were common throughout the region.[10]

At this juncture the IMF, directed by the US Treasury, stepped in. The IMF might have attempted to get the international banks to agree to act together to keep their money flowing into Asia so as to counteract the panicky withdrawal of credit; pouring in money is, after all, the normal remedy for a liquidity crisis: witness the US Federal Reserve in the stock market crash of 1987. The argument for such action is further strengthened when one considers that the underlying problem facing Asian firms was, in the main, the insufficient international demand for their goods, not the inefficiency of their production, let alone their dependence upon (non-existent) government deficit spending. But the IMF was primarily concerned, as it had been during the Latin American debt crisis, to see that US, European, and Japanese banks would be repaid in full. Acting as an instrument of US foreign economic policy, it also sought to exploit this opening to compel the region's economies to liberalize their functioning and open themselves up to foreign penetration. As a condition for the advance of bridge finance to these economies, it therefore called, in Hoover-like fashion, for the tightening of credit and the imposition of fiscal austerity, thereby radically exacerbating the domestic economic and debt crises, and inviting depression. As part of the same packages, which can only be called imperialist, it extracted the agreement from local authorities, most dramatically in Korea, to adopt wide-ranging plans for the reorganization of their economies along Anglo-Saxon lines with the goal of easing the entry of foreign capital.

The crisis in East Asia, which broke out in the summer of 1997, steadily worsened over the following year. Throughout much of 1998, stock markets continued to fall and, as money flooded out of the region, currencies swooned, placing great pressure, direct and indirect, on the rest of the world economy. During the summer of 1998, the crisis spilled over into the less developed world. In August, Russia defaulted on its

[10] Radelet and Sachs, 'The East Asian Financial Crisis', pp. 43–9; R. Wade and F. Veneroso, 'The Asian Crisis: The High Debt Model versus the Wall Street–Treasury–IMF Complex', *New Left Review*, no. 228, March–April 1998.

sovereign debt. The Brazilian economy started to melt down shortly thereafter. The core of the capitalist world system now came under threat, not only a Japanese economy barely emerging from recession, but also a US economy in the midst of an enormous, if highly unstable, boom.

JAPAN'S ABORTIVE RECOVERY

During the second half of 1995, responding more or less immediately to the major fall of the yen engineered by the reverse Plaza Accord, Japanese export growth increased sharply and pulled the Japanese economy from its extended recession, helped out by another in a long line of major government deficit spending stimulus packages. Between 1995 and 1997, Japanese exports in value terms, which had actually declined somewhat between 1991 and 1995, recovered by a total of 23 per cent. Profitability began to rise in sympathy, and so did capital accumulation (see above, p. 39, Figure 1.3, and p. 97, Figure 3.1). Manufacturing investment, which had fallen by 15.6 per cent in 1992, by a further 18.3 per cent in 1993, and another 9.2 per cent in 1994, suddenly blossomed by 12.2 per cent in 1995, 11.9 per cent in 1996, and 11.1 per cent in 1997.[11] In 1996, GDP growth leaped to 5.1 per cent, and the economy appeared to be returning to health.

Nevertheless, the upturn could not be sustained. Over-estimating the strength of the recovery, Japanese authorities, anxious to repair government balance sheets that had gone increasingly into the red as a consequence of massive deficit spending throughout the decade, not only cut back extremely abruptly on the growth of government expenditures, but, in March 1997, also imposed a hefty new value-added tax. The excruciating shock to demand that resulted – which subtracted through increased taxes and reduced public spending the equivalent of 2 per cent of GDP – brought a major slowdown of growth, which was made worse by the government's reluctance to incur new deficits to jump-start the economy,

---

[11] OECD, *Economic Survey. Japan 1998*, Paris, 1998, p. 154, Figure 32; OECD, *Economic Survey. Japan 1999*, Paris, 1999, p. 33.

even as it slid back toward recession. When the government turned to reduced interest rates rather than fiscal stimulus to get the economy moving, the increasing lending that resulted financed not so much new domestic investment as the accelerated flow of money out of the country into US Treasury bonds and US equities.[12] Cheaper borrowing costs brought relatively little new investment because the rate of profit had fallen so very low, its decline very much an expression of the huge build-up of excess capacity that had been accumulating throughout the decade of stagnation, especially in the face of badly lagging exports. The investment boom of the last years of the 1980s bubble had itself left much surplus productive power. So, to a lesser extent, had the abortive recoveries from 1993 and 1997. But, institutionally constrained as they were with respect to layoffs and downsizing, Japanese firms had done relatively little to reduce labour force or capital stock in accord with weakening demand.

Dismissals had been used very sparingly. As a result, excess labour was, in 1998, at least 3.5 per cent of the labour force (the government estimate) and conceivably as high as 11.5 per cent (private companies' estimate), with managers, unskilled office workers, and those in construction trades believed to be in greatest supply. In parallel manner, excess plant and equipment was clearly at a post-war high, with capacity utilization in manufacturing more than two standard deviations below the average for the previous thirty years. According to Ministry of Trade and Industry (MITI) estimates, the steel industry was using just 75–80 per cent of its capacity, and the auto industry not much more. Shipbuilding, construction, oil refining, cement, polyester, and paper were other industries weighed down by superfluous productive power. Finally, as the obverse side of industrial over-capacity, firms were hugely burdened by long-term debt, much of it built up at the height of the bubble, and never much reduced. The upshot was that, in 1998, average returns on equity, at 2 per cent, were less than half the figure for the fifteen years before 1991. The OECD estimated that, in order to bring the rate of return back

---

[12] OECD, *Economic Survey. Japan 1998*, pp. 2–5, 36–45; R.T. Murphy, 'Japan's Economic Crisis', *New Left Review*, new series, no. 1, January–February 2000, pp. 37ff; Bevacqua, 'Whither the Japanese Model?'

up to that level, Japanese assets would have to be cut back by 47 per cent.[13]

While failing, unsurprisingly, to spur stepped-up capital accumulation, reduced interest rates did put ever greater downward pressure on the yen, undermining in turn the Japanese stock market. In autumn 1997 several of the country's leading financial institutions collapsed – including Hokkaido Takushoku Bank, Japan's tenth largest, and Yamaichi, one of the big four securities firms – dealing a devastating blow to business and consumer confidence. Last but not least, an escape by way of stepped-up overseas sales was blocked. Even as total Japanese exports thus continued to expand vigorously throughout 1997, Japanese exports to East Asia, by this point its largest market, were from mid-year already diving under the impact of the deepening regional downturn.

In the past, a falling yen had generally been sufficient to generate a recovery, especially because it made it possible for Japanese exports to gain better access to the huge US market. But, of course, over the previous decade the Japanese economy had sought to extricate itself from the tendency to stagnation that had accompanied the irrepressibly rising yen precisely by reducing its reliance on the US market and redirecting investment, trade, and bank finance to East Asia. In 1985, Japan sent 40 per cent of its exports to the US market, but only 29 per cent by 1996. Over the same period, Japanese exports to East Asia as a percentage of the total had increased from 19 per cent to 37 per cent.[14] Thus, when in 1995, with the help of the US government, Japanese authorities set off the long, deep devaluation of the yen, they could not but thereby cut off the path to economic recovery, the tactic backfiring disastrously in the face of the zero-sum game that had come increasingly to prevail in the struggle for the world market over the 1980s and 1990s.

[13] OECD, *Economic Survey. Japan 1999*, pp. 47–58. 'It would have been no surprise if firms had already engaged in a round of severe cost reductions years ago, in response to disappointing sales and profit outcomes. But this did not occur. . . . Instead, both personnel, and sales and administrative expenses have continued their inexorable rise as a share of sales. The result has been a further dwindling in recurring profit, swamping the rise that occurred in the brief recovery from the post-bubble recession' (p. 55).
[14] OECD, *Economic Survey. Japan 1996*, Paris, 1996, p. 181, Table L; OECD, *Economic Survey. Japan 1997*, Paris, 1997, p. 229, Table L.

At the very moment when the falling yen was restoring competitiveness to Japanese exports and raising hopes of renewed growth, it was therefore destroying the very basis for economic recovery by catalysing the crisis in East Asia. With critical encouragement from the low yen, Japanese exporters undercut East Asian exporters on world markets, Japanese manufacturers stifled East Asian importers to the Japanese domestic market, and, starting in spring 1997, Japanese banks rushed their money out of the region as fast they had rushed it in during the previous two years. Not surprisingly, Japan's leading market, by now of course East Asia, disintegrated under the impact. In 1998, Japanese exports to the region fell by more than 30 per cent, causing Japanese exports to go negative. Profitability fell sharply, as did capacity utilization and investment growth. With GDP growth dropping by 2.8 per cent in 1998, the Japanese economy fell back into its worst recession of the post-war period, delivering still another crippling blow to the already reeling East Asian economies, and thereby the Japanese economy itself.[15]

THE US PROVES VULNERABLE

By the autumn of 1997, the East Asian crisis had only just begun to unfold, and the US economy was at the zenith of its manufacturing-led revival. Increased manufacturing profitability, competitiveness, and exports had, from the end of 1993, allowed a very major acceleration of the economic expansion, which was temporarily slowed in 1995 by Greenspan's credit tightening of the previous year but sprang back once again in 1996 and 1997. The strengthening boom was, moreover, fanned from 1995 by the stock-market-driven boost to investment and consumption growth.

Nevertheless, even by this juncture, US manufacturers were increasingly vulnerable. They were having to confront re-strengthened competition from their leading rivals based in Japan, Germany, and elsewhere in

---

[15] OECD, *Economic Survey. Japan 1998*, pp. 41, 43; OECD, *Economic Survey. Japan 1999*, pp. 9, 33, 38, 52.

western Europe, who were enjoying newly falling currencies, courtesy of the reverse Plaza Accord. The rising dollar was, by the same token, already holding down their profit rates (see above, pp. 134–7). When the Asian crisis hit, therefore, in late 1997 and early 1998, US producers were not only obliged to suffer the further stepped-up assaults of their leading rivals: they had to face, in addition, the shrinking of their hitherto dynamic East Asian export markets and the flooding of the US domestic market by East Asian imports rendered extraordinarily cheap by the sharp fall of their currencies.

Over the course of 1998, the growth of US exports, an essential motor of the boom, virtually ceased, exports of goods falling in real terms from 14 per cent in 1997 to 2 per cent in 1998, from an annual rate of 17.4 per cent in the third quarter of 1997 to −0.5 per cent in the second and third quarters of 1998. US real goods imports, meanwhile, continued to expand at an 11.8 per cent clip in 1998, compared to 14.2 per cent in 1997. With goods export prices and goods import prices falling by 3.1 per cent rate and 5.9 per cent, respectively, in 1998, the US corporate manufacturing profit rate was forced down dramatically, declining in that one year by 14 per cent with respect to 1997.[16]

During the first half of 1998, the sudden 20 per cent drop-off in corporate manufacturing profits (net of interest) with respect to the second half of 1997 severely jolted the equity markets. The smaller companies represented on the Russell 2000 Index were most vulnerable and their share prices fell by 20 per cent between April and the first week in August. By that point, the elite S&P 500 had itself begun to drop, having decreased by 10 per cent from its mid-July peak.[17] In the wake of the Russian default, which came a few weeks later, the S&P 500 retreated a further 10 per cent. The stock market decline threatened a quick end to the US expansion by destroying business confidence and sending into

[16] The data here are for the *corporate* manufacturing sector, rather than for the manufacturing sector as a whole, because revised data for 1998, 1999, and 2000 are available for the former, but not the latter. In fact the two sectors are nearly identical – and can be, and will be here, regarded as interchangable, because almost all firms in the manufacturing sector are corporations. See Appendix on Profit Rates.

[17] P. Coggan and J. Authers, 'Wall Street's Ebb Tide?', *Financial Times*, 6 August 1998; J. Fuerbringer, 'Different Focus, Different Profit Figures', *New York Times*, 21 August 1998.

reverse the rising tide of investment and consumption powered by the wealth effect, which in the wake of the collapse of exports had now suddenly become the boom's main source of support. Since the expanding US economy had been serving as the main driver of the international economy, much of which was already in crisis, a recession in the US threatened to plunge the rest of the world into depression.

The US economy had thus come full circle. In 1985 it had been necessary to forge the Plaza Accord in order to save from devastation a US manufacturing sector that was reeling from record high real interest rates and the elevated dollar. Afterwards, the manufacturing profit rate had achieved a notable recovery and ultimately propelled the revitalization of the US economy as a whole, which grew remarkably from the end of 1993. Nevertheless, because it took place within the context of ongoing international economic stagnation, rooted in over-capacity and over-production in international manufacturing, the revival of US manufacturing profitability, dependent as it primarily was upon zero real wage growth and a falling dollar, had found its counterparts in Japan, Germany, and western Europe in the worst recessions of the post-war epoch, reaching their nadir in the first half of the 1990s. Symptomatically, a reverse Plaza Accord had been necessary to rescue Japanese manufacturing and, with the yen and mark buckling again from 1995, Japan, Germany, and western Europe had begun to recover over the following two years. But, as the dollar shot up, the manufacturing sectors of the US and especially of East Asia were once again subject to strain, and East Asia soon entered into profound crisis, which eventually caught up with Japan, as well, finally, as the US.

By 1998, then, the US economy had, in a sense, returned to the conditions of the first half of the 1980s, as exports proved exceedingly difficult and manufacturing profit rates sustained strong downward stress. Yet the same rising dollar that spelled trouble for US and East Asian manufacturing was now helping to fuel the greatest equity price aggrandizement in US history. The wealth effect of the bubble thus continued to lash the US economy forward, even as the manufacturing sector saw its competitiveness, its international sales, and, above all, its profitability fall away. The stock market boom was now the unquestioned key to US, and international, prosperity. Could it be sustained?

CHAPTER 7

FEDERAL RESERVE TO THE RESCUE

By late September 1998, a major crisis was unfolding in the US. The Russian default triggered a flight to quality in the bond market as huge differentials opened up between the interest rate paid on relatively safe US Treasuries and the interest rates paid on less secure corporate bonds, on LDC sovereign debt, and even on certain European government issues. The shares of commercial banks meanwhile dropped abruptly on fears of big losses on loans to emerging nations. But the greatest losses were sustained by the hedge funds and proprietary trading desks of commercial and investment banks, collectively known as Highly Leveraged Financial Institutions (HLFIs), which lost untold billions of dollars as a consequence of their having accumulated huge long positions in high-risk, poorer-quality, higher-yielding debt instruments, offset by short, supposedly safe positions in developed nations' government bonds.[1]

STOCK MARKET KEYNESIANISM

The climax came on 20 September, when the huge Long-Term Capital Management hedge fund (LTCM) admitted to the authorities that it was facing massive losses. At this juncture the Federal Reserve entered the

---

[1] On the unfolding financial crisis of autumn 1998, see P. Warburton, *Debt and Delusion. Central Bank Follies That Threaten Economic Disaster*, London, 2000, pp. 263–6, as well as OECD, *Economic Survey. United States 1999*, Paris, 1999, pp. 43–55.

fray, bringing together a consortium of fourteen Wall Street banks and
brokerage houses to organize a $3.6 billion rescue of LTCM. The Fed
justified this rescue operation of a non-bank on the grounds that, had it
failed to act, the solvency of the international financial system would have
been put in jeopardy, with credit markets seizing up as LTCM's counter-
parties and their creditors rushed for the exits. In the words of William
McDonough, President of the New York Fed, who orchestrated the
bailout:

> There was a likelihood that a number of credit and interest rate
> markets would experience extreme price moves and possibly cease
> to function for a period of one or more days and maybe longer.
> This would have caused a vicious cycle: a loss of investor confidence,
> leading to a rush out of private credits, leading to a further widening
> of credit spreads, leading to further liquidations of positions, and so
> on.[2]

Alan Greenspan later complained to *Washington Post* reporter Bob
Woodward that he was not pleased that McDonough had involved the
Federal Reserve so openly and explicitly. But it is hard to believe that
Greenspan was really all that vexed about the operation, given that the
best spin that he himself could put on the situation was that '[t]he
probability that LTCM's collapse would unravel the entire world financial
system was significantly less than 50 per cent.'[3]

The Fed then made its famous three successive interest rate cuts,
including one dramatic reduction in-between its meetings. It also encour-

---

[2] 'Statement by William J. McDonough, President, Federal Reserve Bank of New York Before
the Committee on Banking and Financial Services, US House of Representatives, 1 October
1998'. Cf. 'Testimony of Chairman Alan Greenspan on Private-sector Refinancing of the
Large Hedge Fund, Long-Term Capital Management Before the Committee on Banking and
Financial Services, U.S. House of Representatives', 1 October 1998. Both statements at Board
of Governors Federal Reserve website.
[3] Quoted in B. Woodward, *Maestro Greenspan's Fed and the American Boom*, New York, Simon
and Schuster, 2000, p. 206. To get a feel for the wave of panic that was enveloping top
financial circles at this juncture, see the insider's account in M. Mayer, *The Fed*, New York,
Free Press, 2001, pp. 4–14.

aged US Government Sponsored Enterprises – including the FNMA, GNMA, FHLMC, and FHA – to engage in a spate of lending (and borrowing) entirely unprecedented in their history. The immediate aim was to counteract the freezing up of the financial markets. But a broader goal from the start was to revive equity prices, and keep the long-running bull market going. The Fed's interest rate reductions marked a turning point not so much because the resulting fall in the cost of borrowing was all that great, but because it gave such a strong positive signal to investors that the Fed wanted stocks to rise in order to stabilize a domestic and international economy that was careering toward crisis.

Greenspan vigorously denied that his interest rate reductions were designed to shore up asset values. But investors did not have to be reminded that his intervention at this moment was hardly the first of his bailouts of financiers and corporations. In October 1987, he had intervened to counter the stock market crash, and between 1989 and 1993 he had brought down real short-term interest rates from about 5 per cent to near-zero to rescue failing banks and deeply indebted corporations in the wake of the S&L and commercial banks crises and the leveraged mergers and acquisitions debacle. Nor had it escaped investors' notice that the US Treasury and Fed had gone out of their way to safeguard the leading international banks at the time of the Latin American debt crisis of 1982, those investors who stood to suffer huge losses as a result of the Mexican debt crisis of 1994–95, and the international banks once again on the occasion of the crisis in East Asia of 1997–98.

But most directly to the point, despite his remarks concerning 'irrational exuberance' two years previously, Greenspan had done nothing at all to hold down the expanding bubble, let alone threaten to burst it. In particular, he had, during a span of almost four years – since the beginning of 1995 – raised interest rates on only one occasion, and that by a quarter of a point, even though the stock market had, in the interim, been driven ever upward by record corporate equity purchases that had been made possible by record corporate borrowing, enabled by the Fed's easy money. With international economic stability depending on the continuation of the US expansion, few thought that the Fed chair would suddenly change course and let the markets fend for themselves. The 'Greenspan put', as commentators had come to call it – the assumption that Greenspan would intervene to prevent the markets from falling beyond a certain point – had established itself as a fundamental premise of financial market activity. As Ed Yardeni, chief investment officer of Deutsche Bank Securities, would put it not long thereafter, 'Investors are worried about a hard landing. I am less concerned because I believe that the Fed is our friend.'[4]

As it was, in autumn 1998 Greenspan had limited options. The main foundation of the US expansion, the recovery of manufacturing profitability, premised on increasing competitiveness and export dynamism, had fallen apart under the impact of the rising dollar and the worsening of world over-capacity and over-production that had been both cause and consequence of the crisis in East Asia. Neither manufacturing profitability nor manufacturing exports could be expected to increase soon, and in fact neither improved in 1999 over their very already poor performances in 1998, the corporate manufacturing profit rate remaining essentially unchanged and real goods exports lifting by just 2 per cent. During the previous decade, between 1986 and 1997, corporate manufacturing profitability had increased by 61 per cent; export growth had, in national accounting terms, been responsible for almost one-third of total growth of GDP; and the ratio of manufacturing exports to manufacturing GDP had just about doubled. In 1998 and 1999, however, corporate manufacturing profitability dropped by 13.8 per cent and then another 1 per cent with respect to 1997; export growth accounted for only 7 per cent of GDP growth; the ratio of manufacturing exports to manufacturing GDP suddenly fell by 5 per cent; and the manufacturing trade deficit as a percentage of manufacturing GDP doubled. Finally, the fall in the rate of profit in the corporate manufacturing sector brought down the rate of profit in the non-financial corporate economy as a whole, the latter

---

[4] P. Despeignes, '"Greenspan Put" Could Be Encouraging Complacency', *Financial Times*, 8 December 2000. See also M. Miller, P. Weller, and L. Zhang, 'Moral Hazard and the US Stock Market: Has Mr Greenspan Created a Bubble?' Department of Economics, University of Warwick, December 1999.

declining by a total of 7 per cent between 1997 and 1999 (see below, p. 215, Figure 8.9, and p. 263, Figure 10.1).[5]

To make matters worse, while the US was losing the main motor of its boom, much of the world economy was contracting and no economy outside the US was in a position to pick up the slack. Even those regions that had hitherto evaded crisis, notably western Europe, had been depending for their expansions upon the critical assistance of the US import market.[6] If the world economy was to be kept from serious crisis, the US economy had to be kept turning over.

Between 1995 and 1997, the wealth effect that derived from the stock market bubble had served to magnify the cyclical expansion in which the recovery of manufacturing continued, however, to play a fundamental role. But, by 1998, not only was the precipitous decline of manufacturing competitiveness, exports, and profitability removing a good deal of the steam from the economy, but also the government deficits that could, historically, have been counted upon to fill the gap in demand were unavailable. In that year, basically for the first time since the end of the 1960s, the general government financial balance as a percentage of GDP went positive, at 0.3 per cent.[7] As a result, there was simply no alternative to the wealth effect of rising share prices to take over as the economy's driving engine.

In order to keep the US, and the world, economy from serious disruption, the Fed thus had little choice but to depend upon the continued ascent of the stock market to maintain the accelerated growth of domestic US consumption and investment. In effect, the Fed was sustaining a new form of artificial demand stimulus by means of increased *private* debt, both corporate and consumer, made possible by the rise of equity prices and the resulting wealth effect, rather than relying on the

---

[5] 'US Exports Dropped in 1998: Trade Deficit Highest in History', *Los Angeles Times*, 20 February 1999; *Economic Report of the President 2000*, Washington, DC, 2000, Table B-5.

[6] For the unusually large role played by the US market in this European cyclical upturn, see G. Koretz, 'America's Edge in Capital Goods', *Business Week*, 22 September 1997; G. Koretz, 'All Eyes on the US Economy', *Business Week*, 29 September 1997.

[7] OECD, *Economic Outlook*, no. 68, December 2000, p. 238, Table 30. *Economic Report of the President 2001*, Washington, DC, 2001, p. 371, Table B-82. Isolated surpluses were also accrued in 1973 and 1979.

old Keynesian formula based on public deficits. The ongoing expansion would be secured not by a growing gap between government purchases and government revenues, but by growing gaps between household and corporate expenditures, on the one hand, and household and corporate income, on the other – i.e. on increased household and corporate deficits, both made possible by rising share prices. While the public sector, or general government, budget balance as a percentage of GDP had thus gone from a deficit of about 5.9 per cent in 1991 to a small surplus in 1998, the private sector deficit – which represents the extent of household and company borrowing in order to finance their expenditures – had much more than made up the difference, plunging 11 percentage points, from a surplus of around 5 per cent of GDP in the early 1990s to an historically entirely unprecedented deficit of 6 per cent in 2000.[8] Crudely put, rising equity prices were now enabling US economic growth to depend for its expansion to an ever-increasing extent on the growth of US private indebtedness.

Finally, if all went according to expectations, the growth of US debt, now private rather than public, would enable the US economy to suck in imports at a rapid pace, expand the US current account deficit, and keep the international economy turning over. The US deficit-based stimulus would function, in other words, much as it had in the mid-1970s and early 1980s, to haul the world away from recession, only its source would now be primarily the steep growth of private, rather than public, indebtedness, ultimately based on the continuing rise of equity prices.

Although Greenspan had little alternative but to intervene to prop up the stock market in autumn 1998, this does not mean that he was reluctant to act at that juncture to preserve the value of equities. That was far from the case, for he himself saw little reason to question the logic of the stock market's meteoric ascent. Indeed, since the previous spring, Greenspan

---

[8] W. Godley, *Seven Unsustainable Processes*, Jerome Levy Economics Institute of Bard College, Special Report, 1999; W. Godley, 'Drowning in Debt', Jerome Levy Economics Institute of Bard College, Policy Notes, 2000; 'What a Peculiar Cycle', *The Economist*, 10 March 2001. Between 1960 and 1992, the private sector balance was, on average, 1.1 per cent of GDP in surplus; it was never more than 1.2 per cent in deficit and the deficits, when they occurred, never lasted more than a year and a half. W. Godley, 'The US Economy: An Impossible Balancing Act', *Financial Times*, 19 February 1999.

had been publicly promulgating an analysis of the US boom in terms of the 'New Economy', in which the rising stock market was not only fully justified, but also played an inextricable and indispensable role.

As Greenspan had explained in successive appearances before Congress in June and July 1998, at the heart of the economy's increasing dynamism and the continuing repression of inflation was the recent new phase of productivity growth, propelled since 1993 by the sharp increase in the growth of investment, especially in high-tech plant and equipment. Rising productivity growth drove the expansion by setting off what Greenspan, time and again, termed a 'virtuous cycle'. In this vision, expectations of ongoing accelerated productivity increase, rooted in the technological breakthroughs of the New Economy, justified expectations of 'the extra-ordinary growth of profits . . . extended into the distant future'; the latter 'fuelled still further increases in equity values', which themselves 'provided impetus to productivity-enhancing capital investment'. Simply put, the New Economy justified ever higher profit expectations that were naturally reflected in unstoppable equity prices; in turn, rising equity prices, by way of the wealth effect, incited ever higher consumption and investment growth, which sustained New Economy technological advance, which justified higher profit expectations, and so on.[9]

Greenspan acknowledged that the real US economy had indeed been struck hard by international developments from the end of 1997. The rise of the dollar and the depression of the East Asian economies had prompted, he said, a sharp deterioration in the US balance of trade. During the first quarter of 1998, exports of goods and services had actually contracted in real terms, the first such decline in four years, while imports of goods and services had continued to rise very rapidly. These develop-

---

[9] 'Our economy has continued to enjoy a virtuous cycle. Evidence of accelerated productivity has been bolstering expectations of future corporate earnings, thereby fueling still further increases in equity values . . . and rising equity values have provided impetus to spending and, in turn, the expansion of output, employment, and productivity-enhancing capital investment.' 'Testimony of Chairman Alan Greenspan Before the Committee on Banking, Housing, and Urban Affairs', US Senate: The Federal Reserve's semi-annual monetary policy report, 21 July 1998 and in 'Testimony of Chairman Alan Greenspan Before the Joint Economic Committee, US Congress: An Update on Economic Conditions in the US', 10 June 1998, both at FRB website.

ments, according to Greenspan, had subtracted 2.5 percentage points
from the annual growth of GDP. But, as Greenspan triumphantly pointed
out, owing to his virtuous cycle, the US economy nonetheless 'proved to
be unexpectedly robust', with GDP climbing at an annualized rate of 5.5
per cent.[10]

Greenspan did not seem to be concerned that his own analysis generally replicated the ideology of the stock market itself, assiduously propa-
gated by corporations, brokerages, and investment banks alike.[11] Nor did
he betray any worry about the fact that the rise of asset values was so vastly
outdistancing the growth of profits, even in his vaunted New Economy. As
Greenspan pointed out, '*[E]xpectations* of earning growth over the longer
term have been undergoing continual upward revision by security analysts
since early 1995. These rising expectations have, in turn, driven stock
prices sharply higher.'[12] But, as Greenspan failed to point out, while share
prices for the technology, media, and telecommunications (TMT) sector
– the heart of the New Economy – had risen by 126 per cent between
March 1995 and June–July 1998, when he was making these comments,
earnings over that period for that sector had risen by just 22 per cent.
Indeed, during the previous year, although stock prices in the TMT sector
had increased by 41 per cent, earnings had failed to rise *at all.*[13]

This huge and growing gap between equity prices and profits raised
the possibility that what was actually in play on the stock market was no
mere reflection of improvement in the real economy, but rather a financial bubble. In that case, rather than New Economy-driven productivity
growth underpinning reduced inflation and exploding profits that justified runaway equity prices and the resulting amplification of investment
and consumption growth, as in Greenspan's virtuous cycle, runaway equity
prices fuelled by debt-based speculation would be ensuring stepped-up

[10] 'Testimony of Chairman Alan Greenspan', 10 June 1998 and 21 July 1998.
[11] See, e.g., R. Shiller, *Irrational Exuberance*, Princeton, Princeton University Press, 2000.
[12] 'Testimony of Chairman Alan Greenspan', 10 June 1998 and 21 July 1998 (emphasis
added).
[13] Bank for International Settlements, *71st Annual Report. 1 April 2000–31 March 2001*, Basel,
11 June 2001, p. 103, Table VI.1, as well as underlying monthly figures, provided by Bank for
International Settlements, based on data from Datastream. I wish to thank Angelika Don-
bauer of the BIS for sending me this material.

investment growth, rising productivity growth, and reduced inflation, which would all ultimately prove unsustainable – and worse – because unaccompanied by sufficient profits. But, as Greenspan would say, again and again, 'To spot a bubble in advance requires a judgment that hundreds of thousands of informed investors have it all wrong. Betting against markets is usually precarious at best.'[14]

Given the rise of the New Economy, the bubble economy was, for Chairman Greenspan, simply an extraneous hypothesis. As he would continue to insist,

> Something special has happened to the American economy. . . . The synergies that have developed, especially among the microprocessor, the laser, fiber-optics, and satellite technologies, have dramatically raised the potential rates of return on all types of equipment that embody or utilize these new technologies. Beyond that, innovations in information technology – so-called IT – have begun to alter the manner in which we do business and create value, often in ways that were not readily foreseeable even five years ago.

Thus, 'the remarkable generation of capital gains of recent years has resulted from the dramatic fall in inflation expectations and associated risk premiums, and broad advances in a wide variety of technologies that produced critical synergies in the 1990s.'[15] For Greenspan, it was clearly New Economy productivity gains that were generating rising incomes (including profits), and thereby rising equity values, and emphatically not vice versa.

---

[14] 'Testimony of Chairman Alan Greenspan Before the Joint Economic Committee, US Congress: Monetary Policy and the Economic Outlook', 17 June 1999, FRB website.
[15] 'Testimony of Chairman Alan Greenspan Before the Joint Economic Committee, US Congress: High-Tech Industry in the US Economy', 14 June 1999, FRB website; 'Testimony of Chairman Alan Greenspan Before the Committee on Ways and Means, US House of Representatives: State of the Economy', 20 January 1999, FRB website. Cf. '[T]he process of *recognizing* this greater value [of our capital stock] has produced capital gains in the equity markets' (emphasis added).

EQUITY PRICES REACH THEIR ZENITH

Especially in light of Alan Greenspan's endorsement of the run-up of share prices in terms of the New Economy, the Fed's decisive intervention in the equity and credit markets in autumn–winter 1998 naturally gave an enormous fillip to investor confidence. It not only put a stop to the frightening glissade of the stock market of the previous summer, but quickly set off what turned out to be the most violent phase of the equity price bubble, in which the growth of share prices seemed for a time to unhitch itself from any dependence at all on the growth of profits and in which high technology shares scaled unparalleled heights. Over 1998–99, after-tax corporate profits (net of interest) failed to grow, falling by 6.6 per cent in 1998, then increasing by 5.5 per cent in 1999. Yet, the NYSE Index managed to streak upward by 20.5 per cent and 12.5 per cent, respectively, in those years. The more elite firms represented on the S&P 500 index did only slightly better, registering gains in earning of 0 per cent and 17 per cent, respectively, in 1998 and 1999, while their equity prices rose by 27 per cent and 22 per cent, respectively. In the process, not surprisingly, equity prices of New Economy companies, now bearing the implicit imprimatur of the Fed chair, rose at unprecedented speed to incredible levels.

In the latter part of 1999, the Fed jumped in to reassure the financial markets on a still further occasion. In October and November, Greenspan himself had spooked investors not only by continuing with a series of quarter-point interest rate increases that rescinded his interest rate reductions of the previous winter, but also by going so far as to warn banks about the vulnerability of collateral on loans that they held in the form of (over-valued) equities.[16] But, ostensibly in response to concerns about a possible Y2K disruption, he outdid himself in compensating for these steps. During the final quarter of year, the Fed pumped sufficient liquidity

---

[16] T.S. Mulligan, 'Greenspan, Gust of Inflation Pummel Stocks, Spiking Fears', *Los Angeles Times*, 16 October 1999; 'Greenspan and the Markets', *Financial Times*, 16 October 1999; G. Baker, 'Fed Seeks to Reduce the Speed Limit', *Financial Times*, 17 November 1999.

into the banking system to suddenly bring down the Federal Funds Rate from 5.5 per cent to below 4 per cent – the widest deviation from its target rate in over nine years – and thereby paved the way for the last frantic, record-shattering upward lunge in the equity markets, which took place during the first quarter of 2000. Bank loans thus raced ahead at a 19.4 per cent annual pace during the fourth quarter of 1999, the highest in at least fifteen years, after having stagnated at an annual rate of 1.6 per cent during the first three quarters of the year. Simultaneously, the growth of the money supply vaulted to 14.3 per cent, even faster than in the wake of the Fed's moves to calm the crisis of the previous autumn.[17]

Helped out by this series of interventions, reassurances, and rationalizations by the Federal Reserve, the S&P 500, having fallen by about a fifth during summer 1998, catapulted back up by close to 50 per cent between Greenspan's moves of October–November 1998 and March 2000. Over the same period, the technology and Internet stocks that Greenspan touted as transforming the economy's profit-making potential exploded in much more extreme fashion, more than doubling in value, while the Dow Jones E-Commerce Index quadrupled. All of this was, of course, most dramatically reflected in the technology and Internet-dominated NAS-DAQ Index: having fallen by about 30 per cent from July through October 1998, it also took off in the wake of the Fed's three successive interest rate reductions of October and November, almost doubling by May 1999; then, after stagnating throughout summer 1999, it veered sharply upward again in correlation with the Fed's fourth-quarter credit loosening, almost doubling from 2736 at the beginning of October 1999 to just over 5000 in March 2000.

Tellingly, from the time that the Fed intervened to head off the financial crisis of autumn–winter 1998, stocks outside the New Economy ceased to rise, remaining essentially flat. The ascent of the stock market in the final, most fevered phase of the bubble, from November 1998 through March 2000, was thus accounted for entirely by TMT shares. It

---

[17] IMF, *International Capital Markets. Developments, Prospects, and Key Policy Issues*, Washington, DC, September 2000, p. 12; OECD, *Economic Survey. United States 2000*, Paris, 2000, p. 69, Table 11.

was TMT equities alone, in accord with Alan Greenspan's encomium to the New Economy, that carried the bubble to its peak (see below, p. 187, Figure 7.3).[18]

During the first quarter of 2000, the total value of US non-financial corporate equities, their market capitalization, reached $15.6 trillion, up from $4.8 trillion in 1994. The incongruity of this figure, and this ascent, was evident from many angles. Most definitive, of course, was the absurd disconnection between the rise of paper wealth and the growth of actual output, and particularly of profits, in the underlying economy. Apparent wealth thus levitated with little reference to the actual creation of goods and services. Between 1994 and early 2000, the ratio between the market capitalization of non-financial corporations and non-financial corporate GDP leaped from 1.3 to 3, more than 75 per cent above the highest level previously reached during the post-war period (1.7 in 1968); this despite the fact that, in that six-year period, after-tax non-financial corporate profits (net of interest) had risen by only 41.2 per cent. By contrast, it had taken fourteen years, between 1980 and 1994, for the ratio of non-financial corporate market capitalization to GDP to increase from 0.9 to 1.3, even though non-financial corporate profits had risen by 160 per cent in the intervening period (see Figure 7.1).[19]

Equally indicative was the exceptional level attained by the ratio between companies' valuations in terms of their equities on the stock market, on the one hand, and in terms of what it would cost to replace their plant and equipment and financial capital, on the other hand. In the first quarter of 2000, for non-financial corporations, this ratio, known as Tobin's q, reached an all-time high of 2.06 – compared to 1.14 in 1995 and 0.46 in 1986, and to an average of 0.65 for the twentieth century as a whole (see Figure 7.2). Tobin's q in the first quarter of 2000 was thus more than 50 per cent above its previous historic peaks, which came, not

[18] IMF, *World Economic Outlook. Fiscal Policy and Macroeconomic Stability*, Washington, DC, May 2001, p. 59. On the other hand, in March 2000, the price–earnings ratio for non-technology stocks was still a pricey 23:1. Bank for International Settlements, *70th Annual Report. 1 April 1999–31 March 2000*, p. 107.

[19] Board of Governors of the Federal Reserve System, *Flow of Funds Accounts of the United States. Flows and Outstandings* [henceforth FRB, *Flow of Funds*], Table L.213, Corporate Equities (levels); M. Wolf, 'Risking a Hard Landing', *Financial Times*, 6 December 2000.

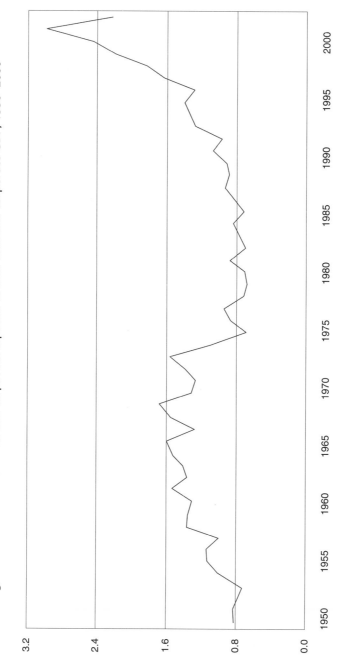

Figure 7.1 Ratio of non-financial corporate equities to non-financial corporate GDP, 1950–2000

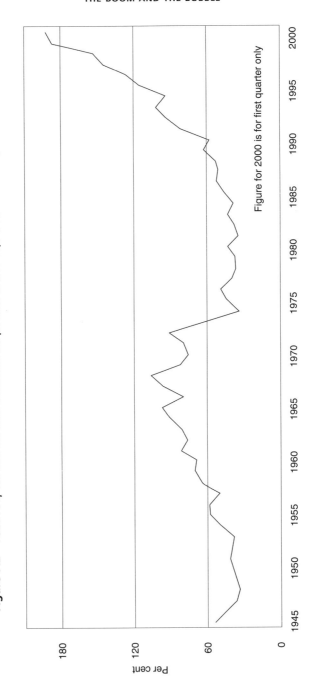

Figure 7.2 Tobin's *q* for the US non-financial corporate sector equities/net worth, 1945–2000

surprisingly, in 1929 (at 1.3) and 1969 (at 1.2), at the very conclusions of the stock market run-ups of those decades. With corporations' shares costing so much more than their actual means of production and net financial assets, it would seem to have been only common sense for investors wishing to secure any given amount of capital to purchase it in the form of new plant and equipment and the like, rather than in the form of equities. That they so often did the opposite was a clear indication that a bubble had taken hold of their senses.[20]

Finally, in March 2000, the price–earnings ratio for the corporations represented on the S&P 500 index – the ratio of what it costs, on average, to buy a share with respect to the annual earnings (profits) that share represents – reached about 32. When one considers the extent to which the rise of share prices had diverged from the increase of profits, it is not surprising that this was again a record – at least one third higher than this ratio's previous high-point during the twentieth century, and about two and a half times its historical average of 13.2. The annual rate of return on equities – the so-called 'earnings yield', which is simply the price–earnings ratio inverted – was thus extremely low in comparative terms – around 3 per cent, compared to the historical average of 7.7 per cent. One might therefore have expected that stocks would have been regarded as an increasingly bad investment.[21] That this was far from being the case demonstrates again that equities were being purchased, for the most part, purely and simply on the expectation that their prices would go up further, irrespective of corporations' rates of return, and one more sign of the bubble dynamic.[22]

The stock market valuations of high-technology companies, and especially Internet firms, were, of course, even more absurd. Despite their tiny place by any measure in the economy as a whole, the market capitali-

---

[20] *Flow of Funds*, Table B.102, Balance Sheet of Nonfarm Nonfinancial Corporations, Line 37; A. Smithers and S. Wright, *Valuing Wall Street. Protecting Wealth in Turbulent Markets*, New York, McGraw Hill, 2000, p. 10, Chart 2.1, and pp. 146–54, 257.

[21] Smithers and Wright, *Valuing Wall Street*, pp. 226 and 227, esp. Chart 22.1.

[22] The foregoing standard, and commonsensical, arguments were quite common, if a minority view, among economic analysts in the early part of 2000. See, e.g., ibid.; Shiller, *Irrational Exuberance*; Warburton, *Debt and Delusion*; S. King, *Bubble Trouble. The US Bubble and How it Will Burst*, London, HSBC Economics and Investment Strategy, 1999.

zation of Internet companies reached 8 per cent of the total. The reality was that most of these companies had made only losses, and the few that were making profits were trading at impossibly high price–earnings ratios. In a sample of 242 Internet companies studied by the OECD, only thirty-seven made profits during the third quarter of 1999, and these traded at an average price-to-earnings ratio of 190. *Two* of these companies alone accounted for 60 per cent of the total profits made by all thirty-seven! The other thirty-five companies traded, on average, at a price–earnings ratio of 270. The remaining 205 companies made losses. For the 168 of these companies for which data were available, total losses in the third quarter amounted to $12.5 billion (at an annual rate). But this did not prevent their market capitalization from reaching $621 billion.[23] Not surprisingly, by spring 2000, in the wake of their continuing losses, many of these so-called 'e-businesses' were on the verge of running out of money. A return to reality on the stock market would not be long in coming.[24]

But the bottom line was that the technology, media, and telecommunication companies (TMTs), at the core of the New Economy, and the darlings of the stock market, failed to perform all that much better, even despite the unprecedented hype and the Federal Reserve Chair's personal endorsement. Between March 1995 and March 2000, the value of TMT stocks grew by a factor of 6.1, their earnings by a factor of just 2.2. In the final, most fevered phase of the equity price run-up – and the US economic boom – between November 1998 and March 2000, the value of TMT equities more than doubled, while their earnings grew by 47 per cent.[25] Powered by information technology stocks, the bubble had taken flight, pulling the economy with it, but leaving profits behind (see Figure 7.3).

[23] OECD, *Economic Survey. United States 2000*, pp. 50–2.
[24] J. Willoughby, 'Burning Up. Warning: Internet Companies are Running out of Cash', *Barron's*, 20 March 2000; J. Willoughby, 'Up In Smoke. Dot.coms are Still Burning Cash, but the Market has Forced Big Changes', *Barron's*, 19 June 2000.
[25] Bank for International Settlements, *71st Annual Report*, p. 103, Table VI.1, as well as underlying data provided by Bank for International Settlements.

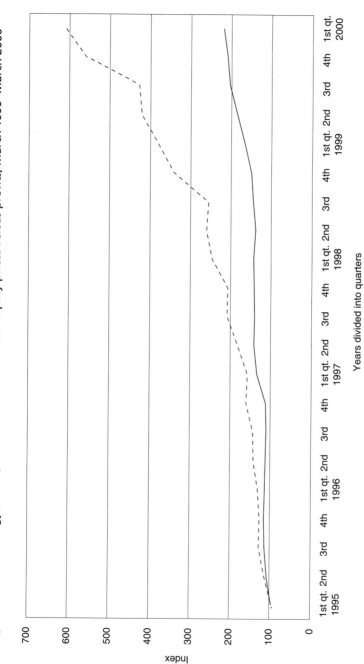

Figure 7.3 Technology, media, and telecommunications: equity prices versus profits, March 1995–March 2000

CHAPTER 8

THE WEALTH EFFECT AND ITS LIMITS

From the end of 1997, the stock market came, in a sense, to exert a greater impact on the real economy than the real economy did on the stock market. After stagnating during the previous two years, the corporate manufacturing profit rate fell sharply in 1998 and 1999, under the impact of the rising dollar and intensifying international competition, worsened by the crisis in East Asia. After having risen in 1996 and 1997 – peaking in the latter year – the rate of profit in the non-financial corporate sector also fell substantially over the next two years. Nevertheless, from 1998 though the middle of 2000, the economy displayed even greater dynamism than it had previously, explicable only as a consequence of the capacity of equity prices to continue their upward flight oblivious to underlying profits, immensely aided in so doing by the Fed and the corporations themselves. The US economic expansion got a new lease on life from the push to both consumption and investment growth derived from the wealth effect of the stock market bubble, and pulled the rest of world behind it. But the economy could defy the gravitational pull of actual returns on investment for only so long.

THE EXPANSION SPEEDS UP

The historic scramble skywards of equity prices gave both households and corporations unprecedentedly easy access to cash. The huge on-paper increases in the value of corporations and in the wealth of households made for vast increases in the apparent collateral of both. That inflated collateral provided, in turn, the basis for the greatest binge of dis-savings in US history, both corporate and household, which was accommodated, with few questions asked, by willing lenders. Meanwhile, corporations in need of capital could also secure it uncommonly cheaply simply by issuing shares at super-inflated prices to ever-more-enthusiastic investors. The resulting explosions of both investment and consumption shot the US, and the international, economy forward as if blown from a cannon.

From rising asset values to easy borrowing and cheap capital: households, corporations, financial institutions

Households

Between 1994 and the first quarter of 2000, the market capitalization of shares held by households snowballed from $4 trillion to $12.2 trillion.[1] As a result, whereas the ratio between household net worth and personal disposable income had increased by just 9 per cent in the fourteen years between 1980 and 1994, it sprang up by 32 per cent between 1994 and the first quarter of 2000.[2] On the basis of this extraordinary stock-market-driven appreciation of their assets, households concluded that they had the wherewithal to decrease savings and help themselves to borrowing to a degree inconceivable before. Between 1950 and 1992, the personal savings rate had never gone above 10.9 per cent and never fallen below 7.5 per cent, except in three isolated years. But, between 1992 and 2000, it plummeted from 8.7 per cent to −0.12 per cent (see Figure 8.1).[3]

It need hardly be added that the households that were responsible for

[1] Board of Governors of the Federal Reserve System, *Flow of Funds Accounts of the United States. Flow and Outstanding* [henceforth FRB, *Flow of Funds*], Table L.100, Household and Nonprofit Organizations (levels): Line 32, Corporate Equities, and Line 33, Mutual Fund Shares.
[2] Ibid., Table B.100, Balance Sheet of Households and Nonprofit Organizations: Line 50, Household Net Worth as a Percentage of Disposable Personal Income (levels).
[3] Recent revisions to the US National Income and Product Accounts have slightly raised the rate of savings during the post-war period over that previously recorded, but the slope of the recent downward trend is unaffected. For the revised data, see the Bureau of Economic Analysis (henceforth BEA) website.

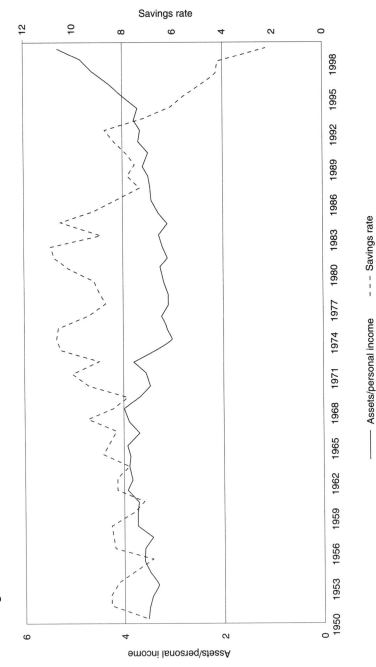

Figure 8.1 US household financial assets/personal disposable income and US savings rate, 1950–99

the huge reduction in the US personal saving rate that took place during the 1990s in conjunction with the run-up of equity prices hailed almost entirely from the ranks of the wealthy. This could be deduced simply from the fact that – contrary to the myth of the broad dispersion of stocks among US households – the ownership of equities, and thus gains from their appreciation, is so highly concentrated. The top 20 per cent of owners of equities thus possesses between 96 and 98 per cent of all assets in the form of stocks (depending on whether pensions are counted or not).[4] Researchers at the Federal Reserve Board have now, however, *explicitly* demonstrated: first, that those in the top 20 per cent by income accounted for 79 per cent of the aggregate increase of the ratio of net worth to personal disposal income that took place in the 1990s; second, that this same top 20 per cent accounted for close to a 100 per cent of the total fall in the US aggregate savings rate that occurred in this period; third, and correlatively, that there was, in the interim, effectively no decline in the savings rate for the bottom 80 per cent of the population, the savings rate of the bottom 60 per cent actually creeping up slightly. The wealth effect was such in more ways than one.[5]

Household annual borrowing naturally followed a parallel trajectory, although as a percentage of disposable income it did not quite reach the record levels of the 1980s, probably because borrowing by working-class families for the purpose of compensating for declining incomes was not as widespread in the late 1990s as in the earlier period. Still, by 2000, households' outstanding *debt* as a proportion of personal disposable income reached the all-time high of 97 per cent, up from an average of 80 per cent during the second half of the 1980s.[6]

[4] L. Mishel, J. Bernstein, and J. Schmitt, *The State of Working America 2000/2001*, Ithaca, NY, Cornell University Press, 2001, p. 265, Table 4.6.
[5] D.M. Maki and M.G. Palumbo, 'Disentangling the Wealth Effect: A Cohort Analysis of Household saving in the 1990s', Federal Reserve Finance and Discussion Series, April 2001 (Federal Reserve website).
[6] *Flow of Funds*, Table D3, Debt Outstanding by Sector (levels); *Economic Report of the President 2000*, Washington, DC, 2000.

Corporations

The easy credit conditions sustained by the Fed initially facilitated, as noted, the stimulation of corporate borrowing that enabled the large-scale corporate purchases that played such a major role in goading equity prices upward. In turn, those same rising equity prices made possible an even further expansion of corporate borrowing by providing the increased assets deemed necessary by creditors to justify further advances. They also opened the way for corporations to secure funding unprecedentedly cheaply – and to an unprecedented extent – through new issues of inflated shares.[7]

Between 1994 and the first quarter of 2000, the market value of equities outstanding of US non-financial corporations sprinted from $4.8 to $15.7 trillion, growing at twice the rate as between 1984 and 1994.[8] This enormous revaluation of non-financial corporate assets opened the way for the greatest expansion in non-financial corporate borrowing ever. Annual borrowing by non-financial corporations as a percentage of non-financial corporate GDP darted from 3.4 per cent in 1994 and 3.7 per cent as late as 1996 to a previously unparalleled 9.9 per cent in the first half of 2000, this during a period when non-financial corporate (nominal) GDP was itself increasing at an average annual rate of 5.7 per cent. As a result, by the first half of 2000, non-financial corporate borrowing on an annual basis had more than quadrupled with respect to 1994 and non-financial corporate debt as a proportion of non-financial corporate GDP had reached 85 per cent, the highest level ever, up from 72.2 per cent in 1994 (see Figure 8.2).[9]

This explosion of borrowing not only allowed non-financial corporate

---

[7] This reasoning is encapsulated in the OECD, *Economic Survey. United States 2000*, Paris, 2000, pp. 48–9, where it is explained that the trend of corporate borrowing would not have been sustainable had it not been the case that 'the overall indebtedness of companies had, up to 1998, been increasing only slightly faster than either [the stock market value of] net worth or total assets.'

[8] FRB, *Flow of Funds*, Table L.213, Corporate Equities (levels).

[9] Ibid., Table F.3 and Table L.3, Credit Market Borrowing by Nonfinancial Sectors (flows and levels); 'Industry Analytical Ratios for Non-Financial Corporations,' folder provided by the Division of Productivity Research, Bureau of Labor Statistics.

Figure 8.2 US non-financial corporate borrowing and debt as a percentage of non-financial corporate GDP, 1950–2000

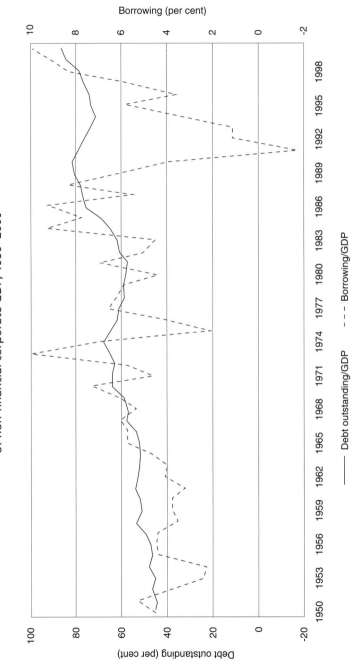

equity buybacks to continue to pullulate, chasing the equity price bubble toward its apogee and the corporate debt–equity ratio to new records;[10] it also enabled non-financial corporations to raise the proportion of their capital expenditures that was financed by borrowing (rather than out of retained earnings) to levels hitherto unmatched during an economic expansion, and thereby amplify an already very powerful investment boom (see below, p. 201, Figure 8.5).

US corporations have tended, historically, to pay for most of their expenditures on new plant and equipment out of internal funds – i.e. profits minus taxes, net interest, and dividends plus depreciation – and this has continued into the present, even though borrowing to pay for capital expenditures did increase notably in the last years of the 1990s, a point to which it will be necessary to return. Between 1950 and 1973, non-financial corporations financed 93 per cent of their capital expenditures out of internal funds, and 87 per between 1973 and 1995. At no time did new equity issues play more than a trivial role in providing finance for the non-financial corporate sector in aggregate, and, after 1980, as has been stressed, the non-financial corporate sector as a whole was generally *buying and retiring* equities rather than issuing them.

Nevertheless, the fact remains that, during the 1990s, and especially its second half, as the stock market ascended into the firmament, there was a startling break from past practice. While the non-financial corporate sector as a whole remained a net *purchaser* of equities – and was so to an historically unprecedented degree – particular firms and sections within the non-financial corporate sector became net issuers in a very big way. Start-up firms and cash-poor corporations seeking to expand rapidly could not resist exploiting astronomical share prices to raise entirely unprecedented amounts of money by way of selling stocks. This was especially true for the technology, media, and telecommunications firms that dominated the last, most fevered phase of the bubble, from November 1998 to spring 2000. A good many of these companies had very limited access to

---

[10] By 1999, the debt–equity ratio of S&P 500 companies shot up to 116 per cent, compared to 84 per cent at the end of the end of 1980s, when the corporate debt crisis had paralysed both banks and corporations, deepening and extending the recession (D. Bogler and G. Silverman, 'US Risky Debt Threat to Banks', *Financial Times*, 22 February 2000).

bond markets or bank finance, so the increase in their stock valuations opened a key channel of funding – and, in turn, investment.[11]

Between 1994 and 2000, then, as equity prices of non-financial corporations rose to levels hitherto unimagined, so did their stock issues. Already in the early 1990s, monies raised by non-financial corporations through selling shares had reached levels 80 per cent higher than their previous (recorded) historic peak. Between 1994 and 2000, these increased every year, more than tripling overall. In the bubble's last phase, in 1999 and 2000, dominated, as has been seen, by information technology companies, non-financial corporate equity issues sped up further, reaching an all-time high of $284 billion in 2000, four times the 1980s peak (see Figure 8.3). Alan Greenspan's 'virtuous cycle' was at the height of its power.[12]

Sales of equities were of course especially critical for start-up firms, and gross proceeds from initial public offerings (IPOs) followed a similar trajectory to that of equity issues more generally, but ascended even faster into the heavens as the information technology bubble peaked. After having averaged less than $3 billion a year between 1980 and 1994, annual gross proceeds from IPOs jumped to about $30 billion between 1994 and 1998. Then, in 1999–2000, proceeds doubled to $60 billion per annum, providing lavish finance for countless New Economy start-ups that would otherwise have had no chance of securing support (see Figure 8.4).[13] Never before in US history had the stock market played such a direct, and decisive, role in financing non-financial corporations, and thereby powering the growth of capital expenditures and in this way the real economy. Never before had a US economic expansion become so dependent upon the stock market's ascent.

---

[11] IMF, *World Economic Outlook. Fiscal Policy and Macroeconomic Stability*, May 2000, pp. 63–4.

[12] Gross equity issues by non-financial corporations, 1984–2000, Federal Reserve Board unpublished time series. I wish to thank Nellie Liang for forwarding these data to me. It must be stressed that these figures, which go back only to 1984, include both public and private issues by non-financial corporations, so are not directly comparable to the data on non-financial corporate net purchases.

[13] 'Annual Report of the Council of Economic Advisers', in *Economic Report of the President 2001*, Washington, DC, 2001, pp. 108–10.

Figure 8.3 Total gross equity issues by non-financial corporations publicly issued and privately placed, 1984–2000

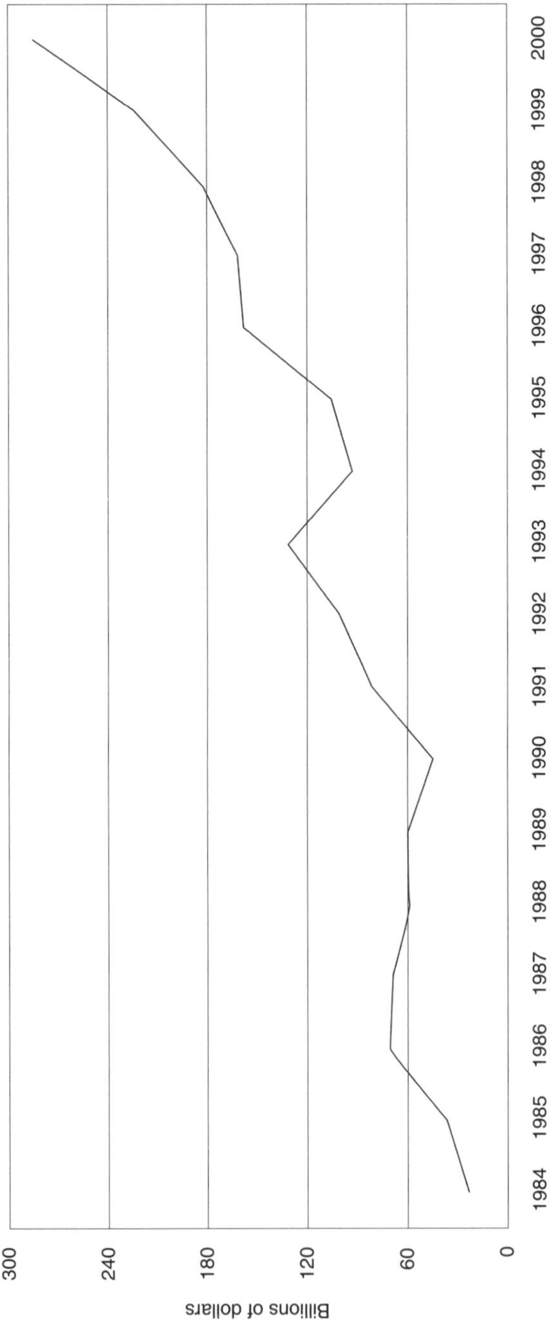

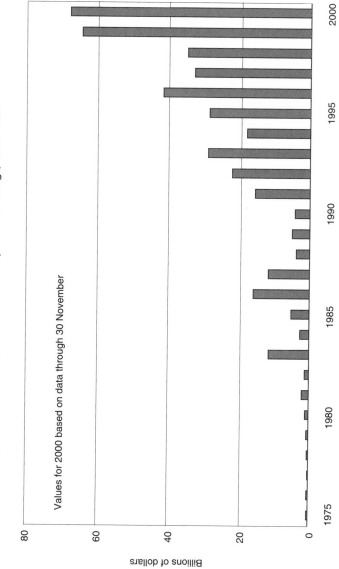

Figure 8.4 Gross proceeds of initial public offerings, 1975–2000

Values for 2000 based on data through 30 November

Financial institutions

In order to respond to the insatiable demand for loans from corporations and households, financial institutions had to vastly enlarge their own borrowing. Between 1995 and 1999, financial sector borrowing increased by two and a half times and averaged just about 10 per cent of GDP, more than double the average of the previous decade (1985–95). During the years 1998–99, helped out by the Fed's three interest rate reductions and its major Y2K loosening of credit, financial sector borrowing averaged 12 per cent of GDP, which was 75 per cent higher than in any previous year on record. In the same two years, just to be sure that available liquidity was great enough to support the enormous bacchanalia of borrowing that was occurring, and to keep the stock market from falling and the economy expanding, the government, through its Government Sponsored Enterprises, lent a cool $0.6 trillion for home purchases and the like. Their own borrowing to do so amounted to almost 30 per cent of total financial sector borrowing in these years.[14] By the first half of 2000, corporate, household, and financial sector debt as a percentage of GDP were all at their highest levels in post-war US history.

From easy access to finance to runaway consumption and investment

Consumption growth

By enabling the sharp increase of household borrowing and the steep rundown of household savings, the runaway stock market made possible a major amplification of the growth of personal consumption, helping to expand the boom, and to sustain it, as manufacturing profitability, com-

---

[14] FRB, *Flow of Funds*, Table F.3, Credit Market Borrowing by Financial Sector (flows); Table F.24, Government-Sponsored Enterprises (flows). Cf. 'The Bulls' Last Charge?' *Economist*, 19 March 1999; D. Noland, 'Capital Markets as Reckless Creators of Money and Credit', *PrudentBear.com*, 7 April 2000 (on-line); P. Kasriel, 'The Unkindest Cut of All: Kasriel Articulates the Consensus View?' *Northern Trust. Daily Economic Commentary*, 10 April 2000 (on-line).

petitiveness, and exports turned down. Between 1985 and 1995, personal consumption expenditures increased at an average annual rate of 2.9 per cent and explained, in growth accounting terms, about 67 per cent of GDP growth. But from 1995 through the first half of 2000, personal consumption expenditures rattled along at an average annual pace of 4.3 per cent and, in growth accounting terms, were responsible for 73 per cent of GDP increase. As the Fed and the Treasury must have hoped, moreover, the growth of personal consumption expenditures sped up sharply between 1997 and the first half of 2000 so as to more than make up for the collapse of overseas sales growth that took place at this time: it achieved the fevered average annual rate of 5 per cent and accounted for 82 per cent of the growth of GDP.[15]

It should not be overlooked in this respect that, accounting as they did for 80 per cent of the gains in household financial wealth and almost the entirety of the dis-saving that took place during the 1990s, the wealthiest Americans were also responsible for virtually all of the increase in households' aggregate propensity to consume during these years.[16] As one pundit wryly put it, the boom of the later 1990s was the first in US history to be driven by yuppie expenditures.

Investment growth

The expanding equity price bubble not only sped up consumption growth, but also – by making possible both the already-noted unprecedented increase of corporate borrowing and the radical reduction of the cost of capital by way of stock issuance – powerfully strengthened an ongoing investment boom that had initially been founded on the recovery of profitability. The big up-tick in investment growth was, indeed, at the heart of the boom of the 1990s. Between 1982 and 1992, real private non-residential investment had increased at an average annual rate of just 4 per cent per annum and accounted for only 12.4 per cent of total GDP

---

[15] *Economic Report of the President 2000*, Table B-5; BEA, 'Gross Domestic Product: Second Quarter 2000 (Final) [and] Corporate Profits: Second Quarter 2000 (Revised)', 28 September 2000 (Press Release, BEA website).
[16] Maki and Palumbo, 'Disentangling the Wealth Effect'.

growth. But between 1992 and 1999, as profit rates (after tax) approached the levels of the 1960s boom, it increased at an average annual rate of 10.3 per cent per annum and was responsible for 31.6 per cent of GDP growth. As in the case of personal consumption expenditures, investment growth was enabled to make its greatest contribution to the economy's expansion by the final explosion upward of the equity price bubble. In the two and a half years between 1997 and the first half of 2000, annual private non-residential investment growth averaged no less than 13.6 per cent per annum and accounted for 37 per cent of the growth of GDP.

Non-financial corporations were, of course, able to raise investment at such a very rapid rate as the stock market bubble reached its climax only because, in the same period, capital was so extraordinarily easily available to them, both through borrowing and through equity issues. Between 1997 and 2000, non-financial corporations were able to finance a full 22 per cent of their capital outlays by borrowing. This was far and away the highest proportion of their investment that non-financial corporations had financed on credit since the Korean War (leaving aside the recession years of 1969–70, 1973–74, and 1979–81, when the bloated fraction is largely explained by shrinking internal funds). By contrast, they had had to cover just 13.3 per cent of their capital outlays with borrowed funds between 1973 and 1995 and only 5.1 per cent of such outlays between 1953 and 1973. To be able to step up their reliance on credit to such a great extent, non-financial corporations were obliged to radically elevate the ratio of their borrowing to non-financial corporate GDP from 6 per cent to 10 per cent between 1997 and 2000, and devote 50 per cent of their total borrowing in those years to capital outlays. (By comparison, in the same period, they devoted about 45 per cent of that borrowing to net purchases of non-financial corporate equities.) They could manage such an increased dependence on debt only because the astounding increase in their stock market capitalization made them appear to be such trustworthy debtors (see Figure 8.5).[17]

---

[17] FRB, *Flow of Funds*, Table F.102, Nonfarm Nonfinancial Corporate Business: Line 58, Financing Gap, and Lines 5 and 7, Internal Funds Plus Inventory Valuation Adjustment. The financing gap equals capital outlays minus internal funds adjusted for inventory valuation. It thus represents the amount of money that must be raised to cover capital expenditures by borrowing (or other means).

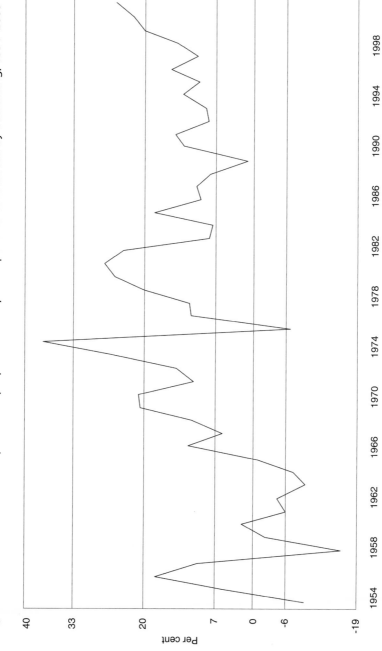

Figure 8.5 US non-financial corporations' proportion of capital expenditures financed by borrowing, 1954–2000

Meanwhile, of course, gross equity issues by non-financial corporations were hitting an all-time high and proceeds from IPOs were going into orbit. The stock market was thus making possible huge increases in expenditures on plant and equipment not only by well-established, credit-worthy corporations, but, as noted, also by companies that would other-wise have been highly constrained in their ability to spend by their constricted ability to borrow, accelerating the investment boom that much further.

Manufacturing

As a result of the powerful quickening of both consumption growth and investment growth that derived from the equity price bubble in its last, most speculative phase, the US manufacturing sector was able to avoid any palpable deceleration, let alone crisis, despite the sharp decline of manufacturing competitiveness from 1995, the flattening of the manufac-turing profit rate from 1995 through 1997, the collapse of manufacturing export growth from the latter part of 1997, and the sharp fall of the manufacturing profit rate in 1998 and 1999. Personal consumption of manufactured durable goods had grown at an average annual pace of 6.5 per cent between 1992 and 1997, but it truly ignited between 1997 and the first half of 2000, springing ahead at an average annual rate of 12 per cent. In 1998 and 1999, manufacturing output growth was therefore able to forge ahead at an average annual rate of 5 per cent, even higher than the 4.35 per cent it averaged between 1993 and 1997. Manufacturing investment growth also gathered steam, averaging 11 per cent in 1998 and 1999 and raising the average annual rate of growth of the capital stock to 3.3 per cent, from 2.4 per cent between 1993 and 1997. As a result, manufacturing productivity growth, which had been powering ahead at 4.4 per cent per annum on average between 1993 and 1997, leaped forward at nearly 6 per cent per annum on average between 1997 and the first half of 2000, the fastest since the early 1970s. By grace of the bubble, the manufacturing sector could ignore, at least momentarily, that the foundations of its hard-won recovery between 1986 and 1995 had begun to crumble.

Non-manufacturing

The non-manufacturing sector was unquestionably the greatest beneficiary of the conditions prevailing during the years of the equity price bubble. After having experienced its most difficult period of the post-war epoch between the mid-1980s and early 1990s, it benefited from the stepped-up demand that emanated from a fast-growing manufacturing sector from 1993 onwards. Moreover, since its output was composed mostly of non-tradables, imports made cheap by the rising dollar from 1995 not only failed to hurt this sector, but also swelled its profits by providing it with lower-cost inputs – just the opposite of what had been happening in the low dollar era between 1985 and 1995. Finally, of course, the sector received a powerful jolt upward from 1995 from the wealth effect of rising equity prices. In every year from 1995 through 1999, the output of the non-manufacturing sector grew faster (if only slightly) than did that of the private business economy as a whole. Capital accumulation in non-manufacturing was also more rapid than in the private business economy as a whole. As the bubble peaked, non-manufacturing investment growth zipped ahead in an extraordinary way, averaging close to 14 per cent per annum between 1997 and the first half of 2000 and lifting the rate of growth of the non-manufacturing capital stock above 4.5 per cent per annum.

All told, between 1993 and 1999, GDP grew at an average annual rate of 3.9 per cent. Between 1997 and the first half of 2000, it accelerated to 4.6 per cent per annum. Of total GDP growth after 1995, according to Alan Greenspan and the US Federal Reserve, about 25 per cent, or 1 per cent a year, could be attributed to the 'wealth effect', i.e. the impact of rising asset prices on the growth of consumption and investment. Put another way, the boost in investment and consumption attributable to the run-up of equity prices raised the growth of GDP by a factor of about one-third.[18] With GDP growth continuing to accelerate, real wage growth

---

[18] 'Testimony of Chairman Alan Greenspan Before the Committee on Banking and Financial Services, US House of Representatives: The Federal Reserve's Semi-Annual Report on the Economy and Monetary Policy', 17 February 2000, FRB website. According to Greenspan, 'three to four cents of every additional dollar of stock market wealth eventually is reflected

finally began to increase substantially in 1998 and 1999, averaging 3.3 per
cent per annum in the business economy, after having averaged 0.3 per
cent per annum between 1986 and 1996, and gave a further major lift to
the growth of consumption in these years.

FROM US BOOM TO INTERNATIONAL RECOVERY

The volcanic growth of US demand, heavily subsidized by the delirium of
the equity markets, not only helped to speed up the US economic
expansion from the end of 1995, while sustaining it virtually single-
handedly between the end of 1997 and the first half of 2000; it also, at
the same time, drove the international economy toward a short-lived
boom between 1995 and 1997 and then enabled it – especially the East
Asian region – to hoist itself out of the serious downturn of 1997–98.

Especially because the dollar's exchange rate rose so rapidly from the
middle of 1995, climbing at an average annual pace of 4.0 per cent over
the next five years in trade-weighted terms, the increase of US domestic
demand ran to an ever greater extent beyond domestic supply (GDP).
Indeed, by 1998 and 1999, the increase in gross domestic purchases was
outrunning that of gross domestic product by 25 per cent. Purchases of
goods produced abroad had to increase to fill the gap. Between 1993 and
1997, real goods imports rose rapidly, at the average annual rate of 11.5
per cent, compared to 5.7 per cent per annum on average between 1985
and 1995. But they expanded even faster, at an average annual pace of
13.6 per cent, between 1997 and the first half of 2000, as the bubble
reached its acme. Over the same two-and-a-half-year period, the ratio of
manufacturing imports to manufacturing value added grew by 20 per
cent.

As US import growth reached its zenith as equity prices and the wealth
effect took their final leap upward and as US exports were held back

in increased consumer purchases', so that 'outlays prompted by capital gains have added
about one percentage point to annual growth of gross domestic purchases, on average, over
the past five years.'

under the impact of the impetuously rising dollar, the US bubble economy in its final phase succeeded spectacularly in pulling the world
economy, and particularly East Asia, from the great crisis of 1997–98.
Between 1997 and 2000, the US manufacturing trade deficit exploded
upward by no less than two and a half times! In this process, the huge
leap skyward of US high-tech capital expenditures between the end of
1998 and the first half of 2000 played the critical role. In that period, US
demand for imports of investment goods expanded at an average annual
pace of nearly 20 per cent, about four times faster than for imports of
consumer goods. East Asian TMT producers, led by Taiwan, Korea, and
Singapore, were able to provide a very major share of the supply response
– spectacularly raising their telecommunications and components exports
to the US by 43 per cent and 22 per cent, respectively, in the year ending
June 2000 – and were thereby enabled to transcend their deep recession
with a velocity that would otherwise have been out of the question. So, of
course, was Japan, which emerged from the doldrums with the significant
assistance not only of the booming US domestic market, but especially of
the rapidly expanding East Asian markets, which owed their own strength
to US demand.[19]

The Euro economies were of course less directly dependent upon the
US market than their East Asian and Japanese counterparts. But their
autonomy from US developments can easily be overstated. The German
economy, constituting about one-third of the Euro economies' GDP,
remains the Continent's dynamo. And it did continue to rely heavily on
exports to the US markets, especially autos and machine tools, to drive its
recovery from the slowdown accompanying the crisis in East Asia. So, in
fact, did Italy. Absent the pull of these two engines, the Euro economies
taken together would have languished. These economies received, moreover, a further, indispensable impetus from the deep devaluation of the
Euro against the dollar in these years, which significantly improved their
competitive position against their US rivals, especially in third markets.[20]

[19] UBS Warburg, *Global Economic Perspectives*, London, 19 April 2001; Bank for International
Settlements, *71st Annual Report*, pp. 13, 43.
[20] UBS Warburg, *US Hard Landing – European Outperformance?* London, July 2000; Bank for
International Settlements, *71st Annual Report*, p. 12.

Nevertheless, the sucking in of more and more imports could not but, simultaneously, bring about growing, then runaway, trade and current account deficits. During the early years of the 1990s, the US current account deficit as a percentage of GDP had withdrawn somewhat from its record highs of the mid- to late 1980s. This was thanks to the declining dollar, which repressed imports and stimulated exports, as well as to the slowed growth of demand due to the recession at the start of the decade and the slow return to growth. But, from 1994–95, as the economy began to expand again, both trade and current account deficits began to widen rapidly once more, reflecting the US economy's high marginal propensity to import with respect to income, especially in the shadow of the rising dollar. When from the end of 1997 export growth faltered and investment and consumption growth sharply gathered speed, the trade and current account deficits exploded and in 1999 and again in 2000 both deficits as a percentage of GDP set new records (see Figure 8.6).

Growing financial dependence on overseas investors

Of course, the US had no choice but to finance its growing current account deficit by incurring growing liabilities to overseas purchasers, especially from 1994–95. But foreign investors hardly needed coaxing to purchase US assets. During the period from 1995 to the middle of 2000, they made ever larger purchases as they rushed to get in on the expanding bubble, and they contributed very significantly to the inflation of the value of US financial assets (see Table 8.1).

The process began in 1995, as has been seen, when foreign purchases of US government securities swelled spectacularly as Japanese and other East Asian governments sought to keep down their exchange rates in the interest of export competitiveness, and private buyers followed suit especially to take advantage of the rising dollar. With the outbreak of the crisis in East Asia in mid-1997, the composition of overseas purchases of US assets did shift notably as governments of the region were obliged to reverse direction and to liquidate dollar holdings in an effort to support their nose-diving currencies. At the same time, however, as an ever greater

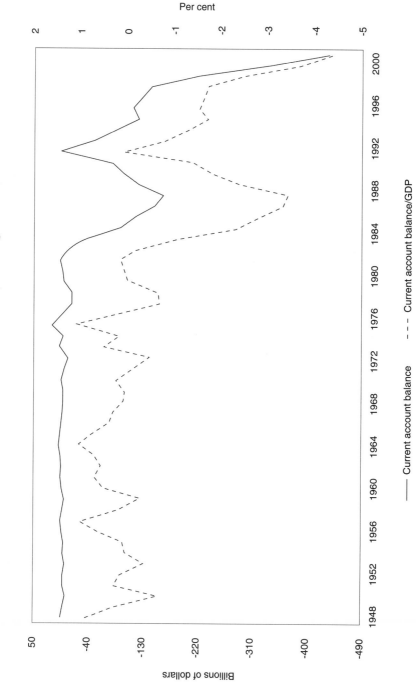

Figure 8.6 US current account balance and as a percentage of GDP, 1948–2000

Table 8.1   Private purchases of US assets by rest of world ($ billion), 1996–2000

	Government securities	Corporate bonds	Corporate equities	Direct investment	Total
1996	191.7	83.7	11.1	89.0	375.5
1997	191.7	84.0	66.8	109.3	451.8
1998	94.5	122.4	43.8	193.4	454.1
1999	51.9	158.9	94.3	282.5	587.6
2000	60.2	175.3	176.35	257.3	669.15
Total	590.0	624.3	392.35	931.5	2538.15

Note: Numbers for 2000 are annualized based on first half of year.

Source: Board of Governors of the Federal Reserve System, *Flow of Funds Accounts of the United States. Flows and Outstandings*, Table F.107, Rest of World (flows).

portion of the world economy became engulfed by recession, private investors abroad increasingly saw the US as a safe haven. They stepped up their direct investments in order to take advantage of the explosion of US consumption and the apparent improvement in business prospects. But, even more, they became central players in US equity and corporate bond markets. By the first half of 2000, they were responsible for no less than 52 per cent of total net purchases of corporate equities – up from 25.5 per cent in 1999, 8 per cent in 1998, and 4 per cent in 1995 – and 44 per cent of total corporate bond purchases – up from 33 per cent in 1999, 20 per cent in 1998, and 17 per cent in 1995.[21]

Foreign investors' growing participation powerfully magnified the US asset boom and encouraged even greater commitments. In effect, overseas lenders directly and indirectly subsidized growing US indebtedness and consumption, so that growing US demand could, in turn, underwrite the exports of their own economies. The fact remains that the large majority of the assets that were purchased by the rest of the world could be liquidated with relative ease, their private purchases of US Treasuries, corporate bonds, and corporate equities between 1995 and the first half

---

[21] FRB, *Flow of Funds*, Table F.213, Corporate Equities (flows), and Table F.212, Corporate and Foreign Bonds (flows).

of 2000 amounting to around $1.6 trillion, compared to around $900 billion in direct investments. By the first half of 2000, gross US assets held by the rest of the world reached $6.7 trillion, or 78 per cent of US GDP, compared to just $3.4 trillion, or 46 per cent of GDP, in 1995 (see Figure 8.7). Of these, $3.49 trillion were composed of privately held US Treasuries, corporate bonds, and corporate equities, compared to $1.2 trillion in direct investments.[22] The dependence of the US bubble, the US boom, and, in turn, the nascent global economic expansion on the unprecedented foreign purchases of US assets could not be more evident. Nor could the vulnerability of the US economy to the more-or-less rapid abandonment of those assets be any clearer.

THE ECONOMY'S ACHILLES' HEEL

Within this general picture of increasing across-the-board dynamism of the US economy in the last years of the 1990s, there was, however, one major trend that did not fit. Between 1997 and 2000, the corporate manufacturing profit rate fell by 20 per cent. In the same three-year period, the profit rate for the non-financial corporate sector as a whole fell by about 10 per cent.[23]

These reductions would have been significant under any circumstances. But what made them especially surprising – and particularly problematic – was that they took place in the face of a powerful US boom that was actually becoming stronger as profitability fell. The question that therefore imposed itself is why the economy was unable to translate into better

---

[22] Ibid., Table L.107, Rest of the World (levels). Between 1995 and 2000, net US assets held by the rest of the world doubled, reaching $1.4 trillion, or 14.2 per cent of GDP, compared to just $0.7 trillion, or 9.4 per cent of GDP, a brief five years before. Net assets here simply means gross assets held by the rest of the world minus liabilities of the rest of the world to US entities (which here includes the market value of foreign equities held by US residents).

[23] It is, once again, necessary to refer to profit rates in the corporate sector, rather than in the private economy as a whole, because, for the most recent period, revised data on profits, or data required to calculate profits, are at this point available only for the corporate sector. See above, p. 169, fn. 16. For the data on the non-financial corporate sector in the following paragraphs, see 'Industry Analytical Ratios for Non-financial Corporations'.

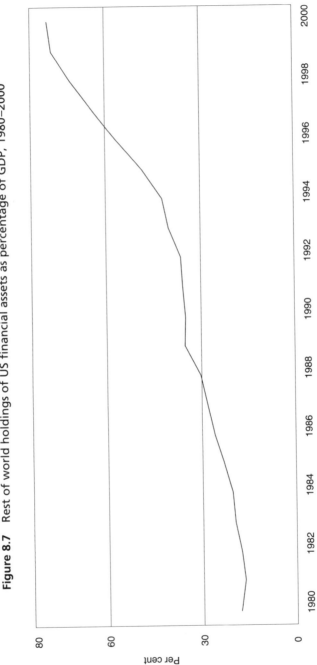

Figure 8.7 Rest of world holdings of US financial assets as percentage of GDP, 1980–2000

rates of return the extraordinary expansion of demand for its goods that took place at the end of the 1990s and the equally impressive growth of productivity that was simultaneously made possible by the rapid growth of investment? This issue was obviously especially pertinent in view of the heavy dependence at this juncture of both investment growth and consumption growth on the runaway stock market. For if profitability was already proving weak, the stock market 'correction' that seemed eventually unavoidable was bound to have devastating effects.

The beginning of an answer is to be found in the unusual pattern of growth of output and growth of prices over the course of the decade. During the economic expansion of the 1990s, the rate of growth of real gross domestic purchases for the economy as a whole increased more or less steadily, year by year, and reached a peak in 1998–2000. The growth of real output in the non-financial corporate sector followed roughly the same pattern and proceeded at a sizzling average annual pace unsurpassed since the 1960s. But, remarkably, in the teeth of this accelerating rise of demand and the rapid growth of output, the annual increase of product prices in the non-financial sector was unusually low in historical terms and fell sharply after 1995, reaching its lowest point during the decade in 1998–2000 (see Figure 8.8).[24]

Now, up through 1997, profitability in the non-financial corporate economy, and indeed the private economy as a whole, steadily strengthened. This was because stepped-up productivity growth combined with exceedingly low nominal (and real) wage growth to yield increases in unit labour costs that were even lower than reduced and declining price increases. But, from 1998 onwards, the non-financial corporate sector was unable to prevent its profit rate from falling notably, despite its improved economic performance. In 1998–2000, average annual productivity growth in the non-financial corporate sector, at 3.4 per cent, reached its highest point during the decade up to that point, indeed the highest level for any three-year period since the early 1960s. Nevertheless, the growth

[24] The average annual increase of product prices in the non-financial corporate sector between 1993 and 2000 was 0.9 per cent, compared to 2.3 per cent for the economic expansion between 1982 and 1990.

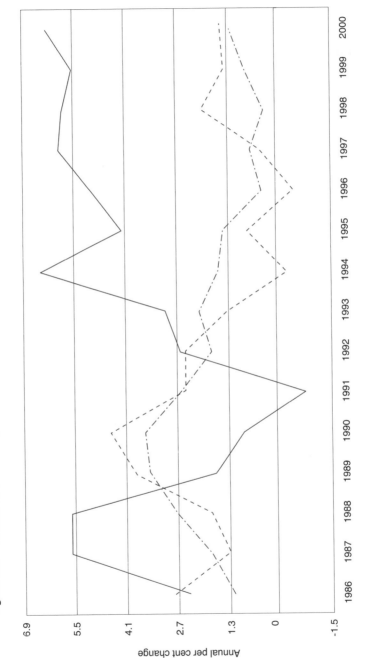

Figure 8.8 US non-financial corporate sector: GDP, unit labour costs, and product prices, 1986–2000

of unit labour costs sped up slightly, because nominal wages finally began to accelerate. Even so, the average annual growth of unit labour costs in 1998–2000 remained a third less rapid than it had been between 1982 and 1990 (and average annual nominal wage growth was no greater than it had been in that period). The problem was that, in the same three years, the average annual growth of product prices in the non-financial corporate sector fell to its lowest point in more than thirty years, and, at 0.8 per cent, was at one third its level of 2.4 per cent between 1982 and 1990. Put another way, the growth of prices was so weak that the growth of product wages (nominal wages deflated by product prices) outran productivity growth, even though nominal wage growth was not particularly rapid (although it did rise in 1998–2000 significantly above its depressed levels of the previous several years), and productivity growth was very strong. It was for this reason that by 2000, the profit rate in the non-financial corporate sector fell by about 10 per cent, compared to 1997 (see above p. 73, Figure 2.11, and below, p. 263, Figure 10.1).

The forces that brought about a fall in the rate of profit in the non-financial corporate economy were concentrated *entirely* in its corporate manufacturing component. From the time that the dollar had begun to rise in 1995, the US manufacturing sector had been subjected to excruciating price pressure from the world market, which, in 1996 and 1997, was already preventing it from translating its accelerating productivity growth into increases in profitability. The fact is that manufacturing profitability would already have begun to decline in these years under the impact of low and falling prices had it not been for manufacturers' extraordinary success in repressing nominal and real wages (see above, pp. 134–7). When the Asian crisis hit in earnest, this syndrome was only extended and accentuated, goods export prices growing at an average annual pace of 0 per cent between 1998 and 2000 (−1.2 per cent between 1995 and 2000) (see above, p. 136, Figure 5.1). In 1998, 1999, and 2000, average annual manufacturing productivity growth reached approximately 5.5 per cent, the highest level for any three-year period since the early 1960s. Nevertheless, corporate manufacturing profitability fell by 20 per cent in the same period, and the explanation is not far to seek. It lay, once again, in manufacturers' incapacity to mark up prices over costs, as can be seen immediately when reference is made to the parallel developments in the non-manufacturing sector.

Between 1997 and 2000, productivity growth in the non-financial non-manufacturing corporate sector, at about 3 per cent, was barely half that in the corporate manufacturing sector, and nominal wage growth was slightly higher. Nevertheless, in the same three-year period, the non-financial non-manufacturing corporate profit rate actually *increased* slightly, extending by three years a rising trajectory that had begun in 1995. This meant that the fall in the corporate manufacturing profit rate was totally responsible for the decline in the non-financial corporate profit rate in those years. What lay behind the divergence in the trajectory of the profit rate between the corporate manufacturing sector and the non-financial non-manufacturing sector is clear. As they had between 1995 and 1997, producers in the non-financial non-manufacturing corporate sector, their output prices largely unaffected by the world market, were able to continue to raise those prices over costs so as to maintain, or increase, their profit rates; but producers in the corporate manufacturing sector, subject to intensifying international competition, were not, even though they absorbed significantly smaller increases in costs (see Figure 8.9). It was for this reason that the corporate manufacturing profit rate and, thereby, the non-financial corporate profit rate fell off between 1997 and 2000.

Between 1997 and 2000, over-capacity and over-production in international manufacturing had worsened as a consequence of the world economic crisis of 1997–98 originating in East Asia. Simultaneously, the dollar had risen significantly higher, its real effective exchange rate climbing precipitously at an average pace of 3.5 per cent per annum, and 5 per cent per annum between 1995 and 2000. US producers were thus squeezed not only by the ongoing revaluation of their currency, but also by East Asian distress selling in their domestic markets, and found it more difficult to penetrate East Asian ones, while naturally being hurt by the general international economic slowdown. Indicative of the stress to which they were being subjected by the world market was the fact that, between 1995 and 2000, world manufacturing prices fell, in dollar terms, at an average annual pace of 4 per cent. This meant that, just to prevent a fall

Figure 8.9 US corporate manufacturing and US non-financial non-manufacturing corporate net profit rates, 1986–2000 indexes

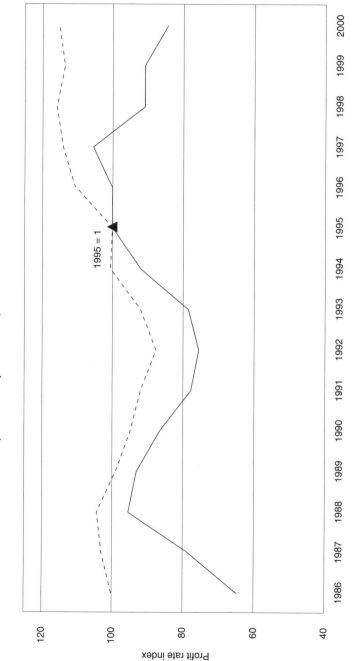

——— Corporate manufacturing   – – – Corporate non-financial non-manufacturing

in their profit rates over this five-year period, manufacturers had to cut their costs at that average annual rate (see above, p. 160, Figure 6.1).

Still, as striking as the intensification of long-standing difficulties in international manufacturing was the impotence of the huge growth of domestic investment and consumption unleashed by the stock market to mitigate the impact of the high dollar and the over-supply of the world market. Between 1997 and 2000, US real consumption of durable goods increased at the torrid average annual pace of 11 per cent. At the same time, as just noted, rising investment growth brought manufacturing productivity increase to its highest level in more than thirty years. But, evidently, the huge leap upward of US domestic demand for manufactures was so fully met by the increase of domestic productive capacity and domestic supply that it failed to compensate for the sharp deterioration of US competitiveness and the over-supply of international markets. It could therefore do little to prevent the consequent fall in the corporate manufacturing and, in turn, the non-financial corporate profit rate – even despite the simultaneous efflorescence of productivity growth.

In sum, the stock market run-up had, through its wealth effect, more than succeeded in extending the US expansion of the 1990s, after the manufacturing sector had ceased to be able to drive the economy forward by way of increasing competitiveness and fast-rising exports, when its profit rate came under ever more severe pressure as a consequence of the rising dollar from 1995 and the crisis in East Asia from 1997–98. But, while furthering the boom, the equity price bubble had signally failed to provide it with a durable foundation. It is difficult to over-stress the point that at the very time that share prices were soaring to their peak, *average* annual profits (net of interest) for the years 1998, 1999, and 2000 fell by 7.5 per cent in the non-financial corporate sector and almost 18 per cent in the corporate manufacturing sector, compared to 1997 (see below, p. 272, Figure 11.1). It was, of course, the extraordinary inflation of assets resulting from those soaring equity prices that enabled already rapid investment growth to accelerate at this point and push the economy ahead. But, since so much of that increased investment clearly was unable to justify itself in terms either of realized or prospective profits, a good deal of it was bound to turn out to be over-investment. The reality of over-investment was manifested as well in the stunning fact that even in 1999 and the first half of 2000, as the boom reached its zenith, manufacturing capacity utilization fell to a level below that for any year since 1994. The bubble could for a time obscure some of this redundant capacity. But, given that firms were already having difficulties making profits in the halcyon days of the end of the century, they were bound to suffer truly excruciating downward pressure on their rates of return when the stock market's wealth effect ceased to subsidize investment and consumer demand, as well as productivity growth. What would at that point drive the economy was the critical underlying issue.

CHAPTER 9

THE CONTOURS AND CHARACTER
OF THE US BOOM

Given the extraordinary hype surrounding it, the contours of the economic expansion of the 1990s and the boom to which it gave rise should be kept in perspective. In autumn 1999, Alan Greenspan gushed, 'It is safe to say that we are witnessing, this decade in the US, history's most compelling demonstration of the productive capacity of free peoples operating in free markets.'[1] But he had clearly become carried away with his own creation – unless, of course, he was taking the historically unprecedented rise in equity prices of the bubble to represent the actual achievements of the so-called 'New Economy'. Greenspan appears to have had great confidence in the projections for future productivity growth and profits of equity analysts and corporate managers. But, considering the data on the real economy, as opposed to the paper one, there are simply no grounds for the finding that a New Economy has emerged – assuming that that term implies, at very least, productiveness and vitality that, in historical and comparative terms, is 'extraordinary', if not unique.[2]

On the other hand, it can hardly be gainsaid that, as the 1990s progressed, the economy displayed significantly greater vigour than it had during the two decades or so after 1973. This is in keeping, I have argued,

---

[1] 'Remarks by Chairman Alan Greenspan, Millennium Lecture Series, Valley State University, Grand Rapids, Michigan: Maintaining Economic Vitality', 8 September 1999, FRB website. Cf. 'Remarks by Chairman Alan Greenspan at the Haas Annual Business Faculty Research Dialogue, University of California, Berkeley: Question: Is there a New Economy?' 4 September 1998, FRB website.
[2] 'Annual Report of the Council of Economic Advisers', *Economic Report of the President 2001*, Washington, DC, 2001, p. 23. See below, p. 220.

with the very major, though still incomplete, manufacturing-led recovery of the non-farm private rate of profit (especially after taxes) across the economy by 1995–97 in relation to the peaks of the 1960s, after more than two decades in the doldrums. The latter steered the economy forward by underpinning a quite significant increase in the growth of investment, a good part of which was in information technology broadly speaking. But the question that is posed at the end of the day is whether this vitality can be sustained over the medium to long run.

A NEW ECONOMY?

'Extraordinary gains in performance'?

When we speak of a New Economy, we have to remember first that the performance of the US economy in the decade of the 1990s *as a whole* did not remotely compare to that of the first quarter century of the post-war era. The last decade's business cycle (1990–2000), which began in July 1990, was stronger than those of the 1980s (1979–90) and later 1970s (1973–79), but only slightly. To the degree, moreover, that it did improve on its immediate predecessors, this was *entirely* due to the acceleration of growth after 1995.[3] Up through 1995, US economic performance in the 1990s failed to better that of the business cycles of the 1980s and 1970s (let alone that of the 1960s and 1950s) (see above, p. 47, Table 1.10). In terms of the growth of GDP, it was weaker.

From the end of 1993, and consistently from the end of 1995, the

---

[3] Indeed, if one considers the *expansion* of the 1990s, the period in the business cycle from the point it hits bottom and turns up (i.e. the trough), 'it has not been the expansion with the highest rate of growth, [and] even during the last four years, average growth only just reached that of the expansion of the 1980s and remained well short of that of the 1960s.' Bank for International Settlements, *70th Annual Report 1999–2000*, Basel, 5 June 2000, p. 13. The reason that the business cycle of the 1990s turns out slightly better than its predecessors of the 1980s and 1970s is that the recession of 1990–91 with which it began was much shallower than those of 1974–75 and 1979–82 with which those began. It should be added that I have included, for practical purposes, what is technically the separate, if very short, business cycle between January 1980 and July 1981 in 'the business cycle of the 1980s'. The business cycle July 1981–July 1990, taken on its own, is a bit stronger than that of the 1990s.

expansion did unquestionably became considerably more powerful. But even the boom of *five years* between 1995 and 2000 was barely able to match the long expansion of *twenty-five years* between 1948 and 1973 in terms of the main indicators of macroeconomic performance – including the growth of GDP, investment/capital stock, productivity, and real wages, as well as the rate of inflation and the rate of unemployment (and that earlier long upturn contained wartime inflations, as well as recessions, that were absent in the recent short one). Of course, the magnitude of the expansion of the US economy during the post-war long boom did not remotely compare to that of Japan or most of western Europe. In its annual report for 2001, published early that year, the US Council of Economic Advisers justifies its designation of the US economy in the second half of the 1990s as 'the New Economy' by reference to its ostensibly '*extraordinary gains in performance* – including rapid productivity growth, rising incomes, low unemployment, and moderate inflation'.[4] But, if the gains of the five years between 1995 and 2000 can be considered 'extraordinary', and indicative of a New Economy, how should we characterize the incomparably more impressive gains of the long post-war boom between 1948 and 1973, and what should we term the economy of *that* long epoch (see Table 9.1)?

The expansion of the 1990s, it should be added, delivered such low rates of unemployment mainly because it started with so little labour market slack compared to its predecessors; it actually created jobs at a significantly slower pace than did the upswings of either the 1980s or 1970s. Moreover, real wages did not begin to grow noticeably until 1998, a full seven years into the expansion: even by 1997, the level of real hourly compensation in the non-farm business economy was no higher than it had been in 1992. For production and non-supervisory workers, the situation was very much worse: by December 2000, the average hourly real wage in private industry had still failed to surpass its level of September 1968, and was still more than 5 per cent below its 1979 peak. Median family income actually fell slightly between 1989 and 1995. By 1998 it had risen to just 4 per cent above its level of 1989 and only 8 per cent above its level of 1979. The distribution of wealth created over the course of the 1990s was notoriously

4 'Annual Report of the Council of Economic Advisers' (2001), p. 23 (emphasis added).

Table 9.1 The US economy: 1948–73 versus 1995–2000 (average annual per cent increase, except for unemployment rate)

	1948–73	1995–2000
GDP	4.0	4.1
Non-farm business net capital stock	3.5	3.8
Non-farm business labour productivity	2.9	2.5
Non-farm business real hourly wages	2.8	2.0
Inflation/consumer price index	2.4	2.4
Unemployment rate (average)	4.2	4.7

Sources: 'Industry Analytical Ratios for the Total Economy' and 'Industry Analytical Ratios for the Business Sector and Non-Farm Business Sector, All Persons', folders provided by the Division of Productivity Research, Bureau of Labor Statistics; Economic Report of the President 2001, Washington, DC, 2001, Appendix B, Table B–42.

skewed: between 1992 and 1999, the top 20 per cent saw their share of total net worth increase from 59.6 per cent to 62.9 per cent, while the bottom 80 per cent experienced a corresponding percentage decrease. By the same token, in the six years between 1993 and 1999, the poverty rate fell by just 3.3 percentage points, compared to 11.1 percentage points between 1960 and 1973. By 1999, moreover, the poverty rate had still failed to fall back to its level of 1979, let alone to that of 1973.[5]

Perhaps most telling of all, the rate of growth of labour productivity, though marking a major step up from that of the previous two decades, fails to demonstrate the emergence of a New Economy in the US. In the non-farm business economy, even during the best years of the expansion between 1995 and 2000, average annual labour productivity growth fell 15

[5] Bank for International Settlements, *70th Annual Report 1999–2000*, p. 14; L. Mishel, J. Bernstein, and J. Schmitt, *The State of Working America 2000/2001*, Ithaca, NY, Cornell University Press, 2001, p. 36, Table 1.1, p. 121, Figure 2A; L. Mishel, J. Bernstein, and J. Schmitt, *The State of Working America 1998–99*, Ithaca, NY, Cornell University Press, 1999, p. 264 Table 5.6; US Bureau of Labor Statistics, National Employment Hours, and Earnings: Series EES00500049, available at BLS website; 'Annual Report of the Council of Economic Advisors' (2001), pp. 21–2.

per cent short of that between 1948 and 1973. In the manufacturing sector, labour productivity growth was unquestionably impressive if taken on its own; however, it was not decisively better than that of its leading rivals. Whereas between 1993 and 2000 manufacturing labour productivity in the US improved at an average annual rate of 5.1 per cent, manufacturing labour productivity in western Germany and France grew at the average annual rates of 4.8 per cent (through 1998) and 4.9 per cent, respectively. During the same period, manufacturing labour productivity growth in Japan lagged behind somewhat, averaging 3.9 per cent per annum, but was clearly held down by serious recession during several of these years (Japanese manufacturing labour productivity growth had averaged 5.3 per cent between 1979 and 1991).[6]

In the economy as a whole, over the course of the 1990s (1990–2000), labour productivity growth (GDP/hour) in the US fell short of that in the Euro area taken in aggregate (1.8 per cent versus 1.7 per cent), and so did multi-factor productivity increase. Nor for the economy as a whole was the performance of labour productivity even during the boom years between 1995 and 2000 at all out of the ordinary in the longest-term historical perspective. Indeed, the average annual growth of total GDP per hour, at 2 per cent during those five years, was palpably below that for the entire century between 1889 and 1989, at 2.2 per cent. The New Economy has failed to generate productivity growth that in either comparative or historical perspective can be called extraordinary.[7]

[6] US Bureau of Labor Statistics, 'International Comparisons of Manufacturing Productivity and Unit Labor Cost Trends, 2000', *News Release*, 31 August 2001 (BLS website), p. 17, Table 1. It should be added that US manufacturing productivity growth for the years 1998, 1999 and 2000 will certainly be revised downward significantly in line with already reported downward revisions of manufacturing investment, when revised data on manufacturing value-added and hours are made available in late 2001 or early 2002. The rate of productivity growth between 1995 and 2000 for the non-farm business sector as a whole was revised downward from 2.9 per cent to 2.5 per cent.

[7] 'Europe's Economies: Stumbling Yet Again?' *The Economist*, 16 September 2000, p. 78, Chart 2; 'New Technologies and Productivity in the Euro Area', *ECB Monthly Bulletin*, July 2001, p. 38, Table 1; A. Maddison, *Dynamic Forces in Capitalist Development. A Long Run Comparative View*, Oxford, Oxford University Press, p. 38, Table 2.2; 'Industry Analytical Ratios for the Total Economy, All Persons', folder available from BLS, Office of Productivity and Technology. I wish to thank Dennis Redmond for calling attention to the ECB study on LBOTalk listserve.

New institutions fostering entrepreneurship, innovation, and the accumulation of intangible assets?

Those who insist that a New Economy emerged in the US during the 1990s, and especially between 1995 and 2000, can do so only by ignoring the basic fact that US economic performance, though clearly better than that of the previous two decades, was unexceptional from an historical or comparative perspective. Failing to acknowledge this fundamental point, many adherents to the idea of a New Economy have gone on to account for the US economy's ostensibly prodigious achievements in terms of a new, putatively more entrepreneurial institutional framework that is peculiarly able to underwrite innovation and cope with risk. That institutional framework has, they argue, brought about, in an amazingly short period of time, a remarkable increase in the assets at the disposal of American corporations, not just tangible assets, in the form of plant, equipment, and software embodying advanced technology, but also and especially intangible ones, in the form of skills, organization, and information. The ability to amass intangible assets, it is said, now constitutes perhaps the single key to the capacity to innovate.

From the foregoing standpoint, the rise of venture capital is at the heart of the emergent New Economy. It has facilitated the funding of those high-technology start-up firms, traditionally lacking capital, that have contributed disproportionately to the stream of innovations behind more rapid productivity growth. Venture capital, it is argued, came to the fore in the 1980s and especially the 1990s by forging an ever tighter connection to the stock market, and especially the market for initial public offerings (IPOs). The IPO market has fostered innovation, it is asserted, by providing capital for new enterprises and, in particular, by offering an attractive exit mechanism for venture capitalists, enabling them to more easily finance high-risk high-tech companies. As the US Council of Economic Advisers puts it, 'The flourishing venture capital market and the dynamic IPO market are unique features of the US economy and may help explain why the New Economy emerged here rather than in Europe or Asia.'[8] What has, finally, enabled firms at the cutting edge of technology to innovate and compete as effectively as they have has been, above all, their ability to mobilize intangible assets. 'Success in the New Economy,' says the Council of Economic Advisers, 'relies on intangible capital. . . . [I]ntangible assets – organizational practices, R&D capability and reputation – are now much more prominent features of a firm's competitive strategy, because they are the foundation for innovations that lead to success.'[9]

It is, however, doubtful whether the actual evidence so far adduced to prove the contribution of New Economy entrepreneurship attests as much to the impact on the US economy of new ways of doing business as of the stock market bubble of the second half of the 1990s. Until recently, the contribution of venture capital has generally been seen as significant, but strictly limited, because investment by venture capital firms has amounted to such a minute fraction of total investment and such an insignificant percentage of what the economy spends overall on research and development. But, according to the Council of Economic Advisers, 'One of the most important factors in the financing of new technology . . . has been the *recent acceleration* in the growth of venture capital, which itself has benefited from a thriving market for IPOs.' According to Mandel, 'Venture capital is the fastest growing part of the financial system . . . [and] has increased to the point where it rivals R&D spending as a source of funding for innovation.' What is the evidence of this increase? According to the Council of Economic Advisers, '[T]otal venture capital investment jumped from $14.3 billion in all of 1998 to 54.5 billion in the first three quarters of 2000 alone.' According to Mandel, 'In the first quarter of

---

[8] See 'Annual Report of the Council of Economic Advisers' (2001), especially Chapter 3, as well as M. Mandel, *The Coming Internet Depression*, New York, Basic Books, 2000. Both of these studies put forward this analysis, and in very similar terms. Quotation is from 'Annual Report', p. 110. For another rendition, see D. Hale, 'Rebuilt by Wall Street: The US's Dynamic Stock Market Has Directed Resources into High-Tech Industries, Giving the Economy a Huge Advantage That Other Countries Must Strive to Match', *Financial Times*, 25 January 2000. Essentially the same argument can also be found in E. Phelps, 'Europe's Stony Ground for the Seeds of Growth', *Financial Times*, 10 August 2000.

[9] 'Annual Report of the Council of Economic Advisers' (2001), p. 136.

2000, venture capital equalled fully one-third of all money spent on R&D, compared to 3 per cent in the 1980s.'[10]

Nevertheless, it could scarcely be more obvious that this dramatically discontinuous character of the increase of venture capital investment and of IPO financing at the end of the 1990s tends to *discount, rather than validate*, their longer term significance for technical change in the US economy. It reflected no autonomous maturation of a new system of financing of technological innovation, but simply the extraordinary returns that could *temporarily* be secured on the IPO market by selling vastly overpriced shares in high-technology, especially Internet, start-ups, as the equity price bubble approached its apex. Before the stock market took off in 1995, and right up to 1999, the magnitude of venture capital investment continued to be rather limited, as it had historically. Mandel's own graph of venture capital investment shows that during the period between 1980 and 1995 venture capital disbursements failed at any point to reach 5 per cent of total expenditures on R&D. Even by the end of 1997, two years into the stock market bubble, venture capital investment had struggled to reach 10 per cent of R&D spending, and in 1998 it amounted to only 15 per cent. As late as 1998, annual investment by venture capital firms was thus a mere $14.3 billion (up from perhaps $8 billion in 1995). Amounting as it did to such a small fraction of R&D spending, it is difficult to see how venture capital could have been a decisive force in transforming the economy before 1999.[11]

In 1999 and the first quarter of 2000, of course, everything changed, as the stock market took its last and greatest flight upward. The NASDAQ index more than doubled, and so did the price of technology stocks more generally. In the process, one after another Internet company enjoyed entirely unprecedented returns on its IPO. In this situation, venture capitalists could hardly have had a greater incentive to involve themselves in Internet start-ups, and in 1999 at least 50 per cent of their total

[10] 'Annual Report of the Council of Economic Advisers' (2001), p. 106 (emphasis added); Mandel, *Coming Internet Depression*, pp. 19–20. Venture capital investment rose to $102 billion in 2000 as a whole. P. Abrahams and E. Luce, 'No Exit: After Five Years of Spectacular Growth Silicon Valley Venture Capitalists are Facing a Shake-Out', *Financial Times*, 26 February 2001.
[11] Mandel, *Coming Internet Depression*, p. 20; 'Annual Report of the Council of Economic Advisers' (2001), pp. 106–7 (emphasis added).

investment went to such companies. Returns on venture capital overall in that year averaged a once-in-a-lifetime 165 per cent.[12]

Nevertheless, as we know, the phenomenal profits secured by venture capitalists in 1999 and early 2000 had little if anything to do with the business-worthiness of the new firms – many of which went out of business a short time later – and everything to do with the prospects for the price of their shares. Since returns to IPOs leaped into the stratosphere in 1999 and the first part of 2000, it is not in the least surprising that venture capital investment followed suit. The Council of Economic Advisers refers with a straight face 'to a new group of promising projects in Internet-related businesses, as the driving factor behind this surge of [venture capital] financing', even though it must be well aware that most of these firms failed ever to return a profit and that many of them went out of business during the spring and summer of 2000. But the Council does call attention to 'the strange behavior of IPO pricing in 1999 and 2000': in those two years, the annual proceeds of initial public offerings climbed to more than double the average of the previous three years, and, in 1999, 'the average first day return on IPO securities (calculated as the percent-age by which the price at the end of the first day of trading exceeds the offering price) was an amazing 69 per cent . . . *three times higher than the average first day return in any year between 1975 and 1999*.'[13] That the surge in venture capital investment resulted from the surge in returns to IPOs seems self-evident, as does the parallel assertion that neither had much to do with the actual profit-making potential of high-technology businesses. It could in no way have been expected to persist in the absence of such inflated returns to IPOs (see Figure 9.1 and above, p. 197, Figure 8.4).

The evidence adduced by the US Council of Economic Advisers for the sharply increased place of intangible capital in total assets in the New Economy is the extraordinary rise of the ratio between the value of

---

[12] Hale, 'Rebuilt By Wall Street'; 'Venture Capital: Under Water', *The Economist*, 5 May 2001.
[13] 'Annual Report of the Council of Economic Advisers' (2001), pp. 106–7, 109 (emphasis added). Amazingly, the Council of Economic Advisers was unwilling to venture an opinion as to whether these returns to IPOs resulted from 'irrational exuberance' or 'persistent under-pricing by the underwriters of these securities . . . [that] is not necessarily the result of market failure' (p. 109).

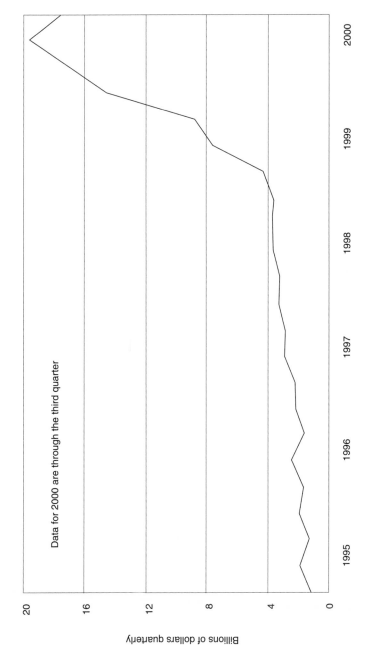

Figure 9.1 Venture capital investment, 1995–2000

Data for 2000 are through the third quarter

Billions of dollars quarterly

non-financial corporations in terms of market prices and the value of those same corporations' tangible and financial assets, measured at replacement cost (i.e. Tobin's q).[14] The relatively much faster increase of the market's valuation of these assets is supposed, by the Council of Economic Advisers, to reflect the fact that the market takes into account *all* of a firm's assets, including, presumably, recently fast-growing intangible ones, whereas the replacement cost measure of that firm's value confines itself, by definition, to the firm's tangible assets (plant, equipment, and software, etc.).

What undermines this argument, however, is, once again, the timing of the relevant trends. As noted, Tobin's q doubled in the very short period between 1995 and 2000 to reach a level that was more than 50 per cent higher than its previous historic peak (see above, p. 185, Figure 7.2). But, since this was precisely the moment when equity prices were outrunning output and profits to an extent entirely unprecedented in US economic history, it is impossible to avoid the conclusion that the impetuous climb of Tobin's q reflects much more the inflation of the stock market bubble than any discontinuous rise in the amount of intangible assets at the disposal of non-financial corporations. On the other hand, were it the case that the market valuation of non-financial corporate assets expressed in Tobin's q did turn out to accurately measure the assets, intangible as well as tangible, actually at corporations' disposal, the logical consequence would be that the actual rate of return achieved by corporations during the second half of the 1990s – profits over tangible plus intangible assets – was in fact greatly lower than the measured rate. In that case, the gains in profitability delivered by the New Economy – already far from impressive – would turn out to be even lower than they appear to have been.[15]

In sum, the stock market's taking centre-stage in connection with venture capital and initial public offerings in the process of capital accumulation during the latter part of the 1990s had a rather different

---

[14] 'One indicator of the importance of intangible capital is what economists call Tobin's q ... Tobin's q for publicly traded US firms rose throughout the 1990s. This is consistent with an increasing importance of intangible capital.' 'Annual Report of the Council of Economic Advisers' (2001), p. 136.

[15] A. Smithers and S. Wright, *Valuing Wall Street. Protecting Wealth in Turbulent Markets*, New York, McGraw Hill, 2000, pp. 315–20.

effect than that attributed to it by the advocates of the New Economy, with their belief in the superiority of the US's unique entrepreneurial institutions. The stock market unquestionably made possible a speeding up of investment growth that would have been impossible without it, as a consequence of the enormous wealth effect that resulted from the runup of equity prices. But since that rise in share prices mainly reflected runaway speculation, it brought about massive misinvestment. Specifically, in accelerating the flow of funds into the high-tech sector, the stock market bubble allocated investment not so much in accord with rising potential profits as in accord with the potential for speculative gains. As a consequence it issued much less in long-term gains in productivity growth than in medium-term over-capacity.

A REAL INCREASE IN ECONOMIC DYNAMISM

To doubt that the US witnessed the rise of a New Economy in the 1990s is in no way to deny that, during these years, it did secure a significant increase in economic dynamism – reflecting substantial technical advance and organizational improvement – in comparison to that which it had evinced during the two decades after 1973. This was expressed in the major, interrelated accelerations in the rate of investment and productivity growth in the non-farm economy that began around 1993 and were sustained into the middle of 2000. Between 1995 and the middle of 2000, as a percentage of GDP, total real business investment and real business investment in equipment averaged, respectively, 17 per cent and 9.7 per cent, compared to 14.6 per cent and 6.0 per cent, respectively, during the eight-year expansion of the 1980s, and 13.4 per cent and 3.4 per cent, respectively, during the nine-year expansion of the 1960s. During the same four-and-a-half-year period, non-farm labour productivity growth averaged 2.5 per cent, compared to 1.6 per cent between 1990 and 1995 and 1.4 per cent between 1973 and 1990.[16]

---

[16] Bank for International Settlements, *70th Annual Report 1999–2000*, p. 13. Figures on the growth of real investment in this period have been called into question because they appear,

Stepped-up productivity growth

In light of the boost in the rate of capital accumulation, the figures indicating a parallel surge in the growth of labour productivity generally carry conviction, despite the understandable controversy surrounding them.[17] The case is fairly clear cut for manufacturing, simply because the speed-up of both productivity increase and investment growth were so pronounced and were located precisely where one would have expected them. In the period between 1993 and 1999, the rate of growth of manufacturing labour productivity was more than 50 per cent greater than that during the expansion of 1982–90, and involved, as already noted, no sacrifice of capital productivity growth. It seems only reasonable to view this incontestable improvement in productiveness, taking into account both labour and capital inputs, as stemming from the doubling of the rate of growth of the capital stock in the same period, compared to 1982–1990. Such a case is reinforced when one bears in mind that, for the first time since the long downturn began around 1973, the manufacturing capital–labour ratio (the growth of plant and equipment per worker hour) was able to grow consistently during an expansion, jogging along at an average annual rate of 2.4 per cent between 1993 and 1999,

---

in part, to be based on the attribution of unrealistically huge declines in prices to components of investment growth (hedonic pricing). However, the fact that the growth of non-farm business investment *in nominal terms* was also so rapid – averaging 9 per cent per annum during the business expansion of the 1990s (1991–2000), compared to 4.9 per cent for the business expansion of the 1980s (1982–90) when inflation was significantly higher – gives credence to the evidence that capital accumulation was indeed quite rapid. *Economic Report of the President 2000*, Washington, DC, 2000, p. 326, Table B-16.

[17] The controversy is rooted partly in the fact that, in the later 1990s, the Bureau of Economic Analysis made a series of significant changes in the way it measured output, which directly affected the measures of productivity by the Bureau of Labor Statistics. The problem is not so much in the methodological changes that were implemented, which generally make sense in themselves, as in the non-comparability of the resulting figures over time and across countries. The methodological changes brought palpable increases in the output/productivity growth numbers for the years 1978–present, but they were not applied to the period before 1978, making for an exaggerated difference between measured growth rates before and after that date, and they have been only sporadically taken up by foreign governmental statistical agencies.

compared to 0 per cent both between 1975 and 1979 and between 1982 and 1990 (see below, p. 235, Table 9.2).[18]

At the same time, the gain in productiveness was concentrated almost entirely in the durable goods sector, where labour productivity growth jumped to 7.1 per cent for 1993–99, compared to 3.9 per cent between 1982 and 1990.[19] The durable goods sector is where one would have anticipated seeing manufacturing productivity gains disproportionately located. It is there that the acceleration of manufacturing investment growth was disproportionately located – with durable goods investment growth averaging 12.3 per cent per annum between 1993 and 1999, non-durable goods investment growth 6.3 per cent per annum. It is there, too, that the leading growth industries were to be found – industrial and commercial machinery, including computers, and electrical machinery, including semi-conductors. In fact, labour productivity growth accelerated markedly across a good part of the durable goods industries between 1993 and 1999, with five of the ten durable goods industries experiencing average annual labour productivity growth that was at least one-third faster between 1993 and 1999 than between 1982 and 1990, one industry experiencing roughly constant labour productivity growth over the two periods, three experiencing productivity growth decline over the two periods, and one lacking data for the two periods.[20]

Productivity growth in the economy beyond manufacturing is more difficult to evaluate because of its extreme discontinuity. In 1995, the level of labour productivity in the non-manufacturing sector was just *10 per cent*

---

[18] In the business cycles of the 1970s and 1980s, gains in the manufacturing capital–labour ratio were made only during the recessions, as a consequence of sharp absolute falls in the size of the labour force, rather than absolute increases in the size of the capital stock.

[19] In non-durable goods, labour productivity growth averaged 2 per cent per annum and 2.3 per cent per annum, respectively, between 1982 and 1990 and between 1993 and 1999.

[20] Labour productivity growth in the durable goods industries, 1993–99/1982–90 (average annual per cent change): motor vehicles and equipment: 3.5/0.5; electric and electronic equipment (including semi-conductors): 20.1/10.4; industrial and commercial machinery (including computers): 12.9/9.1; primary metals: 3.5/0.7; furniture and fixtures: 0.7/0.2; fabricated metals: 2.0/2.1; lumber and wood products: 0.8/1.9; stone, clay, and glass products: 1.8/3.6; miscellaneous manufacturing industries: 2.6/5.5. Data are not available for the years between 1982 and 1990 for instruments and related products. Value added by industry from BEA Gross Product Originating by Industry (BEA website) and hours from Bureau of Labor Statistics (kindly forwarded by John Glaser).

higher than it had been in 1977. But, after having barely grown at all during the previous eighteen years, between 1995 and 1999 non-manufacturing labour productivity cantered forward at an official average annual rate of 2.3 per cent.[21]

The fact that non-manufacturing labour productivity growth did not begin to increase until 1996, well after the growth of output began to gather strength in late 1993, has led some analysts to discount it, interpreting it as simply a by-product of the more rapid growth of unmeasured labour input. By this reasoning, the up-tick in recorded labour productivity growth outside of manufacturing was mainly the result of speed-up, employers responding to the rapid growth of demand during the second half of the decade by burdening their employees with more work per hour rather than increasing the hours of work by means of increased overtime or hiring more workers (which would have suppressed recorded labour productivity growth). This is a phenomenon that has in the past been typical of the later stages of the business cycle.[22]

What calls the foregoing account into question, however, is that, very atypically, the growth of non-manufacturing investment during the 1990s actually accelerated, attaining increased momentum as the business cycle matured, and was accompanied by a significant speed-up in the growth of the capital–labour ratio. The result was a palpable upturn in non-manufacturing *capital* productivity growth (the increase of the real output–capital ratio), as well as labour productivity growth (the increase of the real output–labour ratio). Average annual investment growth in the non-manufacturing sector *in nominal terms* was thus around 10 per cent from the start of the business expansion in 1991 through the first half of 2000 – more than twice as high as in the comparable expansion of the much more inflationary 1980s – and reached its highest point during the first half of 2000. The average annual growth of *real* non-manufacturing

[21] This figure will almost certainly be reduced by several tenths of a point when revised numbers are released in late 2001 or early 2002, for reasons already noted. See above, p. 222, fn. 6.
[22] R. Gordon, 'Does the "New Economy" Measure up the Great Inventions of the Past?' draft of paper for *Journal of Economic Perspectives*, 1 May 2000, website of Robert Gordon, Economics Department, Northwestern University; R. Gordon, 'Not Much of a New Economy', *Financial Times*, 26 July 2000.

investment during the same period was over 12 per cent, compared to 3.8 per cent between 1982 and 1990.

The outcome of this investment boom was that, between 1995 and 1999, not only was the non-manufacturing capital–labour ratio increasing at twice the rate it had grown during the years between 1982 and 1995, but gross output per unit of net capital stock – i.e. capital productivity – was growing much more rapidly than it had at any time since the 1970s – at an average annual pace of 1.5 per cent, compared to 0.6 per cent between 1982 and 1995 (and 0 per cent between 1977 and 1995). This seems strong evidence for the view that the rise of measured output per hour was an expression not just of workers' increased effort, but also the result of the increased plant and equipment that was put at the disposal of workers and, even more important, of increased overall productiveness, the increase of output from any given sum of labour and capital inputs.

In the economy outside of manufacturing, the step-up of both investment and productivity growth was, in fact, impressive across most of the service sector, including in wholesale trade, retail trade and FIRE.[23] Indeed, wholesale trade and retail trade were, aside from durable manufacturing, the most dynamic industries of the economy during the expansion of the 1990s. They built their productive power, in the first instance, by exploiting an extraordinary long-term reduction of labour costs in their industries: by 1993, the real wages (excluding benefits) for production and non-supervisory workers had fallen by 17 per cent below their post-war peak attained in 1973.[24] From this starting point, they were able, between 1993 and 1999, to use high rates of investment growth to achieve the highest rates of productivity growth attained by industries outside of durable manufacturing and, on that basis, to achieve increases in profitability (50 per cent in wholesale trade and 33 per cent in retail trade) that further sustained rapid capital accumulation, and so on. On the other

---

[23] In the services *industry* (which is part of the service sector and includes a heterogeneous array of business and personal service lines), it seems very likely that measured productivity growth is understated by the data, especially given that investment growth was very great, but measured productivity growth *negative*, between 1993 and 1999.

[24] Bureau of Labor Statistics, National Employment, Hours, and Earnings, Series EEU50000049.

hand, the trend was just the opposite in the rest of the non-manufacturing sector, namely the non-manufacturing industrial sector, which includes construction, mining, and transportation and public utilities. In these industries, productivity growth was actually lower between 1993 and 1999 than between 1982 and 1990 (see Table 9.2).

What would seem finally to confirm the view of palpably stepped-up productivity growth across at least significant swathes of the economy is that, over this period, as many have pointed out, the burgeoning of investment growth took the form, to a very great extent, of purchases of high-tech equipment, the cost of which was on a rapid downswing.[25] Between 1990 and 1999, investment on information processing and software as a proportion of total non-residential investment arched upwards from about 28 per cent to 35 per cent (on computers and peripherals and software alone from 14 per cent to 21 per cent). In the end, it is hard to believe that employers, making increasingly large capital expenditures over the period, were not securing increased productiveness from increasing plant and equipment per person. Whether, on the other hand, these investments also redounded in increased *profitability* and whether they are *sustainable*, are, as already noted, entirely different questions to which it will be necessary to return.[26]

The control of inflation

The containment of inflation during the 1990s is in line with the preceding analysis of improved productiveness, but also, it must be stressed, with the strong emphasis throughout on the new rise of the dollar from 1995 onwards, which made for intensifying competition and downward pressure of prices on profits. Accounting for the retarded growth of prices during the first half of the decade is hardly a problem. In those years, real wage growth was effectively zero, so upward pressure from costs on prices was

[25] See, eg., B.P. Bosworth and J.E. Triplett, 'What's New About the New Economy? IT, Economic Growth and Productivity', unpublished paper, available at Brookings Institution website.
[26] *Economic Report of the President 2000*, p. 326, Table B-16.

Table 9.2 Growth of investment and productivity, 1993–99/2000 versus 1982–90

	Real gross output (value-added)		Labour productivity		Real gross output/ net capital stock		Net capital stock		Gross investment		Net capital stock/ labour	
	1982–90	1993–99	1982–90	1993–99	1982–90	1993–99	1982–90	1993–2000	1982–90	1993–2000	1982–90	1993–2000
Manufacturing	4.0	5.3	3.1	4.7	2.7	2.5	1.3	2.5	4.1	7.8	0.5	2.2
Manufacturing durable goods	4.9	8.3	3.9	7.0	3.6	5.0	1.2	2.9	4.0	9.8	0.4	2.0
Manufacturing non-durable goods	2.9	1.3	2.0	2.3	1.5	−0.6	1.4	2.0	4.2	5.8	0.6	3.2
Non-farm private	4.3	4.7	1.7	2.2	1.5	0.9	2.8	3.3	3.9	10.2	0.26	1.2
Non-farm non-manufacturing	4.4	4.6	1.25	1.4	0.9	0.9	3.5	3.8	4.1	11.0	0.37	0.75
Retail trade	4.5	6.5	2.2	4.6	0.3	2.3	4.2	3.8	7.1	7.5	1.9	1.98
Wholesale trade	4.9	7.9	3.0	5.2	−1.2	1.3	6.2	6.5	3.9	14.5	4.3	4.2
Finance insurance, and real estate	3.0	4.1	0.2	2.1	−0.3	3.35	2.7	3.2	7.4	7.4	0.5	0.9
Services	4.8	3.8	−0.3	−0.8	0.0	−2.1	5.0	6.7	9.0	14.7	−0.159	2.5
Transportation and public utilities	4.2	4.6	2.35	1.8	2.3	1.9	1.8	2.7	2.7	8.6	0.6	−0.2
Communications	3.85	6.5	4.8	1.8	−0.07	0.7	3.9	5.95	2.6	12.7	4.9	1.4
Construction	4.8	4.4	0.6	0.01	5.0	6.2	6.5	6.0	9.5	12.7	−3.95	1.4
Mining	2.7	3.2	8.3	5.4	2.8	2.7	0.01	0.5	−7.2	4.7	5.8	2.6

Sources: Bureau of Economic Analysis, 'Gross Product Originating By Industry, 1947 – Present', BEA website; Bureau of Economic Analysis, Fixed Asset Tables, BEA website.

minimal. With GDP increase in these years also so very limited, the growth of demand was even lower than in the 1970s and 1980s. Just to make sure, the Fed hitched interest rates up very sharply in 1994.

What requires more explanation is the economy's ability to keep inflation down over the next half decade, between 1995 and 2000, when GDP grew rapidly, unemployment fell significantly, and wages growth (belatedly) accelerated. No doubt, the weakened position of workers continued to be a critical facilitating factor in keeping down price increases. The already-decimated unionized portion of the private sector labour force actually fell further during the second half of the 1990s to reach an all-time low of 9 per cent in 2000, the efforts of the AFL–CIO under new leadership notwithstanding.[27] Moreover, despite low unemployment, workers' insecurity remained profound. Through 1997, a year of high prosperity, the business failure rate maintained itself at levels that were nearly twice the post-war average through 1980, and turnover/layoffs continued to run correspondingly high (see above, p. 52, Figure 2.1).[28]

In addition, the huge proportion of the labour force in low-wage jobs continued to undercut the bargaining position of those with better pay. No less than one quarter of all employed workers today are thus stuck in jobs paying below the poverty level – defined as $17,029 per year or $8.19 per hour – and constitute what might be called a 'surplus army of employed', functioning along with the surplus army of unemployed to bear down heavily on wages.[29] Ever tighter labour markets did finally issue in more rapid real wage growth in the last three years of the decade (1998–2000), but, even then, the growth of real wages did not, in itself, squeeze profits or force up prices significantly.[30]

---

[27] Y.J. Dreazen, 'U.S. Union Membership [Public and Private] Declined to a Record Low 13.5% in 2000', *Wall Street Journal*, 19 January 2001.

[28] Thus Alan Greenspan's crocodile tears over 'the necessary heightened level of potential dismissal' and 'the evident insecurity felt by many workers despite the tightest labor markets in decades'. 'Remarks by Chairman Alan Greenspan Before the National Governors' Association: Structural Change in the New Economy', 11 July 2000, FRB website (1997 is, unfortunately, the last year for which data are available on the business failure rate).

[29] R. Sharpe, 'What Exactly is a "Living Wage?"' *Business Week*, 28 May 2001.

[30] Between 1995 and the first quarter of 2000, the growth of real hourly compensation in the private business economy averaged 1.7 per cent. Nonetheless, there was no squeeze on profits in the non-manufacturing sector, where businesses were able to increase prices to

The main *active* force in keeping down inflation during the second half of the decade was almost certainly the very slow growth of world manufacturing prices. These stemmed both from the dollar's ascent beginning in 1995 and the emergence of crisis conditions internationally in the last several years of the decade. In 1996, the trend of world manufacturing price increase manifested a sharp break downward—from 10 per cent in 1995 to −2.7 per cent; this found expression in a simultaneous drop in the growth of US import prices, as well as the GDP deflator, making it very difficult for US sellers of tradable goods to raise their prices or to prevent severe downward stress on their profits. Downward pressure on prices only mounted, of course, when the East Asian region, and much of the rest of the world as well, entered into depression from 1997: industrial goods now came onto the market at distress prices and, as demand collapsed, so did raw material prices, especially oil. Between 1995 and 2000, world manufacturing prices fell, in dollar terms, at the stunning average annual rate of 4 per cent (see above, p. 160, Figure 6.1). Changes in world market conditions plus the levitating dollar thus account for a substantial part of the striking reduction of inflation, but made for profitability problems in the manufacturing goods sector while easing import, thus input, costs outside of it (see above, p. 136, Figure 5.1, and p. 212, Figure 8.8).[31]

Even so, one should not discount the additional anti-inflationary impact of the rapid growth of productivity, which played a major part in limiting the average annual growth of manufacturing unit labour costs between 1993 and 1999 to −1.8 per cent. Augmented productivity growth was increasingly important outside manufacturing and the tradable goods sector as well. During the two-and-half years from 1997 through the first half of 2000, although real wage growth in the non-farm business economy averaged 2.8 per cent per year, the growth of unit labour costs over the

---

compensate for increases in nominal wage growth. This is not, of course, to doubt that, in the presence of the emergence of demand-side problems manifesting themselves in the form of the slowed growth of output or prices, the failure of wage growth to adjust downward in sympathy can squeeze profits and/or lead to greater inflation. In this sense, of course, they already had.

[31] See R.W. Rich and D. Rismiller, 'Understanding the Recent Behavior of US Inflation', *Federal Reserve Bank of New York Current Issues in Economics and Finance*, VI, July 2000.

same period averaged only 1.6 per cent per year. This made it possible to
limit the average annual increase of product prices to a low 1.4 per cent
per annum, although, again, doing so did entail a significant sacrifice of
manufacturing profitability (see above, pp. 209–17).

Finally, and crucially, the rapid enlargement of the capital stock, by
preventing capacity utilization from increasing much over the length of
the expansion, despite the accelerating growth of GDP, also had to be
critical in containing costs and prices. Even despite the record-breaking
length of the 1990s expansion, the factory-operating rate at the beginning
of 1999 was more than a percentage point below its average over the past
thirty years. To make the same point another way, capacity utilization
declined significantly between 1997 and 1999 as the boom accelerated
and unemployment fell, and was still a bit lower in the middle of 2000
than it had been in 1994.[32]

NEW TECHNOLOGY, CAPITAL ACCUMULATION,
AND THE FUTURE OF THE US BOOM

In sum, from the end of 1993, the US economy achieved significantly
more rapid growth of output, investment, and productivity than it had
during the previous twenty years. It did so, moreover, while damping
down the growth of prices, despite relatively low unemployment. Fast-
rising demand was thus met much more by fast-rising supply and the slow
growth of prices – i.e. by rising quantities rather than by rising prices –
than had tended to be the case during the 1970s and much of the 1980s.
From the standpoint argued here, what was ultimately most responsible
for this improvement in performance was the impressive speed of investment throughout the expansion, ultimately rooted in the major increase
in pre-tax and after-tax profit rates, with respect to those that had
prevailed for two decades or more from the end of the 1960s. The rise of
profitability originated in the manufacturing sector between 1985 and

---

[32] OECD, *Economic Survey. United States 1999*, Paris, 1999, p. 30; *Economic Report of the President
2001*, p. 337, Table B-54.

1995. It spread beyond manufacturing between 1995 (when the non-manufacturing profit rate finally recovered its level of 1985) and 1997, bringing about a significant further enhancement of profitability for the entire non-farm economy. From 1998, as the profit rate fell off somewhat across the non-financial corporate sector, the wealth effect of spectacularly increasing equity prices drove investment growth even faster. In the last analysis, it is the transformation in the conditions for profit-making, and the sustaining of those conditions, that was responsible for the acceleration of investment growth, in turn of productivity growth, and ultimately of aggregate demand that lay at the heart of the boom of the 1990s, although, again, in its final years, the contribution of the stock market bubble was clearly indispensable.

The sharply improved conditions for profit-making that lay behind the economy's reinvigoration derived from major reductions in absolute and relative costs during the previous decade: the effective wiping out of wage growth; the profound decline in the value of the dollar; and the major diminution of the cost of borrowing, one of the effects of which was the recovery of firms' balance sheets; plus the huge reduction of the corporate tax rate during the early 1980s. At the point at which the economy began to take off in the last quarter of 1993, manufacturers had succeeded in limiting the average annual growth of real hourly wages during the previous eight years to just 0.6 per cent, and during the subsequent four years of rapid economic expansion average hourly real wage increase would actually fall below zero (−0.3 per cent). During the same period, manufacturers had been able to take advantage of an average annual decline in the dollar's nominal effective exchange rate of no less than 4.7 per cent, and they would benefit from a further decline of 8 per cent in 1994–95. Meanwhile, manufacturers had been able to profit from a 50 per cent fall in real long-term interest rates (thirty-year Treasury bonds) from 7.2 per cent in 1985 to 3.6 per cent in 1993, as well as the spectacular collapse of the real Federal Funds rate from 5.31 per cent in 1989 to 0.32 per cent in 1993, thanks to Alan Greenspan's bailout of the financial sector in these years.[33] Finally, in 1993, taxes constituted just 23.9 per cent

---

[33] *Economic Report of the President 2001*, p. 360, Table B-73.

of corporate manufacturing profits, compared to 56 per cent in 1980. It was the huge reduction in their absolute and relative costs, and thus the very major increase in their potential rate of profit, secured for the most part during the decade after 1985, that enabled US manufacturers to ignite the cyclical upturn of the 1990s.

As the economic expansion of the 1990s accelerated, fast-growing investment made for fast-growing productivity, and the latter underpinned rising profitability and rising investment in a virtuous cycle typical of economic booms. There is no reason to deny, in this context, that the availability of more advanced techniques amplified the productiveness of firms' expenditures on new plant and equipment, thus productivity growth. But, from the perspective adopted here, it was fundamentally the improvement in firms' potential profit rate, as well as in their general financial condition, that, by creating the conditions for stepped-up capital accumulation, underpinned the significant increase in economic vitality achieved by the US economy from just before mid-decade – much more than any putative autonomous rise of a New Economy. Grossly put, higher profitability (so long as it lasted) could and did make possible more rapid investment growth, which allowed for the faster adoption, and indeed development, of new technology and thus more rapid productivity increase; but the greater availability and the faster adoption of new technology could not in itself, and did not in fact, make possible increased capital accumulation on a sustainable basis, because it could not in itself, and did not in fact, enable the achievement of a sustainable rise in profitability.

It is thus no more possible to believe that a step-up in the availability of new technology brought about the boom in capital accumulation that began around 1993 than that a putative exhaustion of technological potential around 1973 had been responsible for the slowdown of productivity growth rates and capital accumulation of the subsequent twenty years (see above, pp. 23–4). Technical advance simply does not occur so discontinuously, so rapidly, and with sufficient depth and breadth as to incite the sort of sudden end of investment stagnation and explosion of investment growth that took place at that juncture. The more reasonable hypothesis would be that just as secularly reduced profitability brought secularly slowed capital accumulation, and, as a result, both the slowed adoption and the slowed improvement of new techniques after the early 1970s, the vast increase in potential profits and the business climate of the early 1990s allowed for suddenly elevated levels of investment growth that made the bringing in of new technologies more feasible than it had been over the previous twenty years and opened the way in the process of ongoing capital accumulation for their rapid enhancement.

Powerful technologies had been coming on-line for quite some time, and it seems fairly clear that most, if not all, of the key techniques implicated in the 1990s boom had long been available. This is true of course of the personal computer and the Internet at the heart of the information technology revolution, of computer-aided production and design in industries like auto or retail and wholesale trade, of mini-mills in steel, and so on. In the face of the sharply reduced profit rates, record-high real interest rates, record-high levels of corporate indebtedness, and slowed growth of aggregate demand that prevailed throughout most of the 1980s, firms had been hesitant to invest in such technologies. But, then, as the profit rate finally began to rise significantly, while real interest rates and corporate indebtedness began to tumble, firms were able to rapidly bring them into play by ratcheting up their rates of investment. In turn, as capital accumulation and the growth of output continued to increase rapidly over the course of the 1990s, innovation was further speeded up, not only by the adoption of hitherto neglected advanced technologies, but also by their further enhancement. This took place by means of the stepped-up learning-by-doing (as with computers), the economies of scale (as with semi-conductors), and the network effects (as with all virtually all aspects of information technology, communications, and media) that generally accompany the speedy growth of the capital stock in economic expansions.

Nevertheless, there is a major 'catch' – really two catches – to the foregoing scenario of an investment-driven, profitability-based revitalization of the US economy in the 1990s. Up through 1997, it makes sense to attribute the strong cyclical upturn, and the upward leap in economic energy compared to the previous two decades, to the very major recovery of the economy's underlying rate of profit. But, from the latter part of

1997 if not before, an increasingly internationally oriented manufacturing sector was deprived of much of its initial source of dynamism by the rising dollar and the crisis in East Asia, and ceased to be able to impel the economy forward in the way it had been doing. From that point onward, it is clear that the giddy stock market – via the wealth effect of rising equity prices on investment, as well as consumption – was, to a very large extent, powering the impressive ongoing boom (and keeping the manufacturing sector itself moving forward rapidly) although it cannot be overstressed that it was doing so in increasing defiance of actual profit-making, even despite the rapid pace of technological advance that it was making possible, because the gains from increased productivity growth were going, via reduced prices, disproportionately to users/consumers rather than producers. The question that therefore immediately imposed itself was whether the economic dynamism thus sustained could be maintained, either over the short or longer run, in view of the drying up of both of its two main sources – first, the reversal of the wealth effect with the fall of the stock market and, second, the difficulty of regaining manufacturing competitiveness and export growth in the presence of the high dollar and the apparent persistence of a surfeit of capacity and production on an international scale.

CHAPTER 10

FROM THE END OF THE BUBBLE
TO THE END OF THE BOOM

Whether or not the US economic revival is ultimately sustainable would seem to come down to two closely interrelated questions. The first is whether the excesses of the stock market bubble that drove the economy so far upward will find their necessary counterpart not only in the collapse of the bubble, but also in a sharp, extended down-side over-correction, as they did in Japan. The second, even more fundamental, is whether, despite the bubble, or even partly because of it, the US economy – and the world economy on which it ultimately depends – has so thoroughly transformed itself as to have secured the foundations for an ongoing long boom roughly analogous to that of the first post-war decades, quite aside from whether or not, in the short term, the economy enters into a serious recession. Put simply, the issue is whether the inevitable big stock market reversal that has taken place will have such a profound effect as to seriously reverse the gains of the 1990s expansion and return the economy to the slowed growth that characterized the previous two decades and worse, or whether the underlying strength of the economy will enable it to limit the impact of the fall in equity prices, and continue, after a relatively brief interruption, to put the long downturn definitely behind it and vigorously sustain a new long upturn.[1]

---

[1] As foreseen, e.g., in OECD, *The Future of the Global Economy. Towards a Long Boom?* Paris, 1999.

THE US ECONOMY PEAKS

To prevent the expected equity price 'correction' from having serious negative repercussions for the real economy, US policy-makers counted upon the bubble-driven expansion of US corporate investment and household consumption, before petering out, to place the economy on a qualitatively different footing and thereby to ensure a relatively smooth transition from the international crisis of 1997–98 to a prolonged upturn. By animating export-led cyclical booms throughout the world economy that would permit the increasingly rapid growth of overseas demand for US goods, stock-market-driven economic growth would, in policy-makers' favoured scenario, enable US manufacturers to recover the level of export growth that they were enjoying through 1997. This is what former Treasury Secretary Larry Summers meant when he asserted that 'the global expansion must be balanced up rather than balanced down.'[2] At the same time, policy-makers hoped, the equity price bubble would keep investment turning over sufficiently rapidly to ensure that productivity continued to increase at least at the rate attained during the second half of the 1990s, especially outside of manufacturing. In these ways, manufacturers and non-manufacturers alike would secure higher profit rates, making it possible for the economy to shift to a new basis – to break its dependence on the wealth effect of the run-up of share prices in favour of greater reliance on autonomously expanding investment and rising exports while better justifying elevated equity prices.

As of the middle of 2000, the US economy seemed to be developing in much the manner hoped for by US authorities. It was booming in an extraordinary way, picking up its pace in a manner rarely seen so late in the business cycle. Over the previous twelve months, from mid-1999 to mid-2000, GDP had grown by 5.2 per cent, an annual rate that had last been attained in 1984, at the start of the expansion of the 1980s. In the same period, labour productivity in the business economy had bounded ahead at a 4.1 per cent pace, well above the annual average of 2.35 per

---

[2] 'The Outlook', *Wall Street Journal* (interactive edition), 17 April 2000.

cent achieved during the previous two years. This result was clearly attributable to the ever-steeper rate of non-residential investment growth, which reached 11 per cent for that year and a sizzling 14 per cent on an annual basis during the first half of 2000. Despite the lift in GDP and productivity growth, moreover, real wage growth in the business economy fell slightly, compared to the previous year. Firms in the business economy were simultaneously able to raise prices twice as fast as in the year before (1.85 per cent, compared to 0.9), and in the first half of 2000 business economy inflation jumped to a 2.7 per cent annual pace. Things seemed to be going swimmingly for US capital.

Meanwhile, the ever-expanding US economy did indeed stimulate a new cyclical upturn throughout much of the world economy, especially East Asia and western Europe, and was benefiting in turn from the increased overseas sales made possible by faster growing markets. Korea in particular had, it appeared, emerged from its crisis. Korean exports were growing rapidly, and Korean GDP, having steamed along at an 11 per cent pace in 1999, was projected to almost match that in 2000. Korea's neighbouring Newly Industrialized Countries – Taiwan, Hong Kong, and Singapore – were doing about as well. The Euro economies were expanding more rapidly than they had since the end of the 1980s, at an average annual rate of more than 3.5 per cent, with unemployment finally heading earthwards. Even Japan appeared to be emerging from the depths after two extremely bad years, with export growth projected at 13.6 per cent and GDP increase at 2 per cent for 2000.

In response to this dynamic cyclical international upturn, US exports were able to leap upward, as had been hoped. In the year ending in the middle of 2000, real goods exports expanded by 12.8 per cent, compared to 2.1 per cent in 1998 and 3.9 per cent in 1999. The policy scenario of Greenspan–Summers–Clinton seemed to be in the process of realization, the vista of a new long upturn anything but a fantasy.

To help ensure the desired outcome, from June 1999 to spring 2000, Alan Greenspan put into reverse gear his 1998 policy of reducing interest rates to push up equity prices, instead raising the short-term cost of borrowing by a total of 1.75 per cent. Greenspan's tightening was extremely mild, to say the least. By summer 2000, the Federal Funds rate was just 1 per cent above its level of summer 1998 (since Greenspan had cut interest rates a total of 0.75 per cent in late 1998), and the real rate was a full percentage point – and 25 per cent – lower.[3] Indeed, owing to more rapid price increases, real short-term interest rates were no higher than at the time the tightening had begun.[4] But the Fed Chair apparently hoped that, in the same way that his patent aspiration for equity prices to rise had induced a frenzy in the stock market beginning in November 1998 without the need for dramatically reduced borrowing costs, his unconcealed desire for them now to cease their ascent and sustain a modest 'correction' would generate the desired outcome without further exertion. The intention was explicitly to rein in the growth of household consumption by cooling off the equity markets and thereby holding down the wealth effect.[5]

The bubble had, however, clearly become a good deal more fragile than Greenspan had realized, and correspondingly more dependent upon his patronage and support for it.[6] Already in late 1998, and then again in late 1999, the Fed had had to vigorously loosen credit in order to reverse major stock market downturns and keep equity prices rising. When, by

[3] T. Petruno, 'By One Measure, Rates are New Zero',*Los Angeles Times*, 27 June 2001. The Federal Funds rate in real terms was at 3 per cent in mid-2000 compared to 4 per cent in mid-1998.

[4] Between the first half of 1999 and the first half of 2000, while the Federal Funds rate rose by 1.75 per cent, the consumer price index rose by 3.6 per cent. *Economic Report of the President 2001*, Washington, DC, 2001, p. 343, Table B-60. Cf. 'Rates were finally moved above pre-[1998] crisis levels in February 2000. Overall financial conditions, though, have still not [as of May 2000] become appreciably tighter, though they have stopped becoming more expansionary.' OECD, *Economic Survey. United States 2000*, Paris, 2000, p. 71. By contrast, Greenspan raised interest rates by a full 3 per cent between February 1994 and February 1995.

[5] 'Testimony of Chairman Alan Greenspan Before the Committee on Banking and Financial Services, US House of Representatives: The Federal Reserve's Semi-Annual Report on the Economy and Monetary Policy', 17 February 2000. It is here that Greenspan presents his intention to rein in the run-up of equity prices, and thereby the rise of household financial wealth, which had, of course, increased far in excess of the growth of income.

[6] In his report of 17 February 2000, Greenspan expressed his optimism about the underlying strength of the economy and his confidence that any cyclical downturn could be rather easily controlled. 'It would be imprudent . . . to presume that the business cycle has been purged from market economies. . . . We can only anticipate that we will readily take such diversion in stride and trust that beneficent fundamentals will provide the framework for continued progress well into the new millennium.' Ibid.

contrast, Greenspan continued to insist throughout the first half of 2000 that the Fed would no longer nurture the bubble, equity prices began to drop, even though real short-term interest rates barely moved. E-commerce firms saw their share values collapse first, in spring 2000. From the end of the following summer, the broader markets began to drop alarmingly. By late winter 2001, the technology- and Internet-dominated NASDAQ index, central site of the equity price run-up, had declined by 60 per cent from its peak in early 2000. The S&P 500 was in bear territory, having fallen by more than 20 per cent from its high point. Five trillion dollars in assets had gone up in smoke. The issue immediately raised was whether the negative impact of the equity price decline on the real economy could be contained, or whether it would bring about serious recession by summoning up depressive forces that would work in just the opposite direction as the stimulative ones earlier let loose by the equity price bonanza. This question converged with, and was closely tied to, one more profound: in the absence of the stock market bubble, what forces could be expected to dynamize the economy in the middle to long run?

A VICIOUS CIRCLE

From 1995, when the stock market bubble took off, the US economy had behaved in accord with Alan Greenspan's virtuous cycle (see above, pp. 176–9). Belief in the unprecedented potential of the New Economy to increase productivity made for ever-increasing profit expectations, which drove share prices ever higher; the resulting increase of on-paper wealth allowed for record levels of household and corporate borrowing, leading to fast-rising rates of investment and consumption growth; high levels of investment brought about significantly improved productivity performance and helped to dampen inflation, appearing to justify confidence in the New Economy, and so forth. The glitch, of course, was to be found in the ever-increasing chasm that had opened up between expected profits, on the one hand, and actual profits, on the other, which manifested itself in the stock market bubble. Alan Greenspan displayed at all points a touching faith in the optimistic predictions of equity analysts, who accepted at face value the rosy reports they were receiving from corporate executives. But, as we know, from 1995–96, equity prices in both the New and Old Economies increasingly outran corporate profits and, in 1998 and 1999, as the bubble reached a fever pitch, profits in the non-financial corporate sector did not just lag behind share values, but fell significantly. During the first quarter of 2000, the high-tech/Internet bubble reached its apex as NASDAQ's trailing (past year's) price–earnings ratio reached the absurd figure of 400:1. This, however, was the end of the road: henceforth, the gap between profits and share prices could no longer be overlooked.

The fall in equities: 2000–

During spring 2000, one after another e-business ran out of money and collapsed, setting off the stock market decline, most of them never having made a penny of profits.[7] During the following autumn and winter, almost all of the greatest names in the information technology sector, which had made the running throughout the length of the boom – not to mention the also-rans – were struck by an unending succession of increasingly distressing profit reports and saw the value of their shares whistle downwards, especially as investors gradually came to remember that the bottom line was still the bottom line.[8]

There is strong reason to doubt, moreover, that, even at the time of writing, in mid-2001, the carnage is over, that the stock market has hit bottom. The fall in equity prices has naturally tended to push down hugely inflated price–earnings ratios to more realistic levels. But, because profits have also fallen so sharply, price–earnings ratios have not dropped as much as might have been expected, and, in general, remain far above historical norms. By mid-March 2001, the NASDAQ's trailing price–earnings ratio

---

[7] J. Willoughby, 'Burning Up. Warning: Internet Companies are Running out of Cash', *Barron's*, 20 March 2000; J. Willoughby, 'Up In Smoke. Dot.coms are Still Burning Cash, but the Market has Forced Big Changes', *Barron's*, 19 June 2000.
[8] For a narrative of the equity market swoon, see Bank for International Settlements, *71st Annual Report 1 April 2000–31 March 2001*, Basel, 11 June 2001, pp. 101–6.

had fallen to 154, from its level of 400 a year earlier, but it was still triple its average of 52 for 1985–2000. At the same time, the S&P 500's price–earnings ratio was at 24, not that much below its level of 28.3 a year earlier when the bubble peaked, and far above its long-term average of around 15. It would seem that the depressive pressure on equity prices exerted by insufficient corporate profits still is very much at work.[9]

Downward stress on share prices is, indeed, likely henceforth to increase substantially, in view of the fact that both US non-financial corporations and overseas buyers sharply increased their holdings of equities in the face of precipitously falling share prices during late 2000 and early 2001, thereby cushioning the fall in a way that is highly unlikely to continue. In the final quarter of 2000, US non-financial corporations indulged in the greatest quarterly splurge of net stock purchases in US history, no less than $350.8 billion on an annual basis. This binge resulted, however, from a series of huge merger and acquisition deals that had been completed before share prices began their swoon. It is therefore almost certain to come to an abrupt halt.

Meanwhile, in 2000 as a whole, net purchases of stocks by the rest of the world hit an all-time high, at $172.9 billion. During the first quarter of 2001, moreover, they maintained themselves at just about this same record magnitude, i.e. at $166.6 billion, some two-thirds above the already very elevated level of 1999, when purchases were 40 per cent higher than ever before. It is virtually impossible, however, to believe that overseas buyers can much longer remain oblivious to the stock market plunge, any more than can US non-financial corporations considering new mergers and acquisitions. If they do not, another major support of equity prices will fall away.[10]

On the other hand, in keeping with the equity price decline, and contributing to it in a major way, non-financial corporations *did* reduce their stock *re-purchases/buybacks* to $82.7 billion in 2000, a fall of almost 50

---

[9] G. Zuckerman *et al.*, 'Despite Declines, Stocks Remain Expensive in Relation to Earnings', *Wall Street Journal* (interactive edition), 13 March 2001.
[10] For this, and the previous, paragraph see Board of Governors of the Federal Reserve System, *Flow of Funds Accounts of the United States. Flows and Outstandings* [henceforth FRB, *Flow of Funds*], Table F.213, Corporate Equities (flows).

per cent from the average of the previous three years and the lowest amount since 1995 (see above, p. 149, Figure 5.4). Debt-financed corporate equity re-purchases had of course been a major driving force behind the stock market bubble. But, with profits falling so sharply, and borrowing increasingly difficult, they seem likely to continue to fall off precipitously, removing one more prop to share values.[11]

The wealth effect in reverse

The decline of equity prices has shifted Greenspan's virtuous cycle brusquely into reverse, generating something like an 'equal and opposite reaction' and weighing down the economy. As household and corporate on-paper assets fall, households and corporations can be expected to reduce their borrowing and, in turn, their consumption and investment growth. Indeed, the negative impact of the 'reverse wealth effect' will most likely be magnified by the efforts of households and corporations, with their indebtedness at record levels, to repair their balance sheets by bringing down their debt in the face of a slowing economy that offers declining prospects and looming dangers, especially of bankruptcy and unemployment. It will be amplified as well by banks', and other lenders', increased reluctance to extend credit, both because of the reduced collateral of prospective corporate and household borrowers and because of the deterioration of business prospects.

Above all, much of the hugely increased investment of the bubble years is turning out to be over-investment. This is because it was enabled, and motivated, not by increased rates of profit, but rather, in spite of decreased rates of profit, by the seemingly endless supply of almost costless capital, made possible via stock issues of overvalued equities and borrowing backed up by inflated assets, as well as the illusion of infinitely expanding consumption, especially of high-technology products. The downward stress on prices and sales that is resulting will thus drag down

[11] Unpublished Federal Reserve Board time series on equity repurchases by non-financial corporations. See above, p. 148, fn. 9.

profitability, already under pressure from the declining consumption and investment demand that is resulting from falling equity values. Reduced rates of profit will, in turn, force down capital accumulation, already being hit by the increased difficulty of raising funds for investment in the face of falling share prices and shrinking assets. With investment growth thus slowing because unsupportable by either equity prices or realized profits, productivity growth is likely to decrease over the medium run, inviting a further squeeze on profitability, thus capital accumulation, and so on.

Households

By early 2001, these mechanisms connecting stock market decline and economic slowdown had already started to take their toll. In the short time between the first quarter of 2000 and the first quarter of 2001, the value of household-owned equities – which had risen from $4.1 trillion to $12.7 trillion between 1994 and the first quarter of 2000 – fell back to $8.8 trillion, a decline of $3.9 trillion, or 31 per cent. During 2000 as a whole, moreover, household financial assets as a whole fell for the first time since 1952.[12] The negative wealth effect of this sharp decline in asset values was felt more or less immediately as the growth of real personal consumption expenditures, which had risen at an average annual rate of 4.15 per cent between 1995 and 1999, fell from a 5.7 per cent annual pace in the last quarter of 1999 and the first quarter of 2000 to a 2.55 per cent annual pace in the first two quarters of 2001. Simultaneously, the growth of real personal consumption expenditures on durable goods, which had raced ahead at an average annual pace of 8.8 per cent between 1995 and 1999, fell from a souped-up 16.4 per cent annual pace in the last quarter of 1999 and the first quarter of 2000 to an 8.3 per cent annual pace in the first two quarters of 2001.

It needs to be stressed that the stock market decline has thus accounted for a significant fall in the growth of personal consumption expenditures, even in the absence as yet of any serious downward pressure on wages and

---

[12] FRB, *Flow of Funds*, Table L.100, Households and Nonprofit Organizations (levels); J. Plender, 'A Different Kind of Wealth Effect', *Financial Times*, 16 April 2001.

only a minimal increase in unemployment (as of mid-2001) Personal consumption expenditures thus plummeted, despite the fact that relatively fast-rising real wages and further expanding household debt were still buttressing households' spending power through the middle of 2001.[13] During the first half of 2001, real hourly wages in the business economy actually accelerated, increasing at the annualized rate of 3.3 per cent, compared to 2.7 per cent for 2000 as a whole. Equally to the point, unemployment was only beginning to rise significantly, remaining at close to thirty-year lows during the first half of 2001. By the same token, households managed to maintain their borrowing during the first quarter of 2001 at the same record level as in 2000. The fact remains that wage growth, employment levels, and household borrowing are all likely to drop precipitously in the face of the stunning collapse of the main engine of the system, i.e. corporate investment – which was prepared by the blowing up of the equity price bubble and its implosion, and to which it is now necessary to turn.

Corporations

Corporations have had to confront the same decline in asset values as have households. After having grown from $4.8 trillion in 1994 to $15.7 trillion in the first quarter of 2000, the value of non-financial corporate equities crumbled to $10.5 trillion, a fall of $5.2 trillion, or 33 per cent, and the wealth effect on corporate investment also began to go into reverse as securing funds became much more difficult.[14]

Selling shares to raise money for investment now obviously became much less lucrative. Having peaked in the first half of 2000, non-financial corporate equity issues thus fell steadily thereafter. Meanwhile, in the first quarter of 2001, proceeds from IPOs plunged to $16 billion on an annualized basis, their lowest level since the beginning of 1991, compared to something more than $70 billion in 1999.[15]

---

[13] FRB, *Flow of Funds*, Table F.100, Households and Nonprofit Organizations (flows).

[14] Ibid., Table L.213, Corporate Equities (levels).

[15] 'Feeling the Heat', *Business Week*, 2 April 2001; P. Abrahams, 'End of Second California Gold Rush Leaves the Valley in Shock', *Financial Times*, 9 May 2001.

At the same time, borrowing slowed down as it became both harder and more risky. During 2000, the proportion of banks that implemented stricter credit conditions reached its highest level since the 1990–91 recession. Moreover, over the course of 2000 and into early 2001, corporate bond spreads – the difference between the interest rates paid by the corporations rated most reliable and those deemed more risky – rose precipitously, and became even wider than they had been during the financial crisis of autumn 1998.[16] The enormous debt that corporations had built up during the previous half decade against the apparent collateral of their equities – which, as a percentage of non-financial corporate GDP reached an all-time high of 86.5 per cent in the first quarter of 2001 – constituted an additional discouragement to borrowing, especially as the downswing of equity prices began to raise the ratio of corporate debt to corporate assets and net worth. Already, then, in the first quarter of 2001, non-financial corporations had cut their new borrowing in half (on an annualized basis), reducing it as a percentage of non-financial corporate GDP to 4.2 per cent, compared to over 8 per cent (on average) during the previous three years.[17]

Declining access to funds by means of stock issues and borrowing, resulting from the decline in equity prices and asset values, is bound to dampen corporations' enthusiasm for investment. So is the parallel drop-off in the growth of consumption that has the same root. Still, the main barrier erected by the bursting of the stock market bubble to the maintenance of capital accumulation and economic expansion is the massive overcapacity in multiple industrial lines that the bubble itself left in its wake, the legacy of the unfettered, and unfounded, expansion of investment made possible by unrestricted access to capital.

---

[16] Bank for International Settlements, *71st Annual Report*, pp. 25, 75.
[17] FRB, *Flow of Funds*, Table D.2, Borrowing by Sector (flows).

Worsening over-capacity

As the bubble reached its apogee, the enormous additions to both consumer and investment demand that the explosion of equity prices and asset values made possible did allow, to a substantial degree, for the realization of the huge additions to the economy's stock of plant and equipment that had already been induced by the runaway stock market. Nevertheless, the fact remains, as has already been amply stressed, that, despite the huge subsidies to demand *and* jacked-up growth of labour productivity that were facilitated by the bubble, both the manufacturing corporate sector and thereby the non-financial corporate sector sustained significant declines in their profit rates between 1997 and 2000 of 20 and 10 per cent, respectively, even though capacity utilization maintained itself at high levels (see above, pp. 209–13). Downward pressure on prices, which became ever more intense as the decade wore on, thus squeezed the rate of return even as the expansion of purchases of both capital and consumer goods and the growth of productivity reached their highest levels of the 1990s boom, but were more than counter-balanced by the over-expansion of capacity and output (see above, p. 215, Figure 8.9, and below, p. 263, Figure 10.1).

Especially in the wake of the leap upward of capital accumulation during the first half of 2000, the over-capacity that was already showing itself very clearly in 1998, 1999, and 2000 has become blatantly obvious, as bubble years' over-investment, exacerbated by the reversal of the wealth effect, has hit the economy with ever greater force. Firms across broad stretches of the economy have thus found their hugely expanded plant and equipment much more than sufficient, and have, as a result, faced plummeting prices and fast-declining orders, leading to sharply reduced rates of profit on their capital stock. They are therefore radically reducing investment growth, or ceasing to invest at all, for they see little point in making new expenditures on plant and equipment embodying the latest technology in order to 'keep up with the competition' when they can already meet the market simply by putting into play their plant and equipment. The profound reduction in the growth of investment – or its absolute fall – is thus leading aggregate demand downward for the economy as a whole.

It follows that even though they are cutting back purchases of new plant and equipment, firms are not necessarily cutting back production. Having achieved major reductions in marginal costs precisely on the basis of economies of scale made possible by their enormous investments, they can, even in the face of falling prices, still often make a decent rate of profit on their circulating capital, i.e. the additional outlays on labour, intermediate goods, and raw materials that are required to make each additional good. They thus continue to flood the market, even as their retarded accumulation of capital erodes the increase of investment demand and, by the way of rising unemployment and declining consumer confidence, consumer demand as well. In an ever-growing number of cases, moreover, they are cutting prices in a predatory manner, sacrificing their profit margins in a desperate effort to force their rivals out of business as condition for their own survival.

Given the degree to which the last, most spectacular phase of the stock market run-up focused on technology, media, and telecommunications (TMT), it is understandable that over-investment and, in turn, sharply declining profitability has been especially concentrated in this sector. Here equity values rose most steeply, so here money was easiest to raise and investment cheapest to undertake.[18] Moreover, as share prices in this sector lost all touch with underlying profits (see above, p. 187, Figure 7.3), equity analysts concocted an array of ever more bizarre alternative measures of the value of company shares, such as the growth of sales or the increase of physical output. The latter, however, had the effect of making access to funds for many information technology companies dependent upon their ability to expand, inducing investment without limit and inviting further realization problems in the sector as a whole.

This syndrome has turned out to be most exaggerated, with the greatest

---

[18] For documentation of the 'virtuous cycle', at the height of the stock market bubble, that linked elevated equity prices in the TMT sector to elevated investment to elevated productivity growth and, in turn, elevated equity prices – but with no reference to profits – see IMF, *World Economic Outlook*, May 2001, pp. 63–6.

implications for the economy as a whole, in telecommunications.[19] Tele-communications deregulation, which came in 1996, opened entry to the industry to all comers. At just that moment, the development of the Internet appeared to be offering unprecedented, and unlimited, potential for the creation of efficient, easy-to-use communication networks within businesses, among businesses, and between businesses and customers – and for the inter-connection of these networks to one another. With virtually no restriction on their access to funds, carriers built new fibre-optic networks, locally, nationally, and internationally, as if there was no end to the market, egged on by equity analysts who justified share prices in terms of miles of line laid down. In 2000, no fewer than six companies in the US were building new nation-wide fibre-optic networks, and hundreds more were laying down local ones. Between 1997 and 2000, the telecommunications industry steadily raised annual investment, from around $50 billion to $124 billion. Over the same period, it increased its annual borrowing by almost exactly the same amount, with the result that US and European telecommunications companies are today in debt to the tune of $700 billion.

The outcome of all of this investment is a huge glut in telecommunications, with the utilization rate of telecommunication networks at a staggeringly low 2.5 per cent (April 2001)! Under these conditions, it is hardly surprising that the rate of return in the industry has dived headlong, the return on equity in telecommunications dropping from close to 14 per cent in 1996 to under 6 per cent in 2000,[20] while one after another of the pace-setting telecommunications companies have suffered huge declines in the price of their stocks, the shares, for example, of industry leaders AT&T, Sprint, and Worldcom all dropping by one-half to

---

[19] For this paragraph, and the two that follow, R. Miller *et al.*, 'Too Much of Everything', *Business Week*, 9 April 2001; P. Elstrom, 'Telecom Meltdown', *Business Week*, 26 April 2001; A. Berenson, 'Market Paying Price for Valuing New-Economy Hope over Profits', *New York Times* (web edition), 21 December 2000. I am deeply indebted to Aaron Brenner for helping me to better understand the dynamics of the TMT sector.

[20] Even by 1999, before the enormous splurge in capital expenditures of the first half of 2000 and the subsequent huge drop-off of demand for telecommunications products, the rate of profit (net profits divided by net capital stock) in the telephone and telegraph industry, one of the two component lines (along with radio and television) of the communication industry, had fallen by 20 per cent from its peak in 1996.

two-thirds between January 2000 and January 2001. With their profitability down, assets reduced, and debts at a record high, they have also faced suddenly increased difficulty borrowing money. In this situation, it is obvious that expansion of telecommunication networks must be radically slowed, and many companies must go under.[21]

The implications of what has been called a 'dead zone' in telecommunication industry investment are profound for much of rest of the economy, especially in the TMT sector. Telecommunications accounted for 12 per cent of total equipment spending and one quarter of the total increase in business spending that took place during 2000. Telecommunications companies buy networking equipment to route Internet traffic, computer servers to offer Web hosting, software to provide services, and fibre-optic gear to transport bits of information. Their declining orders have thus hammered the profitability of their suppliers. These include almost all of the leading lights of the high-tech boom, most of which have sustained catastrophic collapses in their share prices and announced large-scale layoffs. Near legendary Cisco Systems, for example, along with such other Wall Street luminaries as Lucent and Nortel, sustained equity price declines of between 75 per cent and 85 per cent between early 2000 and mid-2001 and have announced job cuts in the range of 10,000 to 20,000, or more. Of course, when the leading equipment makers were stymied by the drop-off of demand for their products from the carriers, the companies that provide components to the equipment makers could not themselves avoid being set back disastrously, and that is exactly what happened. Equity market darlings JDS Uniphase and Sycamore, for example, sustained declines from 309 to 15 and 256 to 27, respectively, between early 2000 and mid-2001.

Over-capacity, fuelled by the equity price bubble, is not confined to the telecommunications industry and the food chain of suppliers dependent upon it. According to the Federal Reserve, semi-conductor makers and computer companies, along with communication makers, boosted their capacity by no less than 50 per cent in 2000. The upshot is that chip

---

[21] By one estimate, there were, in spring 2001, about 1300 local and 14 long-distance carriers in the US, whereas the economy can support only about 300 to 500 competitive local and 5 to 7 long-distance carriers. Miller *et al.*, 'Too Much of Everything'.

makers are experiencing their most severe downturn since 1984–85, if not in history.[22] At the same time, computer producers like Dell, Gateway, Hewlett Packard, and the like, have all announced major redundancies, and Dell has declared open price war on its rivals. The problem can perhaps be encapsulated in the observation that, in the years 1998, 1999, and 2000, purchases of high-technology information-processing equipment made up no less than 61 per cent of the total increase of nominal equipment and software investment. But such purchases were not only unable to bring about an increase in profitability in those years, they were also responsible for a good part of the over-capacity that chased manufacturing profit rates downward by 20 per cent between 1997 and 2000. Investment in information-processing equipment cannot therefore but plummet dramatically henceforth.

Nor has the economy beyond the TMT sector managed to remain immune from bubble-driven over-capacity. Initially in response to the growth of output and demand for manufactured goods, especially consumer durables, both wholesale trade and retail trade expanded rapidly from around 1993–94. Of course, growth in these lines further accelerated in response to the enormous speed-up of consumption growth incited by the stock market bubble. In wholesale trade, after having increased at an average annual rate of just 3.9 per cent between 1982 and 1990, investment raced upward at an average annual rate of 14 per cent between 1993 and 1999, with the capital stock increasing by well over 6 per cent a year. In retail trade, investment growth was not quite so fast, but still sped forward at an average annual rate of 9 per cent a year, and 22 per cent in 1999 (the last year for which industry investment figures are available). Between 1992 and 2000, square footage among retailers thus grew five times as fast as the population. This huge expansion appeared justifiable as profitability in wholesale trade and retail trade rose by 50 per cent and 33 per cent, respectively, between 1993 and 1999. But consumption growth is falling back rapidly as the wealth effect goes into reverse, and as unemployment rises and consumer confidence falls. It would therefore be

[22] Bear Stearns E-Week, 2 May 2001. I am grateful to Aaron Brenner for bringing this document to my attention.

surprising if both industries were not made to pay for what turns out to be their over-building. Indeed, by early summer 2001, Standard and Poor's was reporting the outlook in the retail trades as 'bleak', and downgraded the credit-worthiness of twenty-five of them.[23]

Of course, both the auto and steel industries have been plagued by too much capacity for several years, the result of the broader, longer-term trend to over-building on a world scale. The world auto industry can thus sell just 74 per cent of the 70 million cars it builds each year. In the later 1990s, the US auto industry was able to cope successfully with this trend by getting in first on the exploding demand for high-end, high-profit models, especially SUVs and small trucks. But German and especially Japanese producers have caught up, and unleashed a powerful assault on the markets and profits of their US rivals, which now face declining prospects. In steel, the situation is even worse, as shown by the US government's recent protectionist clampdown on steel imports. These are trends to which it will be necessary shortly to return.[24]

Declining productivity growth

Declining investment growth stemming from falling profitability, in turn the result of industrial over-capacity, will, finally, most probably prove self-perpetuating and self-exacerbating as a consequence of its negative effect on productivity growth and thereby profitability. Just as the more rapid productivity growth of the 1990s expansion was underpinned by the more rapid increase of the capital stock, slower productivity growth will probably be entrained by the slowdown of capital stock increase. This is especially the case given the ever-increasing degree to which the accelerating expansion of plant and equipment was itself dependent upon corporations' ever easier access to funds by way of the wealth effect of the stock market run-up, rather than the underlying rate of return – and the near-certainty that this will not soon come back. But, if productivity growth

---

[23] Miller *et al.*, 'Too Much of Everything'; L.P. Weston, 'S&P Paints Dark Picture for Retailers', *Los Angeles Times*, 6 July 2001.
[24] Miller *et al.*, 'Too Much of Everything'.

declines, profitability will be further squeezed by real wage growth that has not yet been made to adjust downward, and this will further undercut capital accumulation.

The slowdown in productivity growth is likely to be aggravated, and extended, by the fact that a disproportionate part of the most recent gains in productiveness accrued to firms in the information technology sector. These tended to enjoy the greatest increase in equity values, thus investment growth, and thus productivity growth. Nevertheless, as has been emphasized, profitability increases corresponding to the increases in productivity failed to materialize. Information technology firms have thus been hardest hit by over-capacity and among those most subject to correspondingly large investment cutbacks. They are therefore among those most likely to experience big reductions in productivity growth, which are, moreover, likely to be long-lasting, since, again, the favourable conditions of the bubble are unlikely to reappear in the foreseeable future.

The productivity growth slowdown will be exacerbated as well by the slashed contribution of venture capital to technical advance. Venture capital came to play a major part in financing innovation in the final stages of the stock market bubble, when it was powerfully driven upward not by the potential profitability of high-technology start-ups, but by the outrageously elevated returns to their IPOs (see above, pp. 225–6). But, with the stock market's return to earth, IPOs cannot but run aground, taking venture capital expenditures with them. This is all the more the case in light of the fact that, as the bubble has deflated, most of the companies with the most successful IPOs have struggled to yield profits on investment, their equity prices dwindling to insignificance. Of the ten companies with the greatest first-day gains for their IPOs between 1 October 1999 and 21 March 2000, only two have managed to sustain equity prices that are above their initial offer price. The remaining eight saw their share prices achieve an average first-day gain of no less than 513 per cent with respect to their initial offer price, but ultimately experienced declines that left them by 7 March 2001 an average 61.6 per cent below that initial offer price.[25] As noted, already

---

[25] K. Kelly, 'Investors Discovery Gravity as IPOs Return to Earth', *The Wall Street Journal* (interactive edition), 7 March 2001.

by the first quarter of 2001, proceeds from IPOs had fallen 80 per cent (on an annualized basis), compared to 1999. Venture capital investment dropped back in sympathy – to $10 billion in the first quarter of 2001, from its peak of $26 million in the first quarter of 2000.[26] The decline in venture capital spending is, once again, almost certain to be structural, not just cyclical, for the high-tech bubble was a once-in-a-lifetime affair. As the head of West Coast investment banking at Goldman Sachs characterized the prospects for US venture capital, 'From August 1995 to March 2000 – the history books will show that five-year period was an aberration.'[27]

The pressures toward serious recession

The over-capacity that is the legacy of the bubble economy – along with the reduction of expenditures and of borrowing by both corporations and households that derives from the reverse wealth effect – has created, in a very short space of time, powerful downward pressure on the economy as a whole. This is especially because, itself heavily focused on, though not confined to, the manufacturing sector, it is making itself felt against a background of already existing over-capacity and over-production in the international manufacturing sector, which it is seriously exacerbating. The latter began to manifest itself once again – and ever more strongly – in the US from the time that the dollar began to once more rise in 1995.

Between the first half of 2000 and the first half of 2001, profits (including net interest) in the corporate manufacturing sector, struck by the double whammy of intensified international competition/over-capacity and the TMT overshoot, declined disastrously, dropping by 46 per cent (without capital consumption adjustment and exclusive of net interest). The fall in manufacturing accounted for about 80 per cent of the simultaneous decline of about 23 per cent in the profits of the non-financial corporate sector as a whole. The general result was that, by the first half of 2001, the non-financial corporate profit rate (with adjustments and including net

---

[26] 'Feeling the Heat'; Abrahams, 'End of Second California Gold Rush'.
[27] P. Abrahams and E. Luce, 'No Exit: After Five Years of Spectacular Growth Silicon Valley Venture Capitalists are Facing a Shake-Out', *Financial Times*, 26 February 2001.

interest) was 23 per cent below its 1997 peak, and had fallen below its level
of 1993, wiping out, for the time being, virtually all of the gains in
profitability achieved in the course of the expansion of the 1990s (see
Figure 10.1).[28]

With profitability plunging, capital accumulation collapsed. Having
rushed ahead at a 14 per cent annual rate during the first half of 2000,
private expenditures on non-residential plant and equipment fell at a 6.9
per cent annual rate in the first half of 2001 (13.6 per cent in the second
quarter). With not only consumption growth but also, and especially,
investment growth, declining so rapidly, the growth of GDP and, in turn,
labour productivity could not hold up. The growth of GDP, which had
reached 5.2 per cent in the year ending in the middle of 2000, fell to just 1
per cent (on an annualized basis) in the first half of 2001. Over the same
interval, non-farm business productivity growth was reduced by more than
two-thirds and manufacturing productivity growth swooned even further,
falling in absolute terms at an annual rate of 1.9 per cent in the first half of
2001. Although unemployment in the economy as a whole had yet to
increase very much, it had jumped up sharply in the manufacturing sector,
the epicentre of the downturn, the employment of manufacturing production workers declining by more than half a million, or 4.5 per cent, between
June 2000 and April 2001.[29]

Already existing investment is proving a bar to further investment.
Expectations, in Alan Greenspan's words, of 'ever increasing profits stretch-
ing into the future' from capital accumulation in New Economy technology
– and New Economy equities – have been rudely dashed. It is not easy
therefore to see how the powerful downward momentum that has already
been unleashed by the transformation of Greenspan's virtuous cycle into a
vicious one can easily be slowed, or prevented from wreaking a good deal

[28] The non-financial corporate profit rate used here is constituted by non-financial corporate
profits (with capital consumption and inventory valuation adjustments) from BEA, NIPA
Table 1.16 and non-financial corporate net capital stock (structures and equipment and
software) from FRB, *Flow of Funds*, Table B.102, Balance Sheet of Nonfarm Nonfinancial
Corporate Business.
[29] BLS, National Current Employment Statistics, Table B-1 (BLS website). Manufacturing
sectoral output fell from 8 per cent in the second quarter to 3.8 per cent in the third quarter
to − 1.8 per cent in the fourth quarter.

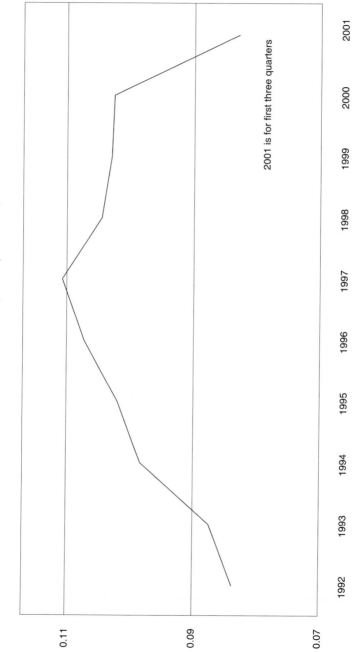

Figure 10.1 US non-financial net corporate profit rate, 1992–2001

of damage. The speed at which GDP growth fell between the first half of
2000 and the first half of 2001 was unprecedented for such a time period
during the post-war epoch. The same is true for investment. Firms are,
therefore, at the time of writing – in mid-2001 – only just beginning to
make the cutbacks in plant and equipment and labour force, as well as
borrowing, appropriate to the state of the market. They are therefore only
now setting off the domino effect, marked by rising bankruptcies and debt
defaults, that is typical of cyclical downturns. Again, unemployment, with
its multiple negative effects, has barely begun to increase outside of manufacturing, but, given the collapse of investment, would seem poised to grow
considerably, forcing down consumer spending and borrowing, both of
which have up till now shown considerable resilience.[30] The economy has
been deprived of, and is now reeling from, the effects of its bubble, as well
as the huge glut of productive capacity left in its wake. A recession has
begun. How serious will be the ensuing downturn would seem to depend
upon the underlying dynamism possessed by the US economy and the
international economy with which it is inextricably connected.[31]

[30] Indicative of the trend, and a harbinger, one would think, of things to come, the personal
savings rate jumped up to 2.5 per cent and then 4.2 per cent in July and August 2001,
compared to 1 per cent for the year 2000.
[31] It is not easy to predict the impact of the macroeconomic stimulus programme that is now
being implemented. An extraordinary series of reductions in the short-term rate of interest
has been under taken by the Federal Reserve. Still, it is difficult to see how easier access to
funds can directly effect that much of a speed-up of capital accumulation, given the
disincentive to investment represented by the mammoth build-up of productive capacity.
With too much plant and equipment already, firms will be loath to borrow for the purpose
of investing, no matter how low interest rates fall. In this respect, the Fed is pushing on the
proverbial string. As in 1998 and 1999, Alan Greenspan appears to be looking to a new run-
up of equity prices, as well as a step-up of borrowing against the collateral represented by the
(still inflated) value of private homes, to once again push up household consumption and
save the day. Whether or not this works in the short run, it seems to risk a new bubble and
an even more damaging stock market drop-off in the medium run. Keynesian deficits,
especially if secured through increased government spending, would be more promising as
they would directly raise demand. However, it is doubtful if they will, in the foreseeable
future, be large enough to make that much of an impact. This is, in the first place, because
in the current political climate, they are likely to be disproportionately constituted by tax
cuts to the wealthy, who will be prone to save rather than consume the bulk of their gains. It
is, secondly, because increased public deficits of the order of magnitude currently in prospect
are likely to be largely offset by corresponding declines in private borrowing as corporations
and households seek to repair their balance sheets.

CHAPTER 11

PROSPECTS: 'IT CAN'T HAPPEN HERE'

For two decades after 1973, the US economy remained mired in worsening stagnation, the long downturn. Indeed, during the first half of the 1990s, the economy performed less well than in any other five-year period during the post-war epoch. From 1993, however, it began to revitalize itself, especially on the basis of the recovery of international competitiveness, exports, and profitability in the long-dormant manufacturing sector, and entered upon a major boom. To avoid returning to stagnation, thereby extending the long downturn even further, the course that the US economy must therefore negotiate is one that would, roughly speaking, return it to the path it had been pursuing up through 1995–97, at which point the rise of the dollar and the crisis in East Asia obliged it to fall back into dependence for its vitality upon the wealth effect of the stock market bubble. This time, however, the US's trading partners would have to sustain sufficiently rapid growth of their domestic markets to support fast-growing US exports, while US producers would have to maintain greater control over the domestic US market without depriving their trading partners of an indispensable outlet. Put another way, the exports of the US and its trading partners would have to be sufficiently complementary that they could all expand in a mutually symbiotic fashion. Equally important, the US non-manufacturing, non-tradable goods sector, having broken from its long stagnation, would have to continue to sustain a virtuous upward spiral of higher profit rates leading to higher investment and productivity growth, making possible better profitability, higher wage growth, and a dynamically expanding domestic market.

Nevertheless, neither the transcendence of the long downturn, nor indeed the avoidance of deepening stagnation or worse, can be expected in the foreseeable future. This is, most generally, because during the length of the late 1990s the advanced capitalist economies taken together were unable to perform even as well as they had during the course of the 1980s, not to mention the 1970s or 1960s. This was so, even despite the enormous stimulus provided by the US boom (see above, p. 47, Table 1.10). It is, more specifically, for two reasons. First, the stock market bubble that was providing the main impetus for US and international expansion in the later 1990s, and especially from 1998 onwards, has burst and cannot make a durable comeback. Second, neither a path of internationally oriented growth characterized by complementarity rather than redundancy in the manufacturing sector, nor a sustainable investment boom in the non-manufacturing sector, will be easy to achieve in either the short or longer run.

NO BREAK FROM THE PATTERN

It must be remembered, to begin with, that, right up through 1998, much as they had through the entire length of the long downturn, the world's leading manufacturing economies – in the US and East Asia, in western Europe and Japan – had continued to find it difficult to expand and prosper together, in the face of incipient international over-capacity and over-production in manufacturing lines. As each cyclical expansion unfolded, national manufacturing sectors enjoying reduced exchange rates would tend to secure increased manufacturing profitability and to grow relatively rapidly, while those with increased exchange rates would tend to be held back. In this context, chronic US budget deficits and US trade and current account deficits typically proved crucial in supplying the demand needed to tug the world economy from recession and keep it turning over. During the first half of the 1980s, the US manufacturing sector was driven into crisis by record high real interest rates that brought with them a rocketing dollar, while the Japanese and German manufacturing sectors were helped to emerge from their recessions by relatively low currencies, as well as record US budget and trade and current account deficits. Between 1985 and 1995, by contrast, US manufacturing prospered via the low dollar, as did East Asian manufacturing, while German and Japanese manufacturing faced increasing difficulties as a consequence of their bloated currencies, difficulties which were ultimately made significantly worse as a result of the US government's decision in 1993 to seek a balanced budget rather than play its accustomed role in subsidizing world demand through accepting increased budget deficits. During the first half of the 1990s, the Japanese, the German, and also the other western European economies sustained their worst recessions since 1950.

Between 1995 and 1997, a new rise of the dollar, paralleled by declines of the yen and the mark, created the potential for economic revival in Japan, Germany, and much of the rest of western Europe. The latter was realized when fast-rising US imports, now amplified by the wealth effect of runaway equity prices, detonated a new cyclical upturn across much of the advanced capitalist world, much as they had done in the wake of the cyclical downturns of the mid-1970s and early 1980s (but had notably failed to do during the first half of the 1990s). Over the same 1995–97 period, the US economy was able to temporarily overcome the effects of the new rise of the dollar and speed up its cyclical expansion, although it could not, even despite falling real wages, prevent the termination of the decade-long ascent of the manufacturing profit rate. This was in part by virtue of its manufacturers' striking success in reducing costs – not least wage costs – sufficiently to compensate for the rising currency, but also in part by virtue of the take-off of the stock market and the stimulative impact of the wealth effect on investment and consumption growth. In 1997, the growth of GDP for the G-7 economies and OECD economies taken together hit a 1990s peak.

Nevertheless, the increased exchange rates that had come to prevail from 1995 in both the US and across East Asia (excluding Japan), which were so essential to economic revival in Japan, Germany, and much of the rest of western Europe, ultimately led in 1997–98 to declining manufacturing competitiveness, shrinking exports, and falling manufacturing and overall profitability in the US and an all-out crisis in East Asia. By autumn–winter 1998 the world economy, including the US, was threatened by a major new recession, or perhaps worse. International over-capacity and over-production, manifested in powerful downward pressure on the profit rate in international manufacturing, had once again reared its ugly head.

In early 1999, according to a survey taken by *The Economist*, '[t]hanks to enormous over-investment, especially in Asia, the world is awash with excess capacity in computer chips, steel, cars, textiles, and chemicals. The car industry, for instance, is already reckoned to have at least 30 per cent unused capacity world-wide – yet new factories in Asia are still coming on stream.' *The Economist* went on to assert, that '[n]one of this excess capacity is likely to be shut down quickly, because cash-strapped firms have an incentive to keep factories running, even at a loss, to generate income. The global glut is pushing prices relentlessly lower. Devaluation cannot make excess capacity disappear; it simply shifts the problem to somebody else.' The upshot, it concluded, was that the world output gap – between industrial capacity and its use – was approaching its highest levels since the 1930s.[1] Clearly, right up to this moment, there had been no definitive transcendence of the conflictive pattern of development that had marked the international economy over the course of the long downturn. Rather, with each passing decade, that pattern had become ever more pronounced and issued in ever more hesitant economic advance system-wide and the increasing risk of ever-deeper crisis.

As we know, from 1998 onwards, with indispensable assistance from the US Federal Reserve, the growth of bubble-driven investment and con-

[1] 'Could It Happen Again?' *The Economist*, 22 February 1999. As the Bank for International Settlements put it several months later: 'In 1998 and early 1999 . . . there was substantial excess capacity globally in many industries. This was particularly the case in Japan and in Asia more generally, but was also true of the United States. Whereas the unemployment rate in the United States trended ever lower, measured levels of capacity utilization in manufacturing fell, contrary to what might been expected. In this environment of heightened global competition, profits began to weaken, sharply in some countries and sectors. . . .' 'The overhang of excess industrial capacity in many countries and sectors continues to be a serious threat to financial stability. Without an orderly reduction or take up of this excess capacity, rates of return on capital will continue to disappoint, with potentially debilitating and long-lasting effects on confidence and investment spending. Moreover, the solvency of the institutions that financed this capital expansion would become increasingly questionable.' *69th Annual Report 1998–1999*, Basel, 7 June 1999, p. 5, 146.

sumption came to substitute for increasing manufacturing profitability, rising international competitiveness, and rising export growth in pushing the US economy forward, enabling it to finesse, for the time being, the problem of international over-capacity and over-production in manufacturing that had manifested itself in the East Asian crisis and resulted in harsh downward price pressure on profits. The exploding boom that resulted, moreover, once again made possible the accelerated growth of US imports that was needed to revive the world economy, and drive a new cyclical upturn from 1999. But the question that loomed ever larger was whether the US economy could ultimately reverse the process through which it had bailed out the world economy. Could the US economy thus give up its dependence on stock-market- and debt-driven growth of consumption and investment and come to rely instead on export growth and autonomous investment growth – at the same time as its rivals and trading partners sustained their own export-dependent expansions? The underlying question was whether the big recessions and crises in Japan, western Europe, and East Asia that had punctuated the 1990s, as well as the rise of new industries all across the advanced capitalist world, had finally rid international manufacturing of its tendency to redundant production and made for the required increase in complementarity. If so, a mutually expanding world division of labour might now, as in the textbooks, endow sufficient gains to all parties to finally support a dynamic international expansion. But if not, the advanced capitalist economies – and the world economy as a whole – risked not only the further perpetuation of the long downturn, but also, once the gravity-defying stock market was pulled back to earth by the dull force of insufficient profits, a return to, or extension of, the great East Asian-cum-international crisis of 1997–98.

In fact, the international economic expansion that gathered force in 1999–2000 offered little reason to conclude that the world's leading manufacturing economies could finally expand together, at least in the absence of explosive increases in US demand, driven either by rising government deficits or the wealth effect of rising asset values, leading to current account deficits that set new records every year. Its pattern failed to diverge significantly from that which characterized the successive cyclical recoveries that have occurred since the long downturn began at the start of the 1970s. As in those previous ones, the US's main rivals and partners in western Europe – especially Germany and Italy – in East Asia, and in Japan thus depended as usual upon a combination of the sizzling growth of the US import market, historically unprecedented US current account deficits, and sharply reduced exchange rates vis-à-vis the dollar (notably the very low Euro) to generate growth, relying in particular on the bubble-driven growth of demand not only for high-technology investment goods, but also for traditional consumption imports, like cars (see above, pp. 204–5).

It is true that US export growth did respond vigorously to the international economic expansion of 1999–2000. But it hardly did so unproblematically. This is because the increase of US *imports* that was required to endow the international economic expansion with sufficient force to enable US exports to grow as quickly as they did had itself to be so extremely rapid. In the year ending at mid-2000, US exports grew by about 13 per cent, but imports increased by about 22 per cent. As a result, by mid-2000, when the boom and bubble peaked, the level of US imports was a full 30 per cent above that of US exports. That meant that exports would have had to race ahead about a third faster than imports just to prevent the trade deficit from widening further.[2] As it was, of course, in 2000 as a whole, trade and current account deficits once against set records – reaching 3.8 per cent and 4.4 per cent of GDP, respectively, compared to 2.8 per cent and 3.7 per cent, respectively, in 1999.

It cannot be over-stressed in this context that, even had high rates of export growth been indefinitely maintainable and record-breaking US current account deficits been indefinitely sustainable, the US manufacturing sector was in no way capable, at the reigning level of the dollar, of returning to its earlier role of providing dynamism to the broader economy. During the first half of 2000, real goods exports climbed rapidly at an annualized rate of 11.7 per cent. Nevertheless, profits (excluding interest) accrued by the corporate manufacturing sector in this half-year

---

[2] J.C. Cooper and K. Madigan, 'Putting on the Brakes Without Crushing the Dollar', *Business Week*, 5 June 2000; 'All Quiet at the Fed, But the Trade Deficit Looms', *Business Week*, 4 September 2000.

on an annualized basis failed still to rise above 80 per cent of their level of 1997. For the year 2000 as a whole, despite real goods export growth of almost 10 per cent, corporate manufacturing profits (unadjusted for capital consumption and excluding interest) fell to 21 per cent below and the corporate manufacturing profit rate to 20 per cent below their levels of 1997. This was so despite the fact that personal consumption expenditures and labour productivity rose strongly for the year as a whole, while manufacturing capacity utilization remained at or near 1990s peaks. As a result of the decline in manufacturing profitability, in 2000 the profit rate in the non-financial corporate sector as a whole was 10 per cent below its level of 1997 (see above, p. 215, Figure 8.9, and p. 263, Figure 10.1).

The problem facing the US, and international, manufacturing sector was the same as it had been throughout the second half of the 1990s. The difficulty was not costs, not even nominal and real wage costs, which now grew relatively rapidly, for, as before, the non-financial non-manufacturing corporate sector was able to sustain, and even slightly increase, its profit rate in 2000, as it had throughout the second half of the decade, despite sustaining greater wage and unit labour cost increases than did manufacturing. It was able to do so because its firms were free to mark up prices over costs in a way that their counterparts in manufacturing could not match (see Figure 11.1; also above, p. 215, Figure 8.9).

What continued to drive down manufacturing profits in the US was the same powerful downward pressure of manufacturing prices that had been squeezing profits with increasing force on a world scale throughout the second half of the 1990s. In the year 2000, world manufacturing prices fell by no less than 6.2 per cent in terms of the dollar and by 2.8 per cent in trade-weighted terms, after having fallen by 2.0 per cent in dollar and 2.8 per cent in trade-weighted terms in 1999. (World manufacturing prices in trade-weighted terms had fallen at an average annual rate of 1.8 per cent between 1995 and 2000, after having risen at an average annual rate of 1.3 per cent between 1986 and 1995.[3]) This was the case, despite the fact that, throughout the advanced capitalist world, demand and capacity utilization rates stayed high throughout the year 2000. The

---

[3] Time series on world manufacturing prices courtesy of IMF.

Figure 11.1 US corporate manufacturing, non-financial corporate, and non-financial non-manufacturing corporate profits net of interest, 1986–2001

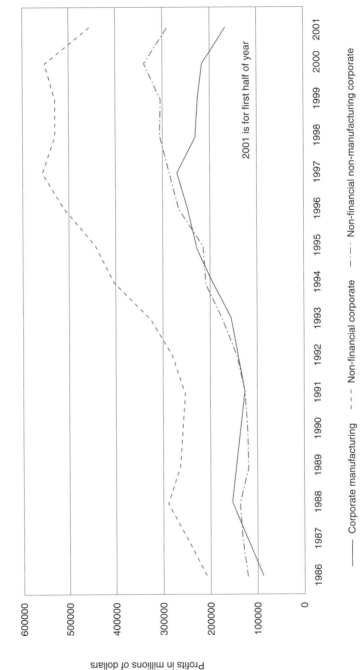

burden of over-capacity and over-production on manufacturing vitality was manifest everywhere, even at the peak of the (short-lived) cyclical boom of 1999–2000 (see above, p. 160, Figure 6.1).

It will be recalled that, in US policy-makers' favoured scenario, a US stock market 'correction' and corresponding reduction of the wealth effect was supposed to somewhat bring down the growth of GDP and of imports, while the GDP growth of the US's trading partners, having previously been jump-started by the stimulus derived from rapidly rising stock-market-driven US imports, would increase so as to coax US exports to ascend. Continued international expansion would thus be secured at the same time as external deficits were reduced, with need for but little slowdown of the US economy. This was the meaning of 'balancing up'. But the lesson of the expansion of 1999–2000 was obviously exactly the opposite. Since, for the world market to expand sufficiently to make possible any given rate of growth of US exports, US imports and the US current account deficit had to grow significantly faster than US exports did, it could be expected that any decline in US import growth would yield a more than proportional decline of US export growth. And that indeed is what happened.

When the US stock market and US economic growth finally fell sharply beginning in the latter part of 2000, import growth did slow very significantly. But, far from picking up the slack, the Japanese, western European, and East Asian economies all experienced major economic slowdowns, with the result that US export growth declined much more rapidly than did US import growth. From the last quarter of 2000 through the first half of 2001, US real goods imports declined at an annualized rate of 5.1 per cent, but US real goods exports declined 50 per cent faster, at an annualized pace of 7.6 per cent, promising still another record trade deficit. In turn, as already noted, during the first half of 2001 US manufacturing profits fell by 46 per cent on an annualized basis compared to the first half of 2000, especially as the growth of US personal expenditures, particularly on durable goods, in the aftermath of the bubble and as a consequence of its deflation, also declined notably. As the US economy thus loses momentum, it cannot be rescued by the rest of the world economy, but can only bring it down with it, further exacerbating its own difficulties. Any recovery from the deepening international down-turn will have to be initiated and driven by the US.

CAN NON-MANUFACTURING DRIVE THE ECONOMY?

It would appear that the future health of the US economy depends heavily on the degree to which the enormous sector of the economy outside of manufacturing can sustain the much increased energy that it displayed during the boom of the 1990s. The non-financial non-manufacturing corporate profit rate rose continuously from 1992 and, after finally regaining its level of 1986 in 1995, it increased a further 15 per cent during the next five years, maintaining itself and even increasing slightly between 1997 and 2000, even while the corporate manufacturing profit rate fell by 20 per cent. (see above, p. 215, Figure 8.9). Rising profitability underpinned rapid capital accumulation, which catalysed rising productivity growth, which helped, in turn, to raise profitability, and did so throughout the decade.

The non-manufacturing sector had experienced an extended period of reduced profitability from the early to mid-1980s through the early 1990s. What had held the profit rate down was apparently the sharp slowdown in the growth of demand emanating from a crisis-bound manufacturing sector during much of the 1980s, as well as the persistently low dollar between 1985 and 1995, which sharply raised the cost of those inputs for the non-manufacturing sector purchased on the world market. The sub-sequently renewed vitality of the non-manufacturing sector was linked, at least in part, to the major speed-up in the growth of manufacturing GDP that took place from the end of 1993 and was then undoubtedly bolstered by the cheap imports made possible by the new rise of the dollar from 1995. From 1995, of course, the non-manufacturing sector was also goaded forward by the ever more rapid growth of demand and ever easier access to capital that derived from the wealth effect of the stock market run-up. The crucial question is: can this sector continue its impressive expansion in the short, medium, or long run?

Given the scope of the improvement in non-manufacturing productivity, the timing of the non-manufacturing productivity take-off, and, finally, the trajectory of the non-manufacturing profit rate, there seems reason for doubt. It will thus be recalled that at least three of the seven non-manufacturing industries – construction, transportation and public utilities, and mining – actually experienced *lower* average annual productivity growth in the years between 1993 and 1999 than they did between 1982 and 1990, and so contributed little or nothing by themselves to increased non-manufacturing dynamism (see above, p. 235, Table 9.2). The improved productivity performance that helped to push up profitability in the non-manufacturing sector was, in fact, confined to the service sector proper – specifically, wholesale trade, retail trade, and FIRE.[4] Moreover, even among this latter group of service sector industries that registered improved productivity growth between 1993 and 1999, none except for wholesale trade began to achieve that stepped up productivity performance before 1996 – until, in other words, both the dollar and the stock market began to take off. Finally, although the non-manufacturing profit rate sustained itself right through 2000 at levels significantly above that of 1995, it was unable to rise after 1997, despite the continuing high levels of investment, consumption, and productivity growth in the sector. It would appear, in other words, as if the revitalization of the non-manufacturing sector between 1995 and 2000 was fatally dependent upon stimuli deriving from the stock market run-up and its wealth effect, and that in their absence it is likely very much to weaken. As not only the subsidy to investment provided by very cheap capital, but also the buttress to profits provided by bubble-driven demand, go by the wayside in the wake of the stock market decline, the non-manufacturing profit rate is likely to fall off and with it the impressive trends of non-manufacturing capital accumulation and productivity growth. If non-manufacturing profitability could not grow under the very favourable conditions that prevailed between 1997 and 2000, it is not likely to avoid a significant drop-off in their absence.

It is certainly conceivable that the US economy holds a trump card that

---

[4] The service industry of the service sector, the seventh and last non-manufacturing industry, is here left aside as the official data on its productivity growth are open to question.

can overcome its apparent weaknesses. It is thus not impossible that the restoration of profitability in the US to the relatively high levels already attained by 1997 will show itself (after a brief, mild recession) to be sustainable in the medium to long run, and ultimately sufficient to sustain solid growth in the US and internationally. It might do so, as it indeed did from 1993 through mid-2000, by underwriting relatively high levels of investment growth that would sustain decent levels of productivity growth for an economy that had already shed, through the crises of the 1980s, the early 1990s, and now the start of the 2000s, much of its outdated plant and equipment. Nevertheless, for this to happen, it would seem necessary that the manufacturing sector prove more vital in the face of the high dollar and absence of the stock market bubble than has here been envisioned. This would seem to require the shakeouts of redundant productive capacity and rise of new industries on a world scale – via the booms and crises of the 1990s – to have brought about a more complementary international world division of labour than was apparent even through 2000. Alternatively, investment growth leading to productivity advance in the non-manufacturing sector could prove more autonomous from the wealth effect of rising equity prices, as well as less reliant on the stimulus deriving from a dynamic manufacturing sector, than I have allowed.

Nevertheless, in the end, it seems to me more likely than either of the above possibilities that, with the bursting of the bubble, the US economy will find itself weighed down by many of the same stagnationist forces that held back the Japanese economy at the end of its bubble. This is, most generally, because, like the Japanese economy at the start of the 1990s, the US economy faces *both* the downward spiral set off by the bubble-in-reverse *and* an international manufacturing sector still constrained by over-capacity and over-production – while remaining burdened itself by an over-valued exchange rate. Like the Japanese economy from 1985, the US economy from 1995 saw its nascent boom, heavily based on the rise of manufacturing competitiveness and profitability, undercut by a rising currency. Like the Japanese economy in the later 1980s, the US economy in the later 1990s papered over its underlying difficulties by means of an historically unprecedented asset price bubble that was nurtured by both its government and the leading corporations. As in Japan in the later 1980s, the wealth effect of the asset price bubble did found a significant boom in the US in the late 1990s, powerfully driven by very rapid capital accumulation. But, because, as in Japan, the growth of investment went unaccompanied by any real improvement in manufacturing profitability – in fact, just the opposite – much of it turned out to be over-investment, which invited the end of both the bubble and the boom.

Hindered, as the Japanese were, by a surfeit of industrial productive power that is the legacy of the bubble-driven mis-investment boom, and confronting greater difficulty gaining access to finance as a consequence of the plunge of asset values, US producers, like the Japanese, will now have little choice but to cut back sharply on capital accumulation, especially in face of the slowed growth of consumption that accompanied the end of the wealth effect. Blocked, furthermore, by the high-priced currency, in the context of an international glut of capacity and production, from successfully returning to a path of growth based on increasing competitiveness, exports, and profitability, the US manufacturing sector will, like the Japanese, be unable to revivify the economy as it had done before the rise of the currency and the blow-up of the bubble, even despite the gains in productivity that had been made possible by massive bubble-driven investment. Put another way, because it can no longer maintain the high levels of capital accumulation that it sustained during the bubble years, it will be unable to sustain the high levels of productivity growth that were required to compensate for the high currency and hold off an even greater squeeze on the rate of profit.

It is possible that the US economy will avoid the banking crisis that has helped to cripple Japan. But it will also lack the enormous savings and current account surpluses that have enabled Japan – so far – to muddle through. The huge indebtedness of US corporations and households, in the context of a darkening business environment, thus leaves the US economy vulnerable to sudden attempts to restore corporate and household balance sheets through sharply increased savings, generating the potential for major, destructive reductions in demand. Such reversions to financial equilibrium brought major recessions to Scandinavia and the United Kingdom, as well as Japan, in the late 1980s and early 1990s. By the same token, the US economy's record current account deficits simultaneously leave it vulnerable to violent withdrawals of domestic investments by foreigners and runs on the dollar that a Japanese economy, with its tendentially rising yen and current account surplus, has rarely had to face.[5] Of course, the US economy would not be held back in responding to any downturn, as has been the Japanese, by the inability to cut back redundant, low profit and low productivity, means of production and labour. Still, a return to the stagnation of the long downturn or perhaps worse would appear to be on the agenda, for, in the absence of both the increasingly vital and profitable manufacturing sector and the stock market bubble which successively drove the expansion, it is not easy to see what forces exist to push the economy forward.

TOWARD CRISIS?

Against a background of loss of momentum resulting from the reversal of its two main engines of the 1990s – manufacturing revitalization and the stock market's wealth effect – the US economy's likely descent into serious recession carries major risks. Most generally, there is the certainty, in light of the decisive role of the growth of US demand in detonating the international cyclical upturn of 1999–2000, that a US recession will set off an international recession that cannot help but be self-reinforcing. In this context, the overriding danger is that the new cyclical downturn represents, in a sense, the continuation of the international crisis of 1997–98, which was temporarily postponed by the last phase of the US stock market run-up but never fully resolved, and that, in particular, East Asia will once again prove the world's powder keg.

In East Asia, the ongoing debility of the Japanese economy remains the heart of the problem. Unlike the rest the region, Japan did not fully partake of the benefits of the international boom of 1999–2000. The underlying reason was that it remained weighed down by massive over-

[5] M. Wolf, 'A Chasm Opens', *Financial Times*, 28 March 2001.

capacity, making for deeply depressed profitability, legacy of the bubble of the 1980s, the stagnation of the 1990s, and the deep recession of 1997–8, plus Japanese firms' profound structural difficulties in ridding themselves of redundant labour and means of production. The proximate cause was that, from late summer 1998 through late autumn 2000, the yen embarked on still another big wave of revaluation, rising by a full 20 per cent in trade-weighted terms. As a result, the rising nominal export growth upon which the economy was depending to haul itself out of its recession was prevented from taking place: exports fell in nominal terms (in terms of the yen) by 12 per cent in 1999 and remained flat during the first half of 2000.[6] In 1999, the last year for which data are available, the profit rate in the Japanese business economy was still more than 50 per cent below its bubble-years peaks of the late 1980s (see above, p. 39, Figure 1.3). To make matters much worse, from mid-2000, Japan's economy had to confront the rapid deterioration of the US market. Since its own cyclical upturn had been so reliant on exports to the US, especially in the form of information technology goods, it now faced the likelihood of falling back into the recession from which it had only recently extricated itself.

Unable to catalyse growth by means of a never-ending series of Keynesian deficit packages, an exasperated Japanese government began in early 2001 to push real interest rates back toward zero in an effort to force the yen lower so as to strengthen exports. But the ensuing 10–15 per cent devaluation of the currency (by mid-2001) posed, and continues to pose, a major series of threats to the world economy and Japan itself, just as it did in 1995, when the yen was forced down for similar reasons.

A declining yen could, first of all, set off a disastrous flight of capital away from Japanese assets, threatening a crash, especially given the dependence of Japanese banks on their holdings of equities for their capital. In this case, Japanese investors would have to sell off their assets abroad and bring their money home to cover their obligations. But the Japanese remain today by far the leading holders of US government securities. Were they obliged to rapidly liquidate them, the resulting rise

---

[6] OECD, *Economic Survey. Japan 2000*, Paris, 2000, pp. 42–3, and Table 3.

in US interest rates could provide a serious blow to hopes for a near-term US recovery. Alternatively, a falling yen, by reducing US competitiveness, could press down even harder on the US current account, and thereby increase the danger of a run on the dollar or a flight from US assets, or both.

Perhaps most immediately threatening, the falling yen has the potential to set off a re-run of the East Asian crisis of 1997–98, by leading to a squeeze on East Asian producers by Japanese manufacturers in both the Japanese market and third markets, as it did from 1995. This is especially possible because this time, unlike the last, when they were cushioned by the ongoing US bubble, East Asian producers are simultaneously being very hard hit by the US economic slowdown. What makes this scenario such a real danger is that the East Asian economies are so very vulnerable, since the big cyclical upturn of 1999–2000 left them so far from full recovery.

In 1999 and 2000, the East Asian economies, notably Korea, did enjoy double-digit GDP growth by means, as before, of fast-rising exports. But rapid expansion, achieved through sharply lower currencies and reduced interest rates, masked underlying weakness. Stock markets throughout East Asia fell through most of 2000 and into 2001, this for the simple reason that profitability had failed to make a comeback. Corporate earnings in the five crisis-stricken economies, above all South Korea, thus languished far below pre-crisis levels, despite the spectacular rise of industrial output. East Asian manufacturers still seemed plagued by over-capacity, some of it attributable to the unwillingness to force effectively insolvent companies out of business. Meanwhile, with labour costs some sixteen times higher than those of their Chinese rivals in high-end computer and electronics lines, Korean and Taiwanese producers had become increasingly vulnerable to ever more formidable Chinese competition. To make matters more difficult, banks remain enfeebled, still heavily burdened by non-performing loans, and loath to lend.[7]

---

[7] G. Koretz, 'Emerging Asia's Shaky Recovery: Scant Profits Point to Growing Risk', *Business Week*, 4 December 2000; B. Bremner *et al.*, 'Asia: The Big Chill', *Business Week*, 2 April 2001; R. Jacob, 'Clouds Gather Again Over Asian Tigers', *Financial Times*, 12 March 2001.

The US slowdown has vastly exacerbated these incipient difficulties by depriving much of East Asia of the main engine that was driving its recovery. It cannot be over-stressed, in this respect, how indispensable for the East Asian economies was the US boom in information technology that was driven by the stock market run-up in its final phase from the end of 1998 to mid-2000. In fact, East Asia is today even more reliant on the expansion of the US market than it was during the first half of the 1990s at the peak of its boom. In 1994 and 1995, as the US economy finally emerged decisively from its recession, and as the dollar and the won plummeted together, Korean nominal manufacturing exports to the US grew by 18 per cent per year, after having fallen every year between 1988 and 1992. Then, between 1995 and 1998, as the dollar rose sharply along with the won, Korean nominal exports fell to an average annual rate of −1 per cent, and the Korean economy entered into crisis. But even at the rapid rates of growth of manufacturing exports to the US achieved earlier in the 1990s, Korea could not have secured the sort of return to rapid growth it achieved in 1999 and 2000. What made that striking recovery possible was that in those two years, Korean manufacturing exports to the US grew at a 31 per cent annual rate.

Korea was hardly unique in East Asia in its dependence both on information technology exports and on the US market. Electronics goods constitute a third of Taiwan's exports, as they do Korea's, and Singapore is in a roughly similar position. Rapid increases in US technology spending in 1999 and the first half of 2000 dramatically raised export growth in Taiwan, Singapore, and Korea. But, after increasing to a 30–40 per cent annualized rate in the first half of 2000 as the high-tech equity price bubble reached its zenith, the growth of new US electronics orders from East Asia sank to 10 per cent in the second half of the year as the stock market went down, and began to fall in absolute terms during the first half of 2001.

In 1997–98, as they collapsed into crisis, especially under the stress of the falling yen (and a devalued Chinese renminbi), the East Asian economies were cushioned by an impetuously expanding US market. But now, with the yen declining again (and Chinese authorities threatening to again devalue the remnibi in the face of the precipitous fall of the

Chinese trade surplus), the US import market is disappearing. If, as thus seems unavoidable, devaluation plus contraction comes to Japan and recession to the US, it is hard to see how a new East Asian crisis can fail to follow. If it does, it is bound, as in 1997–98, to boomerang back upon a Japanese economy that is now more than ever oriented to East Asia, with depressing consequences for the US.[8]

Today, then, the film appears to be running backwards. The deflation of the stock market bubble is propelling a US economy, heavily burdened by manufacturing over-capacity, toward a serious recession, and in the process detonating further recession all across an advanced capitalist world that is similarly held down by superfluous productive power. The resulting downturn is weighing particularly heavily on the triangle of inter-linked economies in East Asia, Japan, and the US itself, so that a mutually reinforcing downturn seems in prospect. Still, given the enormous financial imbalances that have been left over from the bubble, and which hang like a dark cloud over the US and the world economy – the still over-valued US stock market, the huge US current account balances, massive US overseas debt, and the record-breaking US private sector deficit – there is no assurance that economic difficulties will end even there.

If the US real economy does thus continue to fall, and US equity prices do fail to recover and decline further, US assets in general would lose much of their attractiveness to foreign purchasers. This is especially the case in view of how unsustainably fast foreign buying of US assets has been increasing over the last two or three years – and indeed the significant increase in the size of these holdings even during the second half of 2000 as US equities plummeted and US economic growth ground toward a halt (see above, p. 249). But, given that foreign ownership of US gross assets amounts to some 67 per cent of GDP (end of 2000), and in view of the fact that the great bulk of these assets are in the form of privately held government securities, corporate bonds, and corporate equities, all of which can be more or less easily liquidated – if not all at

---

[8] For this, and the previous, paragraph, Jacob, 'Clouds Gather Again Over Asian Tigers'.

once – any serious attempt to flee these assets would put enormous downward pressure on the dollar.

Were the latter to happen, the Fed would be caught in a double bind. It would need to continue to reduce interest rates to provide the liquidity to keep the economy ticking over and defend the value of US assets; but it would, even more, need to raise interest rates so as to attract a continuing inflow of funds from overseas to maintain the dollar, thus making it possible for the US to fund its historically unprecedented current account deficit. Yet how high would interest rates have to go to counteract the enormous downward pressure on the dollar that resulted from foreign investors trying to liquidate their portfolios? Could interest rates be simultaneously kept high enough to allow for the funding of the current account deficit and to prevent a flight of capital, and also low enough to avoid choking off growth?

Just the foregoing sort of scenario seemed on the agenda in the mid-1980s.[9] At that point, a vastly overvalued dollar, which had spurred an enormous financial expansion over the previous several years, had issued in a series of decreasingly supportable current account deficits, which made a major adjustment unavoidable. But when the dollar was finally nudged downward by way of the Plaza Accord, there followed a series of runs on the currency that ultimately brought about the stock market crash of 1987. At that point, interventions by the Japanese saved the day. Not only did the Japanese government play a major part in the bailout of the stock market, but, over the next several years, it also encouraged Japanese corporations to step up their investments in the US, while lowering Japanese interest rates to make that a more profitable proposition. It may be doubted, however, if the Japanese could assume a similar role today.

In sum, the US economy is vulnerable, through any one of a series of alternative channels, to a self-reinforcing international recession in the real economy that could set off, in a variety of ways, a financial explosion. It is liable as well to mutually exacerbating declines in asset and currency

---

[9] The threat of crisis that it potentially posed was limned out in S. Marris, *Deficits and the Dollar. The World Economy at Risk*, Washington, DC, Institute for International Economics, 1985.

markets that could carry devastating consequences for the real economy. The situation is made all the more dangerous – in view of the huge role of borrowing in driving the economy during the second half of the 1990s and the resulting build-up of debt – by the potential for a sudden shift toward saving instead of borrowing by households and especially corporations running for cover as the economy turns down.[10] These are the sort of processes that ushered in the East Asian and international crises of 1997–98. But, of course, it could not happen here.

---

[10] See J. Eatwell and L. Taylor, *Global Finance at Risk*, New York, Norton, 2000, pp. 131–5.

POSTSCRIPT TO THE PAPERBACK EDITION

Economic developments since this book went to press in summer 2001 have generally vindicated its analysis.[1] My bottom line was, and is, that, even today, there is little evidence that either the world economy, or its US component, has succeeded in transcending the long downturn, the very extended period of slowed growth that began around 1973. As a consequence, the US and world economies have had, and will continue to have, a difficult time avoiding a return to stagnation, or perhaps worse.

The reason the global system will struggle to regain its dynamism is quite straightforward. A lasting decline in the rate of profit in the international *manufacturing sector*, caused by the persistence of over-capacity and over-production, has been, and continues to be, fundamentally responsible for reduced profitability and slow growth on a system-wide scale over the long term. Successive attempts by government and corporations to restore profitability, especially by way of elevated interest rates and reduced wage and social spending growth have failed, tending to exacerbate the problem by holding down the growth of demand. Over-capacity actually worsened in the second half of the 1990s, not only becoming more severe in manufacturing, especially in high technology industries like computers and semi-conductors, but spreading to other sectors of the economy, especially key non-manufacturing New Economy

---

[1] I wish to express my profound thanks to Aaron Brenner and Tom Mertes for much indispensable help on matters both of content and style.

lines such as telecommunications. Thus, even as economic growth accelerated and the stock market took flight in the last years of the decade, profitability fell sharply, with the rate of return on capital stock in the non-financial corporate economy dropping by nearly 20 per cent between 1997 and 2000 (according to recently revised government figures). Despite the decade's record-long economic expansion, the non-financial corporate profit rate for the business cycle of the 1990s remained roughly the same as it had been for the business cycles of the 1970s and the 1980s, *decisively lower* than during the long boom of the 1950s and 1960s. It is because over-capacity leading to falling profitability had already become so intense even while the economic boom and stock market run-up of the second half of the 1990s were still gaining momentum that the cyclical downturn that ensued has been so difficult to surmount. It is because there was no profitability recovery to speak of during the 1990s as a whole that it is unlikely there will be any return to economic dynamism in the foreseeable future.

Non-Financial Corporate Net Profit Rate
(net profits/net capital stock)
(per cent)

Periods correspond to business cycles

1948–1959	1959–1969	1969–1979	1979–1990	1990–2000
11.6	13.1	9.6	8.8	9.7

Sources: Bureau of Economic Analysis website, NIPA 1.16 and Fixed Asset Tables

The recession that began early in 2001 distinguished itself from all of the others of the post-war epoch. Whereas previous recessions began with macroeconomic tightening by the Federal Reserve to rein in overheating and inflation, the current one began with the bursting of an equity price bubble and the onset of widespread over-capacity making for downward pressure on prices. It has therefore proved more intractable than most economic analysts expected. The majority failed to appreciate that the same mechanisms by which the stock market drove the economy upward as equity prices ascended would drive the economy downward as equity prices fell. They also failed to grasp how the build-up of over-capacity that took place during the stock market-led boom would serve to hold down the economy once the expansion ended and the economy entered recession. Finally and most generally, they failed to take on board how the freeing up of markets that has taken place during the past two decades has restored patterns of capitalist development reminiscent of the whole epoch before World War I.

The economy's continuing underlying weakness has been manifested in the fact that, as of the middle of 2003, it had responded hardly at all to an unprecedented economic stimulus unleashed by the government – an historic loosening of credit by the Fed, skyrocketing fiscal deficits courtesy of the Bush administration, and a declining dollar helped down by the Treasury. Non-residential investment had fallen significantly in every quarter but two since autumn 2000. Capacity utilization languished at or near post-war lows. Unemployment was continuing to rise. Profitability still remained well below its level of boom. The economy was left dependent for its vitality to a very large extent on the growth of consumer spending, itself made possible by mounting household debt, which was in turn dependent on a combination of hyper-low interest rates and rising housing prices, neither of which seemed sustainable for very long.

The Official Story of the Boom

The official story of the 1990s expansion can be found in the Council of Economic Advisers' *Economic Report of the President 2001* (issued in early 2001), as well as the speeches and testimony to Congress of Alan Greenspan. According to this view, the US economy's free markets, especially its unfettered financial markets – and in particular the pivotal role played by the US stock market in allocating capital – make it uniquely capable of technical advance and, in turn, rapid economic growth. It was thus the stock market's capacity to hot-house a technological revolution that enabled the US, in contrast to its laggard rivals in Europe and Japan, to escape from decades of stagnation and achieve an unprecedented boom. Share prices, on this view, succeeded in rising to unprecedented levels because they were able to anticipate the ever increasing profits that would be endowed by New Economy productivity growth. The underlying assumption was, of course, that 'markets know best' and that the equity market is able to pick out the most promising firms, for the most part to be found in the technology, media, and telecommunications sector (TMT). By virtue of their rising stock prices, such firms were thus enabled to finance stepped-up capital accumulation in advance of actually making profits. They could do this, either by issuing highly priced shares or borrowing against the huge collateral apparently represented by their inflated market valuation. Fund managers and lenders supplied the cash, so as not to miss out on the extraordinary growth opportunities the companies supposedly represented. The outcome, so the story goes, was a dynamic investment boom, making for accelerated productivity growth, leading to even higher expected profits, even greater investment, and so forth – what Alan Greenspan termed a 'virtuous cycle' of economic growth.

In reality, however, as this book argues in some detail, the process worked more or less in the opposite direction from that posited by the theorists of free capital markets and the New Economy. Far from rising on the wings of a productivity revolution, profitability in the non-farm economy fell sharply after 1997 as the expansion ascended to its peak, initially driven down by the precipitous rise of the dollar in the context of worsening over-capacity in the international manufacturing sector. Nevertheless, defying the downward trajectory of the profit rate, equity prices rose in an unprecedented manner, as the stock market systematically *mis*-directed equity purchases toward high technology firms despite the ever-increasing downward pressure on their rates of return. It was the growing disjuncture between the trajectory of profitability and of asset prices that shaped the economy through the second half of the 1990s, opening the way to disaster.

The run-up in stock purchases and share values was made possible in the first instance by a major loosening of credit. The original impetus for reduced borrowing costs came from the 1995 Reverse Plaza Accord among the governments of the US, Japan, and Germany, which had as its goal to drive up the dollar. This stimulated a huge influx of foreign funds onto US money markets, especially from East Asia, bringing about a sharp reduction in the cost of long term borrowing. But what kept the market on its upward path was the Fed's steadfast refusal to raise interest rates for the subsequent four years, even as asset prices went through the roof. Indeed, the Fed loosened credit at every sign of financial distress – the outbreak of the Mexican Peso crisis in winter 1994–5, the onset of the East Asian crisis in summer–fall 1997, the freezing up of international financial markets in autumn 1998, and even the Y2K computer adjustment at the turn of the millennium. And the result in every case was a new surge of the stock market. As Alan Greenspan well understood, with the elimination of the Federal budget deficit under Clinton and the steady rise of the dollar, the healthy growth of both investment and consumer demand had become dependent, at least for the time being, on the wealth effect of rising equity prices, and he had no intention of risking the economy's dynamism by allowing that to wane.

With their share prices skyrocketing, corporations were able to access funds with unprecedented ease through share issues or borrowing. By the end of the decade, annual borrowing by, as well as total indebtedness of, non-financial corporations had reached record levels. Firms that could not borrow cheaply turned to the equity market for their financing to an extent unheard of in the post-war epoch. On this basis, investment did leap ahead between 1995 and 2000, drove a powerful boom, characterized by a notable rise in productivity growth and, in turn, a brief breakout from a long period of wage stagnation. But, investment growth rested not on the reality of rising profits, actual or potential, but rather on corporations' access to essentially cost-free finance made possible by their soaring share prices, which itself came courtesy of the *mis*-information provided by the equity markets. As a result, it could only issue in over-investment. In this way the scope of over-capacity came to extend well beyond the manufacturing sector and especially into information technology. Supercharged investment growth did bring about a significant increase in productivity growth in a number of manufacturing and high-tech industries, but also gave rise to over-capacity in those very same lines. Over-supply thus trumped greater efficiency. The reductions in the growth of costs that resulted from increased productivity were more than offset by reductions in the increase of prices that stemmed from over-capacity. Consumers thus turned out to be the primary beneficiaries of a self-undermining process that brought ever lower profitability for non-financial corporations. As the end of the millennium came nearer, both the increase of investment and the rise in share prices proceeded in ever greater defiance of the gravitational pull of the falling rate of profit.

From Bubble to Bust in Telecom

The foregoing evolution was most dramatically evident in what were supposed to be the leading sectors of the US New Economy, information technology in general and telecommunications in particular.[2] The passage of the Telecommunications Act of 1996, which deregulated the telecommunications market, opened the industry to all comers, and paved the way to the telecommunications bubble. A phalanx of new entrants rushed in, hoping to capitalize on what they took for granted would be the endless increase of demand for their equipment from the infinitely expanding Internet. By expanding through mergers and acquisitions with the greatest speed possible, these companies sought to win the approval of equity markets bedazzled by growth and size, drive up their share prices, and secure the finance needed for economies of scale and rapid innovation. By virtue of what they assumed would be their resulting technological superiority, they expected to wrest market share from such firmly established behemoths as Deutsche Telekom, NTT, AT&T and Verizon. It was just one of the multiple Ponzi games that helped drive the economy in the second half of the 1990s.

The emerging telecommunications companies were soon laying down tens of millions of miles of fiber optic cable across the US and under the oceans, with the indispensable assistance of America's leading financial institutions, above all its greatest banking conglomerates. These 'one stop' financial supermarkets had emerged from an ever deepening process of

---

[2] For much of this section, and some of what follows, see my 'Towards the Precipice,' *London Review of Books*, 6 February 2003.

financial deregulation, closely overseen and patronized by the Clinton administration, which ultimately allowed them to combine investment banking and commercial banking. They were therefore supremely well placed to garner the fees for underwriting the share issues, floating the bonds, and organizing the mergers and acquisitions of the newly deregulated telecom industry. It is only natural that, in their role as investment bankers, they encouraged – and enabled – the telecommunications firms' drive to expand. In support of the effort, and to attract customers to their investment banking business, they were only too happy, in their role of commercial bankers, to lend their clients as much money as they wanted. Meanwhile, their ostensibly independent 'stock analysts' stoked the prices of their clients' shares by touting them to a gullible public, on the basis not of their profits, but their growing size or some other 'New Economy metric,' such as the number of optic lines they had laid down. The grateful companies then rewarded the investment banks with even more business.

In the processes of stock promotion, Salomon Smith Barney, the investment banking arm of Citigroup, played the vanguard role, led by their communications analyst, the appropriately named Jack Grubman. After passage of the Telecom Act, Salomon helped eighty-one telecom companies raise some $190 billion in debt and equity. It received hundreds of millions in underwriting fees and tens of millions more in mergers and acquisitions advice. Salomon's in-group of rising telecom stars included the soon to be notorious World.Com, Global Crossing, and Qwest. But Salomon and Grubman were hardly alone in such efforts. In the half decade after 1995, the top ten banks organized 1670 mergers and acquisitions valued at $1.3 trillion for telecommunications companies, receiving from them $13 billion in fees.

Money managers who stayed away from the action in telecom risked performing less well than their rivals and losing their jobs. As a result, institutional investors ended up buying telecom shares as if there was no tomorrow, driving their values into uncharted territory. Meanwhile, manifesting the sheep-like behavior for which they are rightly infamous, commercial banks showered the telecommunications industry with more funds than it could sensibly invest, virtually force-feeding expansion and guaranteeing over-capacity.

By spring 2000, at the apex of the stock market's ascent, the telecommunications companies produced less than 3 per cent of the country's GDP, yet their market capitalization, the value of their outstanding shares, had reached a staggering $2.7 trillion, or close to 15 per cent of the total for all US non-financial corporations. With such enormous apparent collateral, telecommunications firms could borrow without limit. Between 1996 and 2000, they took on $800 billion in bank debt and issued an additional $450 billion in bonds. On this basis, they were able to increase investment over the period in real terms (i.e. measured in 1996 dollars) at an annual average rate of more than 15 per cent per year and to increase jobs by a spectacular 331,000.

The problem, of course, was that everyone was doing it, thanks to unregulated product and financial markets. In 2000, no fewer than six US companies were building new, mutually competitive, nationwide fiber-optic networks. Hundreds more were laying down local ones and several additional firms were constructing lines under the ocean. All told, 39 million miles of fiber optic line now criss-crossed the planet, enough to circle the globe 1566 times. A mountainous glut was unavoidable, with the utilization rate of telecommunications networks hovering in 2001 at a staggeringly low 2.5–3 per cent, that of undersea cable just 13 per cent. This mass of sunk, fixed capital cannot but weigh on the rate of return for the foreseeable future, in a manner analogous to the bubble-driven build-ups of railroad equipment during the nineteenth century. There could hardly be clearer evidence that the market – and especially the market for finance – does *not* know best.

Making a profit became virtually impossible for telecom companies. Even as their equity prices soared into the heavens and their purchases of new plant, equipment, and software mounted, their profits collapsed. Having reached a peak of $35.2 billion in 1996, the year of the telecommunications deregulation, profits (after the payment of interest on company debt) in the communications industry sank to $6.1 billion in 1999 and *minus* $5.5 billion in 2000, especially as interest payments on the industry's climbing debt exploded. This set in place the conditions for a crash and recession driven by collapsing profits and share prices – a domino effect beginning with the dot.coms and proceeding to the telecommunications carriers, then to their suppliers the telecom equipment makers, then to their suppliers the component makers, and finally to their suppliers the chip producers.

Before the downturn hit, it must be noted, the huge rise in US demand that resulted from the speeding up of the US economic expansion in the last years of the decade, especially in telecommunications, plus the still rising dollar, rescued not just the US but the world economy from the international crisis of 1997–1998, and incited a new international economic upturn in 1999–2000. The rapid growth of US imports was most strongly felt in East Asia, especially Singapore, Korea, and Taiwan, where the unprecedented call for high-tech components practically single-handedly drove the region from deep recession to rapid growth. But US imports were also indispensable for western Europe, where US demand for cars, machine tools, and other products fueled the rapid comebacks of both the German and Italian economies, while the low Euro eased the area's producers' access to third markets. Developing countries like Brazil were also granted a brief reprieve. Simply put, the entire global expansion was driven by the US stock market bubble.

The Crisis of Profitability

The stock market collapse began in spring-summer 2000, set off by a never ending series of horrific corporate profits reports, especially in the New Economy. It quickly precipitated a sharp cyclical downturn, first by reversing the wealth effect of rising equity prices and then by revealing the mountain of corporate indebtedness and the mass of redundant productive capacity that constituted the dual legacy of the bubble-driven investment boom. The resulting recession was made much more serious by virtue of the fact that it unfolded within the context of a long downturn that was itself the expression of a longstanding and now much exacerbated problem of manufacturing over-capacity and over-production.

With their on-paper assets sharply reduced, firms not only found it more difficult to borrow, but less attractive to do so, especially since declining profits and the growing threat of bankruptcy led them to look to repair their over-burdened balance sheets. With far more plant, equipment, and software than they could profitably set in motion, they were obliged either to reduce prices or leave capacity unused, sustaining falling rates of return either way. To cope with falling profitability, they cut back on capital expenditures, while reducing employment and wages so as to bring down costs. Across the economy these moves placed downward pressure on productivity growth and decreased the growth of purchasing power, which, in turn, forced down capacity utilization and further undermined productivity growth – a mutually reinforcing squeeze on both the cost and the demand side. A deepening crisis of profitability – seriously exacerbated by the relentless burden of interest payments on the huge overhang of corporate debt – further intensified the equity price plunge, setting off the rapid fall into recession.

In the communications industry, corporate profits net of interest fell to *minus* $5.8 billion in 2001 and *minus* $11.7 billion in 2002. By the middle of 2002, telecommunications shares had lost 95 per cent of their value, with the result that about $2.5 trillion of market capitalization (and shareholder wealth) had disappeared. Because telecommunications had accounted for such a disproportionate share of the economy-wide increases both of market capitalization and of capital accumulation during the last years of the expansion, the reverberations of the collapse of profits and equity values in this sector were immense. In 2000, the industry was responsible for 12 per cent of the US economy's equipment spending and one-quarter of the increase in such spending. In 1999–2000, telecommunications investment grew at an annual rate of around 10 per cent. But in 2001, it probably fell by more than 20 per cent. Telecommunications debt meanwhile stood at around $525 billion, equal to the value of both the outstanding junk bonds at the end of the 1980s and the cost of the Savings and Loan bailout. In the very brief period between the end of 2000 and the middle of 2002, more than sixty companies went bankrupt and the telecommunications industry laid off more than 500,000 workers, 50 per cent more than it hired in its spectacular expansion between 1996 and 2000. By comparison, it had taken the auto industry two full decades to shed 732,000 jobs.

The precipitously declining orders of the telecommunications companies devastated the profitability of the equipment makers who supply them. These include many of the leading lights of the high-tech boom, most of whom sustained catastrophic collapses in their share prices and financial conditions, notably including the once legendary Cisco Systems, as well as Lucent, Nortel, and Motorola. When the leading equipment makers were stymied by the drop-off of demand from the telecommunications carriers, they could not avoid dealing a heavy blow to their components suppliers, including the makers of semi-conductors. Such stock market darlings as JDS Uniphase and Sycamore descended into oblivion. The semi-conductor industry, hard-hit by the steep drop-off in computer sales, as well as the telecommunications crash, entered into its worst downturn since the early 1980s, with sales decreasing by 50 per cent in 2001 and failing to rise at all in 2002. All told, the chain reactions set off by the fall of the telecommunications industry accounted for about a quarter of the decline in economic growth between the first half of 2000 and the first half of 2001.

The crisis of over-production and equity values in telecommunications and related industries partook of a broader crisis in the high technology sector more generally, prominently including computers and semi-conductors. After having averaged $14 billion and $21 billion respectively from 1995 through 1997, profits net of interest in the industrial machinery and equipment industry (including computers) and the electronic and other electrical equipment industry (including semi-conductors) fell to $7.2 billion and $3.4 billion, respectively, in 1999 and *minus* $6.6 billion and *minus* $3.2 billion, respectively, in 2001. The depth and breadth of this crisis is revealed in a *Wall Street Journal* analysis, published on 16 August 2001, of 4200 companies listed on the NASDAQ Stock Index, home of the New Economy. For these companies, losses in the twelve months between 1 July 2000 and 30 June 2001 totaled no less than $148.3 billion. This was a little more than the $145.3 billion in profits these same companies had reported during the entire period from September 1995 through June 2000! As one economist pithily put it, 'What it means is that with the benefit of hindsight, the late '90s never happened.'

The crisis in information technology occurred in connection with, and constituted one indispensable element of, the long maturing crisis of the manufacturing sector, which was the main force driving the economy down into recession. Already between 1997 and 2000, increasing international competition leading to worsening global over-capacity and an inexorably rising dollar had brought down the manufacturing profit rate by 15 per cent, detonating the profitability crisis of the broader economy. With aggregate demand declining, these pressures very much intensified, as evidenced by US manufacturers' cutting back of their foreign direct investment by 37 per cent in 2001, and by that amount again in 2002. In 2001, world manufacturing prices fell 2.1 per cent, after having declined at an average annual pace of 4 per cent between 1995 and 2000; the US manufacturing import share rose by 10 per cent, compared to 1999, and 20 per cent compared to 1995; US manufacturing exports fell by 7 per cent; and US manufacturing imports rose to 150 per cent of manufacturing exports, compared to just 120 per cent as recently as 1996–97. In this context, in 2001, US manufacturing output (real value-added) declined by a staggering 6 per cent, employment (measured in hours) fell by 4.8 per cent, and capacity utilization declined by 7.1 per cent, to its lowest level since the recession of the early 1980s. Meanwhile, investment fell sharply, by 5.4 per cent. With output and capacity utilization, as well as expenditures on new plant, equipment, and software, falling off so rapidly, there was no way employers could reduce the labor force fast enough to prevent a huge fall in productivity growth. The growth of output per hour in manufacturing plunged from 6.1 per cent in 2000 to *minus* 0.4 per cent in 2001.

Manufacturing firms responded to these excruciating pressures by brutally cutting back employees' compensation, and the growth of real wages fell from 3.9 per cent in 2000 to *minus* 1.2 per cent in 2001. But with productivity and capacity utilization diving as they did, employers could not prevent unit labor costs from rising by 2 per cent. Nor could they stop manufacturing prices from falling by 0.4 per cent, after a 2 per cent drop in 2000. The outcome was that, in 2001, the rate of profit for the manufacturing sector fell a further 21.3 per cent, or a total of 33.5 per cent from its 1997 peak. Manufacturing profits net of interest declined by 31 per cent in 2001, a total of 44.4 per cent from the 1997 high point, with motor vehicles profits leading the way down, at *minus* $9.4 billion.

The manufacturing sector, *by itself*, was responsible for the entire fall in the rate of profit for the non-financial corporate sector as a whole in 2001. That is, if the manufacturing sector is left out, the non-financial corporate sector experienced roughly the same rate of profit in 2001 as in 2000 (This does not, of course, mean that there were not parts of the non-manufacturing non-financial corporate sector that experienced profitability crises, like telecommunications, but that their losses were compensated for by other industries' gains). The fall in manufacturing profits (before the payment of interest) accounted for well over 100 per cent of the profits decline experienced by the non-financial corporate sector in 2001, which would have achieved an increase in profits of 6 per cent in that year had manufacturing been excluded. As it was, however, the profitability crisis in manufacturing was severe enough in 2001 to inflict a 10 per cent fall in the rate of profit on the non-financial corporate sector. As a result, by 2001, the non-financial corporate profit rate, having already experienced a 19 per cent decline between 1997 and 2000, had fallen by 27 per cent from its 1997 peak.

From Corporate Crisis to Corporate Scandals

Against the background of profitability crisis and collapsing equity values, an unending succession of accounting scandals has wracked a growing number of the country's leading corporations, casting a further shadow on business prospects. These frauds have been marked by top managers' systematic cover-up of company expenditures and corresponding inflation of company profits, as well as their personal appropriation of company assets. Many of the firms affected were only recently among the top high-tech stars of the equity markets, including not only Enron, but also the telecommunications giants Global Crossing, Qwest, and World.com, as well as AOL Time Warner, Bristol Meyers, Kmart, Lucent Technologies, Merck, Reliant Services, Rite Aid, Vivendi, and Xerox, plus the two leading US banks, Citigroup and JP Morgan Chase, along with Merrill Lynch and others.

The scandals bore witness not just to the staggering level of individual corruption characteristic of American-style crony capitalism, but to the systemic problems plaguing the real economy. Their raison d'etre has thus been entirely straightforward: to cover up the reality of an increasingly desperate corporate profits picture. As profitability declined, corporations depended to an ever greater extent on their rising equity prices for access to the investment funds to compete and cover fast-climbing interest payments. But, rising equity values are themselves, sooner rather than later, dependent upon rising profits, and rising profits were precisely what the corporations lacked. Confronted with this patent failure of 'fundamentals,' corporate executives faced mounting pressure to keep stock prices aloft by any means necessary. Since their own compensation had become so dependent upon the value of their stock options, they also faced an apparently irresistible temptation to cook the books.

As the economy entered the new millennium and the profits crisis intensified, bringing powerful downward pressure on equities prices, one after another great corporation – especially in the New Economy technology, media, and telecommunications sector – thus falsified its accounts so as to exaggerate short term earnings in order to sustain the value of their shares. In so doing, they received aid bordering on the heroic from the country's largest banks, which were only too willing to employ the latest innovations in 'structured finance' to improve the appearance of their clients' corporate balance sheets.

These same banks were also more than pleased to advise the ostensibly independent 'stock analysts' whom they employed – despite the patent conflict of interest thereby entailed – as to how to value the shares of their clients, in the unlikely event that those analysts were mesmerized by the fact of insufficient returns. Nor were they above straightforwardly bribing their corporate customers, by handing their chief executives millions of dollars worth of shares, often in red-hot initial public offerings, in order to secure their financial business – especially since doing so is not illegal unless it can be proved that the forwarding of the bribe was the explicit condition for contracting the service. Meanwhile, the country's largest and oldest accounting firms, which had come increasingly during the last two decades to double as investment consultants for the very same companies whose books they were supposed to be auditing, kept the game going by turning a blind eye to their clients' financial shenanigans.

A study by SmartstockInvestor.com compared the profits announced quarterly to shareholders and media, with those later reported to the Security Exchange Commission, by the corporations listed on the NASDAQ 100 for the first three quarters of 2001. The former were calculated on a so-called 'pro-forma' basis, which allow firms exceedingly wide latitude. The latter, as legally required, were calculated according to strict Generally Accepted Accounting Principles (GAAP). These one hundred corporations reported earnings of $19 billion to the public. However, they could not avoid later communicating *losses* of $82.3 billion for the same period to the Securities and Exchange Commission – a difference of $101 billion!

For sheer scale and scope of corruption, US crony capitalism clearly has no equal among developed economies. As the *Financial Times* recently demonstrated, executives and directors from the twenty-five largest US public companies to go bankrupt since January 2001 – whom the *Financial Times* calls 'the barons of bankruptcy' – came away with no less than $3.3 billion as their companies went under. But this only scratches the surface of the titanic redistribution of wealth accomplished by US corporate leaders over the course of the last decade or so. Between 1997 and 2001, insiders in the telecommunications industry cashed out some $18 billion in shares, unloading more than half this total in 2000, the year the price of telecom shares peaked. Between 1995 and 1999, the value of stock options granted to US executives more than quadrupled, from $26.5 billion to $110 billion, a figure equal to one fifth of non-financial corporate profits (net of interest) in the latter year. Whereas in 1992, corporate CEOs held 2 per cent of all equity outstanding of US corporations, by 2002 they owned 12 per cent. This must be the among the most spectacular acts of expropriation in the history of capitalism.

Recession and the Response of Government

Under the impact of the collapse of equity prices and the crisis of profitability, the economy as a whole decelerated faster than at any other time since World War II, with the growth of output and investment falling between mid-2000 and mid-2001 at their fastest annual rates of the postwar epoch. This is all the more understandable in view of the fact that, according to the Council of Economic Advisers, the information technology sector, which constituted just 8 per cent of GDP, had accounted for almost a third of all growth of GDP between 1995 and 2000. GDP growth dropped from 5 per cent for the year ending in mid-2000 to -0.1 per cent for the year ending mid-2001. Non-residential investment growth fell from 9 per cent to -5 per cent over the same interval. In response, US corporations began cutting wage growth and reducing their labour forces in an effort to restore competitiveness, placing huge pressure on their rivals to respond in kind. In 2001, non-farm employment (measured in hours) fell by 1.2 per cent. Simultaneously the growth of real wages which had reached 3.5 per cent in 2000 was cut back to *minus* 0.1 per cent in 2001, and total nominal compensation remained at virtually the same level in both 2001 and 2002 as it had been in the fourth quarter of 2000 (on an annualized basis). The ensuing shock to aggregate demand set off a powerful downward spiral in which pressure on prices resulting from worsening over-capacity led to falling profitability, which issued in declining investment, making for rising unemployment and bankruptcies, as well as downward pressure of wages, and, in turn, reductions in aggregate demand that fed back into further repression of price increase and profitability, and so on.

As the US entered its cyclical downturn, the rest of the world followed suit. The stock market's last upward thrust had rescued not only the US, but also the world economy as a whole, setting off a short-lived boom. But with US equity prices and investment collapsing, especially in high technology, the process was reversed. Under the impact of plummeting US imports, the economies of Japan, Europe, and East Asia lost steam as fast as the US, while much of the developing world, notably Latin America, was plunged, after a brief honeymoon, back into crisis. A mutually-reinforcing international recessionary process was thus unleashed, a chain reaction rendered all the more problematic by the degree to which the rest of the world had, in the face of stagnating domestic demand, oriented their economies to exports over the previous two decades – and thus perforce toward an expanding US domestic market that had itself relied upon a stock market bubble. Because the economies of the US's trading partners are so much more dependent on exports in general – and exports to the US in particular – than vice versa, and because the US possesses a far greater propensity to import than do its trading partners, especially with the dollar as high as it has been, the descent into cyclical downturn reduced the capacity of the rest of the world to absorb US imports much more than vice versa. The ratio of US import growth to export growth thus increased, widening the US current account deficit, and it became even more difficult for the US to rely on export increase to support its own growth. Whereas US real exports and real imports had increased by 9.7 per cent and 13.2 per cent, respectively, in 2000, they increased by *minus* 5.4 per cent and *minus* 2.9 per cent, respectively, in 2001 and *minus* 1.6 per cent and 3.7 per cent, respectively, in 2002. As the rest of the world, deprived of its US motor, sank ever further into recession, the US could look only to itself to launch an economic recovery upon which the whole global economy depended.

To stem the plunge of the US and the world economy from the latter part of 2000, the Federal Reserve lowered the cost of borrowing sharply and rapidly, reducing interest rates on 12 occasions between January 2001 and November 2002. But, as the Fed has discovered, while rate cuts can restart economies slowed by rate increases to stem inflation, as they have in all the post-war cyclical downturns prior to this one, they do not work anywhere near as well to revive an economy driven down by over-capacity and the resulting downward pressure on prices.

With respect to investment, the key to economic health, the Fed has, in Keynes's famous phrase, been 'pushing on a string,' unable to stem continuing decline. With far more plant and equipment than they can possibly use, non-financial corporations have had little incentive to increase investment, no matter how low interest rates have fallen. On the contrary, their staggering debt, which rose from 73 to 90 per cent of their GDP between 1995 and 2001, has given them every motivation to mend their balance sheets, and their so doing has made it that much more difficult for them to invest. Having increased their indebtedness at the sizzling pace of 10.5 per cent per year during the last three years of the boom, non-financial corporations raised this by just 5.4 per cent and 1.4 per cent, respectively, in 2001 and 2002. Non-residential investment, in plant and equipment, has thus fallen like a stone, pressing the economy downward. From an average annual rate of 12.5 per cent in the first half of 2000, it dropped to 0.1 per cent in the second half of 2000, to −5.2 per cent in 2001, to −5.7 per cent in 2002, to −4.8 per cent (on an annual basis) in the first quarter of 2003.

Although they failed to stem the slowdown of capital accumulation, the Fed's historic interest rate reductions were able to cut short the economy's frightening downward spiral of 2001 by driving up consumer spending, returning the economy to growth, however sluggish, from the turn of the new year. Primarily by borrowing against homes, households increased their indebtedness at a significantly faster pace than even during the boom. The average increase in household debt was 25 per cent greater in 2001–2002 than between 1995 and 2000. And on this basis consumers succeeded in sustaining their spending. The growth of consumer expenditures, itself dependent on the growth of household debt, has been the decisive factor in keeping the economy turning over, raising GDP growth from a mere 0.3 per cent in 2001 to a more respectable 2.4 per cent in 2002 and a less respectable, but still positive, 1.9 per cent (annualized) in the first half of 2003. It is Washington's hope that it will hold up long enough for corporations to work off their excess capacity and begin investing again.

While the Fed implemented its monetary stimulus, the Bush administration added what seemed to be a major fiscal stimulus modeled after that of Ronald Reagan, forcing through Congress enormous cuts in taxation and major increases in military spending. But these measures are less potent than they look, and are likely to have a declining impact on the economy. The administration did throw a few small bones to the mass of the population, reducing taxes on married people, increasing the child care tax credit, and moving forward in time reductions in rates called for by tax act of 2001. The resulting stimulus amounts to perhaps 0.5 per cent GDP. The remaining tax reductions decrease the levy on dividends and therefore benefit the very rich almost exclusively. As a consequence, they will go much more to increase savings and the purchase of financial assets than consumption, doing little to improve aggregate demand. The fact that tax cuts at a federal level will have the effect of reducing revenue to money-strapped state governments, forcing them to cut back on spending and in some cases to increase taxation, is likely to counteract much, though not all, of what stimulus they do impart.

In the wake of 9/11, the growth of military spending reached 6 per cent in 2001 and 10 per cent in 2002, and enabled the equities of the nation's nine largest defence contractors to perform 30 per cent better than the average firm listed on the S&P 500 index in the year following 9/11. Amounting to about 65 per cent and 80 per cent respectively of the total increases in Federal spending in these years, defence spending did unquestionably help to push the economy forward. Nevertheless, the growth of military expenditures was responsible for an increase of GDP of no more than 0.75 per cent *in total* during 2001 and 2002. Beginning in the second quarter of 2003, ballooning costs for Iraq caused military expenditures to explode upward and to significantly raise the rate of (otherwise lagging) GDP growth. Whether such high levels of defence spending can be sustained for very long is, however, an open question.

The Contradictions of Policy

The Fed's turn to ever easier credit – supplemented by the government's greater fiscal deficits – has brought a semblance of order. But it has also, precisely in so doing, inflated the value of financial assets across the board, exacerbating three enormous 'imbalances' that originated in the second half of the 1990s – overpriced corporate equities, an unsustainable boom in the housing market, and record current account deficits. The sustenance and expansion of these bubbles poses an ever increasing threat to the health of the underlying economy.

Equity prices have, of course, fallen sharply. Paradoxically, however, their decline has failed to bring stock values back into line with profits, because these have fallen just as far. By September 2002, the S&P 500 composite index had declined by about 40 per cent from its average level in 2000, the last year of the bubble. However, profits at those 500 firms fell just as far, with the result that their price earnings ratio failed to decrease at all. It could hardly be more obvious that, in the absence of the Fed's cheap credit policy, share prices would have fallen a great deal further with respect to underlying earnings. The Fed has made the business climate sunnier. But, in so doing, it has, in a very real sense, sustained the stock market bubble in the face of economic recession. A serious 'correction' now could wreck the economy.

While share prices have been declining over the past two years, the price of housing has skyrocketed. Home prices increased 7 per cent in 2002, and by more than 33 per cent over the past four years (compared to less than 10 per cent for the GDP deflator). Just as the Fed's easy credit inflated the stock market bubble of the late 1990s, its rock bottom interest rates have fueled the current run-up in real estate. Major fund transfers from ailing equity markets into the red-hot housing market have also been essential. While stock market capitalization was falling by $6 trillion between 2000 and 2002, the value of real estate was rising by $3 trillion, with stimulative consequences quite analogous to those of the wealth effect of the stock market between 1995 and 2000. As the collateral represented by their houses has risen higher and interest rates fallen lower, homeowners have been able to increase their borrowing and, in turn, their expenditure. Last year, as home sales reached a record $6.4 million at record prices, homeowners extracted an unprecedented $350 billion in capital gains through the sale of their houses, covered by the increased indebtedness of the buyers. At the same time, homeowners who kept their houses took advantage of lower borrowing costs and the increased value of their real estate to refinance their mortgages and 'cash out' a record $200 billion of equity (such extractions had averaged around $40 billion annually between 1995 and 2000). Meanwhile, homeowners were netting a still further $130 billion by taking out home equity loans.

As Alan Greenspan calmly summed up this titanic process in his March 2003 speech on 'The Home Mortgage Market,' 'the amount of previously built-up equity extracted from owner occupied homes last year . . . totaled $700 billion . . . or more than 10 per cent of estimated equity at the beginning of the year . . . [an amount] similar to the increase in mortgage debt.' Mortgage equity withdrawals amounted to no less than 4 per cent of disposable income in the year ending June 2003, and obviously played a huge role in driving up consumer spending in that period. But given that it depended upon bubbling home prices and falling interest rates, it is hard to see how such cashing out can fail to decline significantly in the not-too-distant future, since inflation in real estate seems bound to slow and interest rates, already near post-war lows, seem more likely to rise than fall. If it does, the growth of consumer expenditures, the main source of the economy's current economic dynamism, is bound to be hard hit.

Finally, by enabling consumer spending to continue to increase, the Fed enabled Americans to keep raising their imports right through the recession, even as US exports stagnated as a result of the international cyclical downturn and the decline of purchasing power in most of the rest of the world. By 2002, US imports had risen to 142 per cent of exports compared to around 125 per cent as recently as 1999 and 110 per cent in 1996–1997. The US current account deficit thus set a new record in 2002, reaching 5 per cent of GDP, and seemed to be on its way to breaking it again in 2003. The ongoing expansion of the US current account deficit has provided an indispensable stimulus to the rest of the world economy, keeping it turning over. In particular, it has enabled overseas manufacturers to take an ever greater share of the US market at the expense of US producers, all the more so to the extent that the dollar remained so over-valued. But the rise of the current account deficit has itself depended on the willingness of the rest of the world to finance the increase of US consumption, thereby enabling its own exports and manufacturing output to continue to grow.

Until recently, overseas investors had been more than happy to fund the US current account deficit, making huge direct investments in the US and buying up enormous quantities of corporate equities and bonds during the late 1990s boom. But as the American economy slowed and the US stock market declined, the rest of the world found US private assets decreasingly attractive. Purchases of corporate and Treasury Bonds, as well as bonds sold by US agencies such as Fannie Mae and Freddy Mac, have continued to grow smartly. But both equity purchases by the rest of the world and foreign direct investment have collapsed – the former dropping from an average of $106 billion for 1998 through 2000 to $18.6 billion in 2002, the latter declining from an annual average of $190 billion for 1998 through 2000 to $66.6 billion in 2001 and *minus* 6.8 billion in 2002. Indeed, purchases by private overseas investors were able to cover a shrinking proportion of the US current account deficit, with rapidly increasing purchases by foreign central banks required to cover the rest. As a result of this disenchantment with US assets on the part of foreign buyers, as well as the disparity in the cost of borrowing between the US and Europe, where interest rates have failed to fall as quickly, pressure on the dollar has continued to mount, with the result that the dollar fell by 37 per cent against the Euro between the start of 2001 and the middle of 2003, 27 per cent over the last year.

The dollar's decline against the Euro would tend, all else equal, to make exporting easier and importing more difficult. But, under current conditions, it may fail to bring about all that much improvement in the US current account deficit, while seriously undermining the European economy. The shock of a skyrocketing Euro will likely exacerbate the already serious slowdown in Europe, perhaps pushing key economies, like Germany, further into negative growth. European recession could reduce European demand for US goods, offsetting much of the expected benefit for US exporters from the decline of the dollar. In any case, were the dollar to continue to fall, the Federal Reserve could soon be faced with an excruciating choice: either let the currency drop and risk a wholesale liquidation of US properties by foreign investors – which might not only wreak havoc in the asset markets but also set off a real run on the dollar – or raise interest rates and risk pushing the economy back into deep recession.

In fact, so far, the overall decline in the dollar's exchange rate has been relatively limited. It has taken place almost entirely in terms of the

Euro and to only a small extent in terms of the currencies of East Asia. This is the case, even though trade with East Asia has been primarily responsible for the growth of US trade and current account deficits. The reason that the dollar has held up against East Asian currencies is that, led by Japan and China, East Asian governments, in order to sustain their countries' exports to the US, have entered the currency markets to an ever increasing extent to prevent the dollar value of their currencies from rising and have gone on to re-cycle their mounting current account surpluses into dollar denominated assets, mainly financial assets, especially US Treasury and agency bonds. Without these official purchases, returns to US assets, especially interest rates on corporate and/or Treasury and agency bonds, would have had to rise significantly. Alternatively, the dollar would have had to fall precipitously, forcing down the value of US assets. By closing the rising financing gap that would otherwise have resulted, East Asian governments have thus enabled the Fed and the administration to pursue hyper-expansionary policies that would, in their absence, very likely have already been cut short by rising borrowing costs and/or a downward spiral of currency and asset prices, inviting a new recession across the globe.

The Fed's ever easier credit has, with the help of effectively subsidized loans from East Asian governments to US entities, not only enabled US asset price and current account bubbles to continue to inflate. It has also had the effect of slowing the adjustments that are normally indispensable to enable a productive economy to emerge from cyclical downturn and embark on a new growth path. The sharply reduced cost of borrowing, as well as the increased consumption that this has made possible, has enabled high-cost low-profit firms to stay in business. This has kept superfluous and inefficient means of production in operation, inflating supply, depressing prices, and slowing the recovery of profitability. In the second quarter of 2003, after three years of cyclical downturn, capacity utilization in the manufacturing sector, at 72.7 per cent, had fallen to its lowest level of the entire post-war epoch – down not only from 83.5 per cent in the second quarter of 2000, but from 75.7 per cent in the second quarter of 2002. Capacity utilization in information technology was far lower – with telecommunications equipment at 53.4 per cent and semi-conductors at 64.6 per cent. Even by the first quarter of 2003, annualized profits (net of interest) in manufacturing remained about $73 billion, or 40 per cent, below their 1997 peak, while those for communications, at *minus* $11.3 billion, were $46 billion below their 1996 high point. In just three years, between June 2000 and June 2003, the manufacturing sector had shrunk by about 15 per cent in terms of employment, losing almost 2.7 million jobs. This accounted for virtually all of the jobs lost in the entire non-farm sector in that period. Nor was there any sign that the hemorrhaging had ceased. In the quarter ending in July 2003, the non-farm economy lost a further 192,000 jobs, of which 183,000 were in manufacturing.

The contrast between the manufacturing sector, plus a handful of non-manufacturing high-tech industries, and the rest of the economy could hardly have been greater. Most of non-manufacturing has, so far, come through the cyclical downturn relatively unscathed. By the first quarter of 2003, annualized profits (net of interest) for the non-financial sector, excluding both manufacturing and communications, were only about 5 per cent below their level of 2000, 10 per cent off their 1997 peak, with profits in retail trade having grown more or less steadily between 1995 and 2003 and those in wholesale trade and other services remaining more or less flat over that period. The performance of finance was most spectacular of all. Leaving aside the crisis year of 1998, financial profits had, from the mid-1990s, enjoyed a virtually unbroken ascent, and in the first quarter of 2003 they were more than 35 per cent above their level of 1996. Between June 2000 and June 2003, the service sector as a whole had gained two million jobs. Clearly, for this large swath of the economy, the Fed's interest rate reductions had worked wonders. Consumer spending, based to a large degree on household borrowing against home equity, not to mention runaway housing prices, had kept retail trade, wholesale trade, and other services turning over smartly. Profits stemming heavily from mortgage related business, as well bond trading and underwriting – all tied to declining interest rates – enabled banks and securities firms to continue to achieve dramatically increasing prosperity, even despite the huge fall in equity prices and big reductions in the growth of corporate borrowing. But the big question that obviously imposed itself was how long could the economy move forward by way of the expansion of service and financial sectors that were based directly or indirectly on the growth of domestic consumption, itself dependent upon the vertiginous growth of household and government debt, when key goods-producing sectors remained weighed down by over-capacity and reduced profitability, when overseas producers were grabbing ever greater shares of the US goods market, when exports were falling ever further behind imports with no hope of closing the gap at current exchange rates by way of stepped-up sales abroad of either goods or services, and when the US could not come close to funding its current account deficits without ever increasing assistance from East Asian governments?

*

Between the middle of 2000 and the middle of 2003, the Fed decreased its short term interest rate from 6.5 per cent to a post-1958 low of 1 per cent (including its further 0.25 per cent reduction in June). At the same time, the government's fiscal position moved from a surplus of 1.4 per cent to a projected deficit of 4 per cent of GDP, or $450 billion. During the same interval, the trade weighted value of the dollar fell by more than 10 per cent. Nevertheless, despite this gargantuan governmental stimulus, the economy barely budged. During the first half of 2003, annualized expenditures on plant, equipment, and software still languished 12 per cent below their peak of 2000. In the same period, annualized growth of GDP fell to 1.9 per cent, and a mere 1 per cent, if the huge leap in military spending on Iraq is left out of account. Meanwhile, unemployment rose to 6.2 per cent, and jobs were continuing to disappear at an alarming rate. As the Fed was obliged to acknowledge in June 2003, 'the economy has yet to exhibit sustainable growth.'

It is true that, by mid-summer 2003, with the administration's tax cuts starting to take effect and military expenditures for Iraq rising fast, there was mounting evidence that the government's ever more expansionary policies were finally issuing in stepped-up economic activity. As important, radical cut backs of wage growth and employment had brought about a major increase in corporate profits, offering the hope of a desperately needed investment turnaround, although the implications for growth remained uncertain, as the repression of wages and job reductions simultaneously held down aggregate demand. Yet, even if the economic acceleration turned out to be real, there remained serious doubts about its sustainability, for, driven mainly by the debt-dependent consumption and expanding bubbles that were resulting from the government's reduced interest rates and yawning decifits, it appeared to be taking up where the expansion of the late 1990s had left off, with similar vulnerabilities.

During the first six months of 2003, long term interest rates had plummeted to near post-war lows, as the economy floundered, as investors assumed greater risk in their search for higher yields, and as the Fed seemed to promise to hold down the cost of borrowing until deflation was definitively defeated. A bond market bubble blew up. But, when, apparently in the midst of an intensifying campaign to head off falling prices, the Fed suddenly revealed its belief that the economic outlook was improving, the hitherto over-bought bond market violently reversed itself, and long term rates shot up with a rapidity unseen for many years. The worry was that this was only the beginning, that interest rates would not only further correct themselves, but continue to rise, as the more rapid growth of demand brought higher prices and greater demand for loans. Were they to do so, the housing bubble might very well cease to inflate and mortgage equity extraction begin to fall, seriously undermining the ongoing growth of consumption that had driven the economy since the end of 2000.

Meanwhile, from early 2003, even as bond prices rose and interest rates fell, apparently as an expression of the economy's underlying weakness, equity prices took off on a new, uninterrupted ascent. Defying the disinflationary trend that appeared to be worrying the bond market, the stock market conveyed ever more optimistic expectations, as the S&P500 rose by 18 per cent in five months. This was no doubt as the had Fed hoped. Nevertheless, by late June 2003, according the *Financial Times*, the price-earning ratio of the S&P 500 had reached 33:1 compared to an historical average of about 14:1. A month later, Thomson Financial Network reported that for the equity market as a whole, the ratio of sales to purchases by corporate insiders was running $11.32:1, that for NASDAQ a shocking $1177:1. It was beginning to have the feel of the late 1990s bubble.

Over the same half year period, as exports effectively stagnated, imports leaped upward at an annualized rate of almost 10 per cent, with the result that the level of imports came to outdistance that of exports by an astonishing 50 per cent. This meant that exports would have to rise 50 per cent faster than imports simply to prevent the trade deficit from rising. The current account deficit naturally broke still further records, but overseas private investors were proving less willing than ever to cover it by way of purchasing US assets. During the second quarter of 2003, according to the *Financial Times*, Japan and China were obliged to cover an estimated 45 per cent of the US current account deficit, buying about $39 billion and $27 billion worth of dollars, respectively, compared to a current account deficit of approximately $147 billion. These purchases did assure international economic stability in the short term. But they raised serious questions about its sustainability in the medium or long term.

To the extent that the East Asian governments continue to buy dollars to keep their own currencies relatively cheap, they will drive up the US current account deficit even further, by holding down US exports and making possible increased US imports, which are themselves pushed upward by the continued availability of the Fed's cheap credit to US consumers. They will also find themselves obliged to continue to invest their own countries' correspondingly increased surpluses in US denominated assets, with ominous implications for the world economy. On the one hand, the influx of East Asian funds onto US financial markets, by pushing down the cost of borrowing, will tend, directly or indirectly, to fuel the further expansion of ongoing asset price bubbles in equities and real estate. On the other hand, the growth of East Asian exports puffed up by both the high dollar and government subsidized US demand will continue to undermine US industry, while exacerbating over-capacity in manufacturing on a global scale. This is, of course, much the same syndrome that has plagued the world economy and its US component, throughout the bubble-driven boom and into the cyclical downturn. It is a self-undermining process in which the inexorable rise of US obligations to the rest of the world enables the rest of the world to grow through exports at the expense of US productive power and therefore of the capacity of the US to honor those obligations ... opening the way to rising interest rates, faling asset prices, and a plummeting dollar that would undercut a US and global recovery. In the middle of 2002, Alan Greenspan announced that the recession was over. But the economy is still far from out of the woods.

10 August 2003

APPENDIX I

PROFIT RATES AND PRODUCTIVITY GROWTH: DEFINITIONS AND SOURCES

I. PROFIT RATES

THE RATE OF PROFIT IN THE PRIVATE ECONOMY AND ITS COMPONENT INDUSTRIES

Unless otherwise stated, the rate of profit always refers to the net rate of profit, defined, standardly, as net profits over the net capital stock. Net profits = net value added minus the sum of compensation and indirect business taxes, with net value-added equivalent to gross value-added minus depreciation or capital consumption. So: $r = P/K$.

The profit share (P/Y) is the ratio of profits (P) to output or value-added (Y). The output–capital ratio (Y/K) is the ratio of output or value-added (Y) to the capital stock (K). By de-composing, the profit rate equals the profit share times the output–capital ratio. So: $r = P/Y \times Y/K$.

Unless otherwise stated, both compensation and wages mean wages plus benefits. It should be noted that compensation in the context of the calculation of the profit rate includes not only compensation of employees, but also 'compensation of the self-employed'. The self-employed are thus attributed compensation at the same rate per hour or per person as employees in their industry, or the relevant aggregate. Self-employed compensation thus equals employees' compensation per hour or per person times the number of self-employed hours or self-employed persons (full-time equivalents).

Profit is thus defined as the surplus after depreciation, compensation, and indirect business taxes. This means that it includes net interest paid. The term 'profits' in this text therefore is always meant to include net interest, unless it is explicitly stated otherwise, as in 'profits net of interest', or 'profits minus interest', or 'profits excluding interest'.

The rate of profit is generally given for the 'private economy' or a given major industry. The private economy is, unless otherwise stated, always *non-farm* and *non-residential*, meaning that the value-added of farms and that attributed to the residential sector is excluded. The value-added of government enterprises is also excluded.

US PROFIT RATES: THE PRIVATE ECONOMY AND SPECIFIC INDUSTRIES

The sources for the calculation of profit rates for the US private economy and specific industries, notably manufacturing, are:

- Bureau of Labor Statistics, folders on the business economy and non-farm business economy, available on request;
- Bureau of Economic Analysis, 'Gross Product Originating by Industry', which is available at the BEA website; and Bureau of Economic Analysis, Fixed Asset Tables, available at the BEA website.

US PROFIT RATES: THE CORPORATE SECTOR, THE NON-FINANCIAL CORPORATE SECTOR, AND THE CORPORATE MANUFACTURING SECTOR

Sometimes, the rate of profit is given for the corporate sector, or for the non-financial corporate sector (i.e. the corporate sector with the financial sector excluded), or for the corporate manufacturing sector, or the corporate non-financial non-manufacturing sector (i.e. the non-financial corporate sector minus the corporate manufacturing sector). These profit rates are also net profit rates, defined as above. Unless otherwise stated, profits are always after capital consumption adjustment and inventory valuation adjustment. They are always pre-corporate tax, unless otherwise stated.

The source for the calculation of the net profit rate for the corporate sector and the non-financial corporate sector is Bureau of Economic Analysis, NIPA Table 1.16. Profits here are given after adjustments for capital consumption adjustment and inventory valuation. 'Net profits' are here defined as above – i.e. as value-added minus the sum of compensation, capital consumption, and indirect business taxes – but they are *net* of interest. It is thus necessary to sum 'net profits' and 'net interest' to get a measure of profits as defined above for the private economy and its component industries. The corporate and non-financial corporate profit rates are always 'net profits' plus 'net interest' over net capital stock, unless otherwise stated. Corporate and non-financial corporate taxes are also provided in this table. Net capital stocks for the corporate and non-financial corporate sector can be found in Bureau of Economic Analysis, Fixed Asset Tables, available at the BEA website.

Calculating profit rates for the corporate manufacturing sector poses certain difficulties, since 'profits' for the manufacturing sector provided by the Bureau of Economic Analysis – on an establishment basis in 'Gross Product Originating By Industry' and on a company basis in NIPA Table 6.16 – are without capital consumption adjustment. Since changes in the tax law made over the course of the post-war period affected how much manufacturing corporations declared as their capital consumption allowances, the corporate manufacturing profit figures are not consistent with one another over time; more specifically, the corporate manufacturing profits provided are, over time, increasingly too low. I have therefore calculated the corporate manufacturing profit rate 'from scratch', using the numbers in 'Gross Product Originating by Industry' for the corporate and quasi-corporate sector, i.e. excluding self-employed. This is made viable by the fact that virtually all firms in the manufacturing sector are corporations. Put another way, virtually all manufacturing firms that are not owner-operator firms are corporations. This was confirmed by comparing profit rates calculated 'from scratch' with profit rates calculated using corporate manufacturing profits on an establishment basis, from 'Gross Product Originating by Industry' (without capital consumption adjustment), for the early years of the post-war epoch (before significant changes in the tax law) and finding that these were nearly identical. Time series on corporate manufacturing capital stock and capital consumption are kindly provided by the Bureau of Economic Analysis. I wish to thank Shelby Herman for forwarding these to me.

PROFIT RATES FOR GERMANY AND JAPAN

The sources for the calculation of profit rates for the private economy and individual industries for Japan and Germany are:

- OECD, *National Accounts*, Volume II, Detailed Tables; OECD, *Flows and Stocks of Fixed Capital*. These have been updated in the new '*STAN*' series.

The profit rate series for the Japanese manufacturing sector depend on three sets of unpublished data, provided by the Bureau of Labor Statistics and the Ministry of Finance:

- Manufacturing net capital stock, current and constant prices, 1955–91. 'Data on Japanese Manufacturing Capital', 28 February 1996: I wish to thank Edward Dean of the BLS for making these series available to me.
- Manufacturing net capital stock, current prices (1990–97), in Japan, Ministry of Finance, Financial Statements Statistics of Corporations by Industry, Historical Data, Assets. Available at Ministry of Finance website, *http://www.mof.go.jp/English/files.htm*. I wish to thank John Rodgers for this material and calling my attention to the Ministry of Finance website.
- 'Underlying Data for Indexes of Output per Hour, Hourly Compensation, and Unit Labor Costs in Manufacturing, Twelve Industrial Countries, 1950–1999.' Available on request from BLS, Office of Productivity and Technology.

II. PRODUCTIVITY GROWTH

Productivity is always labour productivity, unless otherwise specified. It is defined as real value-added per hour or per person.

Unless otherwise stated, the productivity measures given for the US private economy or, equivalently, the private business sector are for the *non-farm non-residential* private economy.

Productivity measures for the US private economy and for individual industries, such as manufacturing, are based on real value-added indexes provided in 'Gross Product Originating by Industry' and hours provided by the Bureau of Labor Statistics.

Figures on US productivity are often given for the 'business economy', which always means *non-farm business economy*. These are provided by the Bureau of Labor Statistics in its folder on the business economy. Real value-added for the business economy is virtually equivalent to that for the private economy as defined above, with the difference that it *includes government enterprises.*

Unless otherwise stated, productivity measures for the German and Japanese private economies or private business sector use real value-added figures or indexes and figures for all persons (FTEs), provided in OECD, *National Accounts*, Volume II, Detailed Tables.

Figures on US, German, and Japanese manufacturing productivity are provided directly by the Bureau of Labor Statistics, Program on Foreign Labor Statistics, in 'International Comparisons of Manufacturing Productivity and Unit Labor Cost Trends', news release, available on the BLS website.

The Bureau of Labor statistics publishes data on US manufacturing productivity going back only to 1977. For the years 1950–77, I have therefore relied on an unpublished, unofficial series on manufacturing real value-added, data provided by Bill Gullickson of the BLS Office of Productivity and Technology. I wish to thank Bill Gullickson for forwarding me this series.

APPENDIX II

MAIN SOURCES OF DATA

This list contains the source for all of the variables to be found in the book, unless otherwise stated. There is some overlap, as the same variable is to be found in more than one source. See also above, Appendix I on Profit Rates and Productivity Growth.

I. DATA ON THE NATIONAL DOMESTIC ECONOMIES OF THE UNITED STATES, GERMANY, AND JAPAN

UNITED STATES

(i) US Department of Commerce, Bureau of Economic Analysis (BEA), 'Gross Product Originating Industry', current dollars, 1947–present, and chain dollars, 1977–present, BEA website: nominal value-added, nominal compensation of employees, indirect business taxes, proprietors' income, output of government enterprises, corporate profits (plus capital consumption and inventory valuation adjustments), real value-added, all persons (FTE) employees (FTE).

(ii) US, Department of Labor, Bureau of Labor Statistics, 'Industry Analytical Ratios' and 'Basic Industry Data': for the Non-farm Business Sector; for Manufacturing; for the Non-Financial Corporate Sector; and for the Total Economy, all persons and employees, 1949–present (numbers and per cent change): nominal value-added, nominal compensation, real value-added, hours at work, hourly compensation, real hourly compensation, value-added per hour (labour productivity), consumer price index, employment.

(iii) US Department of Commerce, Bureau of Economic Analysis, National Income and Product Accounts, at BEA website (numbers plus annual and quarterly per cent change): GDP nominal and real, gross private fixed non-residential investment (structures, equipment, and software) nominal and real, personal consumption expenditures (durable goods, non-durable goods, services) nominal and real. Also: contributions to per cent change in real gross domestic product by personal consumption expenditures, by gross private non-residential investment, by exports of goods and services.

(iv) US Department of Labor, Bureau of Labor Statistics, manufacturing index of real value-added, 1950–present. Unpublished series provided by Bill Gullickson. (See above, Appendix I, on Profit Rates and Productivity Growth.)

(v) US Department of Commerce, Bureau of Economic Analysis, Fixed Asset Tables, BEA website: net capital stock current and constant prices, consumption of fixed capital current and constant prices, gross investment current and constant prices. I wish to thank Edwin Dean, Bill Gullickson, Mike Harper, Phyllis Otto, and Larry Rosenblum of the BLS and Mike Glenn, Shelby Herman, Ken Petrick, and Bob Yuskavage of the BEA for help with these data.

(vi) *Economic Report of the President,* Washington, DC (annual): unemployment rate; manufacturing capacity utilization; real government consumption expenditures; consumer price indexes; money supply; interest rates; federal, state, and local government current receipts and expenditures.

GERMANY AND JAPAN
(see also above, Appendix I, on Profit Rates and Productivity Growth)

(i) OECD, National Accounts, Volume ii, Detailed Tables, 1960–94: by industry: value added, current and constant prices; compensation of employees; indirect business taxes; all persons at work; employees.

(ii) OECD, Flows and Stocks of Fixed Capital, various issues back to 1960: for private business economy, manufacturing, and services: gross and net capital stock current and constant prices; consumption of fixed capital current and constant prices; gross investment current and constant prices.

II. BASIC COMPARATIVE DATA ON THE DOMESTIC ECONOMIES OF THE UNITED STATES, GERMANY, AND JAPAN

(i) OECD, *Economic Outlook*, Paris: annual per cent change: GDP nominal and real, private consumption deflators, real gross private non-residential fixed capital formation; also unemployment rates, government financial balances, government structural balances.

(ii) US Department of Labor, Bureau of Labor Statistics, 'International Comparisons of Manufacturing Productivity and Unit Labor Cost Trends', 12 countries, 1950–present, at BLS website: manufacturing: total hours, employment, real output per hour, real output per person, real hourly compensation in national currency, nominal hourly compensation, hourly compensation in US dollars, unit labour costs in national currency, unit labour costs US in dollars.

(iii) US, Department of Labor, Bureau of Labour Statistics, 'International Comparisons of Hourly Compensation Costs for Production Workers in Manufacturing', 29 countries, 1975–present, at BLS website: hourly compensation costs in US dollars for production workers in manufacturing;

annual per cent change in hourly compensation costs in US dollars for production workers in manufacturing.

(iv) US Department of Labor, Bureau of Labor Statistics, 'Comparative Civilian Labor Force Statistics, Ten Countries, 1959–present', BLS website: civilian labour force employment and unemployment; civilian labour force by economic sector.

III. DATA ON INTERNATIONAL VARIABLES

(i) Data Archives of the International Monetary Fund: The United States, Germany, Japan, 1950–94: growth of real exports of goods and services; growth of real imports of goods and services; rate of increase of export prices; rate of increase of import prices; per cent share of world exports; nominal exports of goods and services/nominal GDP; exports of goods and services/GDP (price adjusted); growth of exports to and imports from one another in dollars (trade balances with one another).
Korea, Taiwan, Singapore, and Hong Kong, 1950–94: growth of real exports, per cent share of world exports, growth of exports to the US, per cent share of total US imports, growth of exports in US dollars to US, Germany, Japan; growth of imports in US dollars from the US, Germany, and Japan.
(I wish to thank Staffan Gorne and Pete Kledaras of the IMF for forwarding these data to me.)

(ii) IMF, *International Financial Statistics*, Washington, DC (monthly and annual): The United States, Germany and Japan: nominal effective exchange rates, exchange rates vis-à-vis dollar, goods exports values and volumes, services exports values and volumes, goods and services exports values and volumes, goods imports values and volumes, services imports values and volumes, goods and services imports values and volumes, goods export prices, goods import prices, goods and services prices.

(iii) US Department of Commerce, Bureau of Economic Analysis, National Income and Product Accounts, at BEA website: exports of goods nominal and real; imports of goods nominal and real; exports of goods and services nominal and real; goods exports prices; goods and services exports prices.

(iv) *Economic Report of the President*, Washington, DC (annual): US merchandise exports, merchandise imports, balance of trade, current account balance, real effective exchange rates.

(v) Department of Commerce, Office of Trade and Economic Analysis, 'US Manufactured Exports and Imports to Individual Countries, 1981–present'.

(vi) OECD, *Economic Outlook*, Paris (semi-annual): relative unit labour costs, shares of world goods exports and imports, current account balances, current account balances as per cent of GDP.

INDEX